Mountains of True Peace

A Guatemalan Journey, Volume 1

KelLee Parr

Published by KelLee Parr, 2021.

MOUNTAINS OF TRUE PEACE

First edition. December 4, 2021.

ISBN: 978-0997849219

Written by KelLee Parr.

To my K'ekchi' brothers and sisters who taught me what it means to be true servants of God.

Acknowledgement

It is hard to believe that the events in this book took place over 40 years ago. Still to this day, the three years spent in Guatemala remain special to me and have made me the person I am today. First, I must thank Randall Loucks for being an amazing friend and my coworker for the three years we worked together in Guatemala. The experience would not have been the same without you. I appreciate all your input in this book and your reminders of things that I had forgotten.

I want to thank Margaret Heisserer and her amazing editing skills in helping to bring this book to fruition. Your encouragement means the world to me. I can never thank you enough for your advice and friendship.

The cover design created by Trista Gorrell is a true work of art. With very little direction and a couple of my meager ideas, you always come up with the most amazing design. Thank you for your patience and willingness to tweak things over and over until it is just perfect. You are truly gifted and greatly appreciated.

I must thank my mother and sister Jane for saving each of my letters and putting them chronologically in a binder for me to read. It took 40 years for me to read them but this book would not have happened with the detail without these letters.

My deepest appreciation for our three fellow travelers and MCCers Ken Ekström and Carman and Carolyn Albrect. Sharing the experience with you and the friendship we developed was very special. I especially thank Ken for his incredible memory and helping to get the story in this book as factual as possible after so many years.

Thank you to Linda Witmer, a fellow Guatemalan worker so many years ago. It was such an honor to work with you and to now have you edit and give me feedback on this book. Your knowledge of K'ekchi' and the history is invaluable. All the work you continue to do for our K'ekchi' brothers and sisters is amazing and you are a true gift from God.

To all the Guatemalan missionaries that Randall and I had the pleasure to work with and get to know, your inspiration, friendship, and care is something for which I can never say thank you enough. I hope this book, which covers only the first nine months of my time in Guatemala, will help shed light on the role each of you had in our lives and in the lives of our Guatemalan brethren.

Finally, to my K'ekchi' family (Chepe, Matlide, Óscar, Rolando, Fidelina, Esperanza, and Rigoberto), my Antigua family (Doña Rosa, Angélica, Luis, Patti, Mario and Marito), the men and women of Campat, and all the people Randall and I met along our journey, I must thank you for the kindness, love, patience, and hospitality you showed toward us each and every day. Your Godly spirits taught me forever what it means to be true children of God.

Prologue

It is interesting how life progresses.

At times "things/people" are our breath, and then they are not.

Time or circumstances or fate change it, change us.

Then we are able to move into our next breath or source of oxygen.

We live, we adapt, we grow, all better for having had the experience.

—My friend, Rachelle Mengarelli

Chapter 1
Caxlan Cuink

"Ma cuancat?"

I was lying in bed after just starting to wake up. *Did I hear something?* It was still early and pitch dark. I looked at my watch and the fluorescent hands showed it was 5:45 a.m. It was a mid-April morning and chilly. Inside my sleeping bag was the warmest place to be. I waited, not making a move, to make sure I wasn't just hearing things.

From outside a soft and slightly nervous tone broke the silence with the same words. "Ma cuancat? (Are you there?)" once again chimed with a little more volume and force. The words I heard were the Mayan language *K'ekchi'*—or *Q'eqchi'*, which is the more common spelling used today. My colleague Randall and I had been learning K'ekchi' during the year and a half since we arrived.

The voice wasn't one I immediately recognized but it was a young man or boy's voice. I was alone in my little one room house in the Guatemalan mountain *c'alebal* or village of Campat. Defining a c'alebal as a village isn't really a very good English translation or description. Possibly a community or neighborhood would be more accurate since it was a bunch of huts connected by foot paths and scattered randomly across the mountains and valley. I was by myself because Randall was on his way to Guatemala City, taking his visiting parents from the States back to the airport to return home. He had not seen them since we had left on our adventure of a lifetime. It was going to be hard to say goodbye to them again.

This unexpected visitor outside my door startled me. Nothing like this had ever happened before. People were never out visiting this early unless they needed something urgent. It was especially strange at sunrise for someone to call on the c'alebal *caxlan cuinks* (or *gringos* as the *ladinos*—non-indigenous Guatemalans—referred to

4

us). I never quite understood how they came up with the term *caxlan cuink*, which meant a foreigner. *Cuink* was easy, it meant "man" in *K'ekchi'*. But caxlan? Caxlan meant "chicken"—the bird not being afraid. *Chickenman? Really? Definitely not the same vibe one gets from action heroes like Batman or Superman.*

What the heck? Who could that be? I wondered as I opened my sleeping bag sprawled out over my foam mattress. The three-inch foam was on top of rough planks, which was my bed and part of the handmade bunk beds that I shared with Randall. Turning on my flashlight kept near my pillow to give me a little light, I grabbed my jeans and shirt hanging on the nail at the side of the bunk bed and swung my legs around, carefully placing them on top of my hiking boots sitting alongside the bed. This is the same ritual played out every morning as the dirt floor was always cold and damp. One's warm feet would end up coated with a clay sludge on the bottom otherwise. I leaned back and slid my jeans on over my bare legs and pulled on my t-shirt. The heavy woolen socks were tucked inside my shoes. One always shook out the socks and shoes before putting them on to make sure no creepy crawly thing had found its way in over the night. I put them on and then slipped my feet into my hiking boots.

"Ma cuancat?" rang out a third time a little louder and with a little more urgency. We still hadn't completely mastered the language by any means, but we had made considerable progress and could hold conversations. I knew this phrase to be a polite greeting when one approached someone's house. No knocking on the door. I replied back in K'ekchi' with the acknowledgement that I had a visitor, "*Cuanquin* (I'm here)."

An encouraged "Ma cuancat, *Herman Keli*?" sounded back. Working as agricultural/literacy missionaries in the c'alebal, all of the people referred to us as *Herman Rolando* and *Herman Keli* (*hermano* in Spanish or "brother" in English). The K'ekchi' over the years had given up their indigenous first names and used Spanish names. Neither of our names translated into Spanish but Rolando was close to Randall so he went by that. We just went with a phonetic translation of mine.

I went to the door with my flashlight in hand, slid the metal hook latch and opened it to find the young boy Antonio, about thirteen years old, standing at my door. His sister Erlinda was one of my students that I had been teaching how to read. We had lessons three times a week, and she was bright and learned quickly. If Antonio wasn't off working in the fields with his family, he often sat and listened while Erlinda read with me. He sometimes would read passages with us. He said he had attended the school at the end of the valley for a few years where he picked up his reading skills.

The early morning sky was just beginning to lighten. The sun was still not peeking over the tall mountains that blocked the sunrise in the east. With my flashlight pointed at the ground, there was enough light to clearly see Antonio's concerned face. I asked him to come in but he politely declined. Instead, he urged me to come to his home immediately. "Erlinda is having her baby," he said in a stressed tone. I knew Erlinda was married to José, but finding out she was having a baby was quite a shock. I had no idea she was even pregnant. This was her first baby. I always thought it interesting that Erlinda, being twenty years old, didn't have any children. At twenty most young K'ekchi' wives had one or two children. It was unfathomable coming from my world to see these young people married at such a young age and having babies already.

Erlinda's husband José was a quiet, nice guy. I didn't know him well because he didn't go to the Mennonite church and wasn't one of our students. This young couple didn't have much land or means to make a living and were poor. But José was a hard worker and often was gone for months at a time because he left to work at one of the *fincas* (large plantations) in the coastal areas to make money for his family to survive.

"Something is wrong," Antonio tells me. "It has been too long. She started having the baby yesterday and the baby doesn't want to come into the world. José asked me to come get you. We need your help."

My K'ekchi' still wasn't great but I was able to get the gist of what Antonio was saying, and the fear on his face and tone of voice came through. I'm sure if he could have seen the look on my face, the fear would have mirrored his. The famed words of Prissy from *Gone with the Wind,* crossed my mind. *I don't know nothin' 'bout birthin' babies!* Antonio reached out and grabbed my wrist pulling slightly and saying, "*Banu usilal* (Please), Herman Keli!"

Though completely caught off guard, I said, "*Us, junpatak* (Okay, just a bit)" and stepped back in to get my jacket since the spring morning air was quite chilly. I slid on my jacket and slung my colorful, handwoven *bols* (*bolsa* in Spanish)—purse-like bag—over my shoulder. Every good K'ekchi' man carried with him his bols, which held his important documentation in case he got *chapoc'*ed (or grabbed) by the army to be "enlisted." Married men, as long as they had their papers, were usually released, but single men were quite wary and hid if the rumor of "chapoc"ing was going on. I shut the door and we left with me not having a clue as to what I was getting myself into.

The air was crisp as we headed out on the trail going up the mountain. Thankfully the early light made the narrow dirt path cut along the mountainside more visible and easier to navigate. The morning dew made the path wet and slippery. One had to watch for little mud puddles where the lack of drainage stored the water from the daily rains. Other parts of the path were gravel-like or had rocks jutting out where the clay soil was worn off or washed away. It always amazed me at how the K'ekchi' navigated these treacherous trails with such grace. Often the men and boys wore rubber boots as they walked the rocky and muddy paths. How the men tolerated wearing those sweaty, thick rubber boots with no socks was mind boggling. However Antonio was barefoot on this chilly morning, as if he hadn't taken time or thought to put on his boots.

Antonio was making quick time with his calloused feet on the rugged path. I tried to stay close to him as he moved with urgency. It was a struggle to keep up but my much longer legs did help. Antonio was small and thin like most boys his age. The K'ekchi' men were very short in stature, most standing no more than about 5' 2" and my 6' 3" frame towered over them. Not helping was my much higher center of gravity which provided a huge disadvantage when it came to keeping my balance on the treacherous mountain paths. Hiking the trails of Campat, I came to the conclusion this was a good reason gymnasts were usually not very tall.

The path to José and Erlinda's hut was quite familiar. I had made the trek many times over the past months after Erlinda came to me and said she wanted to learn how to read. When we first moved to the c'alebal of Campat, Randall and I began teaching adults to read in K'ekchi'. However, this had never been our intended reason for being there.

When we first approached the c'alebal elders of Campat and asked if we could live in the c'alebal, we told them we were *agriculturas* (agriculturists) and would like to help in any way we could. Expecting them to jump at the chance to have our vast college-educated, agricultural wisdom poured upon the valley, we were elated when they said, "*Us*" (which is pronounced "Ew-s" and means "good or okay"). Except it wasn't our expertise in agriculture that interested them but another thing we offered, teaching adults to read. We told the elders we would be delighted to teach reading. They were very happy and welcomed us to Campat. This early morning when Antonio came to our door, it had been nearly a year since Randall and I had moved to Campat.

Chapter 2
Na'chin and Erlinda

The cool morning air was quite refreshing. Any sleepiness I had possessed was long gone now, which was a good thing since walking the path could be dangerous if you were not paying attention. One had to be sure to duck for the banana tree limbs, dodge any sisal plants with mini teeth on their sword-like leaves, and not trip on the jagged rocks that protruded sporadically along the path. One slip on the wet clay soil could result in a perilous tumble down the side of the mountain before reaching the bottom, unless a boulder, tree or someone's hut got in the way.

As we passed huts along the up-and-down trail, I could see flickers of light through the porous walls of the huts. They didn't have fancy kerosene lanterns like the caxlan cuinks had brought to the c'alebal and electricity was definitely not available. The K'ekchi's' ingenuity showed through as they would create their own lights by taking a medicine bottle purchased at the market and filling it with kerosene. Creating a wick out of handmade sisal plant rope, they tied a sisal string around the bottle's neck and hung the bottle from the rafters. Once lit, the little kerosene apparatus provided sufficient light and lasted for many nights.

Each family had a tiny, thatch-roofed hut. The walls were either made from crooked posts placed side by side or with rough wood planks. Once in a while one of the more affluent families had a tin roof.

The huts' dimensions varied with the norm being about ten feet by twelve feet. It might be just one large room or maybe divided by a wall made from woven mats. The more established families might have two huts next to each other with a couple of wooden beds. However, more often than not, a family had one bed or just mats on the dirt floor. A family with four or five children all slept together. An open fire in the center of the room kept them warm. The huts where fires were lit had a mix of steam rising off their thatched roofs from the dew evaporating and smoke emanating through the cracks. As Antonio and I trekked onward in the early morning hour, I could hear voices in one hut. The parents and children began singing a familiar church hymn. *Amazing Grace* sung in K'ekchi' was beautiful. I thought, *What joy I hear in their voices.* This "chickenman's" initial viewpoint, coming from a rich man's world, was how sad the people of Campat's lives were. They were so impoverished and lived in conditions I had never fathomed existed. However over time, I came to realize just how loving, happy, giving and spiritual these people were. They would selflessly give you their last *cua* (tortilla) or cup of *cape* (coffee) without even thinking about themselves. I began to ponder how the wealthy people where I came from with all our material things were truly the impoverished ones.

As we approached José and Erlinda's hut, my anxiety kicked in even more. Antonio gave his *"Ma cuanquex?"* announcement to let the family know we had arrived. A woman's voice meekly responded back. The elderly woman opened the door and whiffs of smoke billowed out into our faces. Antonio nodded and respectfully said, *"Na'chin,* we have arrived." Na'chin is the word for a highly respected, older woman in the c'alebal.

I had never seen this woman before but assumed she must be Erlinda's mother. She was thin and looked worried and quite worse for wear. She moved from the door to allow us to enter and stood beside the rocks surrounding the fire pit. Antonio motioned for me to enter the hut. Being much taller than the doorway, I had to bend way over to go through, something I had gotten used to doing. Once inside I still had to be hunched over to not hit the ceiling made of sticks that provided a place for storage of corn and beans below the rafters and thatch roof.

Antonio encouraged me to sit on the split log that had been hand-planed smooth with a machete and turned into a bench. It was about five feet long and sat about a foot off the ground. Wooden peg legs were pushed into carved-out holes on both ends of the half log. I had sat on this bench many times teaching Erlinda. My back was against the post wall and my long legs were bent with my knees practically under my chin. Antonio sat right next to me, using my body heat and the fire to help warm himself.

Antonio told me the woman I had met at the door was his and Erlinda's mother. Another woman sitting by the firepit was introduced as Erlinda's aunt. The reason I had never seen them before was because they lived on the other side of the mountain. Erlinda had moved to Campat after marrying José. Na'chin stoked the fire, bent down and blew on the smoking, red embers and the fire came to life in a burst of flames and more smoke filled the air. She added a couple more pieces of firewood to build a larger fire. It was from this indoor fire pit where the women spent the day bent over cooking and breathing in the smoke that gave them respiratory problems, which led to early deaths. My eyes began to water a little and I wiped a small tear with my jacket sleeve.

It was then I noticed Erlinda. She was in the far corner of the hut. José was there too helping her to stand and she was holding onto a vertical post. She looked worn out and her face showed the pain she was in, but she wasn't making a sound. A woven mat about four feet tall was partially hiding her. I could see she had been squatting on her haunches with a rope tied under her arms. The rope was flung over a beam in the rafters to give her support. It was like a crude sling. Later I found out this was the normal birthing position for the K'ekchi' women. Erlinda was barefoot as was Na'chin. She was clothed in her *uk* (skirt) and only her under blouse that women wore beneath their hand-embroidered *huipil* (blouse). Her beautiful huipil was hanging over the woven mat.

The K'ekchi' women were masters at embroidery work. Erlinda's huipil had fine stitching in a diamond pattern in several rows with black thread around the neckline. These diamonds were filled with different colors and there were small, multi-colored flowers along the edges of the diamonds. Each c'alebal had its own pattern and one knowledgeable about the patterns could easily discern from what c'alebal each woman originated. I noticed Na'chin's and Erlinda's aunt's blouse had a different pattern since they lived in the neighboring c'alebal.

A K'ekchi' woman's uk was made of eight yards of material. Erlinda's beautiful red, blue, and green skirt was cinched around her waist with a drawstring-like rope. Once the rope is pulled taut, the rope is wrapped several times around the waist. That makes K'ekchi' skirts "one size fits all" and falls to just above the ankles. The skirts with so much material are quite heavy and even more so when they become damp from the misty rain that frequents the mountainous region from November through April. The skirts give the women a full-bodied look and was probably what helped me to not realize Erlinda was even pregnant.

Erlinda was obviously very uncomfortable and as she noticed I had seen her, she uttered in my direction a slight whisper, "*Chan xacuil?*" This was the standard polite greeting in K'ekchi' and literally translates into "How do you see yourself?" I replied back, "*Mac'a' naxye, bantiox acue.*" Which basically means "I'm doing fine, thank you for asking." She gave a very small whimper that was almost inaudible and grimaced as another contraction must have happened. I am shocked in disbelief and contemplating, *What am I supposed to do now?*

With what seemed a lack of concern for Erlinda, her mother took care of my question for me. With her tough as nails, calloused hands, she reached for the hot can that had been sitting next to the fire. In her other hand she held a carved-out gourd that was used for a cup. She poured her homebrewed coffee into the gourd and handed it to me. "*Uc' an* (drink up)," she said.

First thing I must admit, I never ever liked the taste of coffee. I loved the smell of coffee brewing but the taste, not so much. Maybe it was because my mother never liked it and never made it unless for company. Not even in college did I indulge when one needed that extra boost of caffeine that all college kids used to pull all-nighters studying for the final exam. For me it was like drinking muddy water. However, one of the first lessons we were given in our training before going to a foreign country was to treat the people with respect and to accept their gifts of food no matter how badly we didn't want it. So as they say, once in Guatemala, do as the Guatemalans do, right?

With utmost respect, I accepted the hot drink. "*Bantiox acue* (thank you)," I said. It was the most humbling experience to be treated with such graciousness. The K'ekchi' people were incredible. Here the poor woman's daughter was in labor and it was more important to give me coffee. Talk about a lesson in putting the needs of another person before your own.

I had learned in the past after being offered the brown elixir to make sure it wasn't too hot. I had seen too often the embarrassed smile on my hosts' faces when I grimaced from burning my tongue. I blew into the gourd and watched the steam rise as Na'chin handed Antonio a gourd with coffee as well. Carefully I took a sip of the sugary coffee. More often than not, the coffee was very watered down compared to American coffee. Here was real Guatemalan coffee.

The coffee beans were probably picked right outside the door of the hut. Na'chin had roasted the beans, ground them, added water, and proceeded to boil the heck out of the liquid. I learned that the K'ekchi' always sweetened their coffee with sugar cane juice or if they had the money, sugar bought at the market in town. This made the drink very tasty without the bitterness of our strong black coffee back home. It was actually delicious. "*Mas sa* (very good)," I shared with my hostess and she smiled a huge smile. This was the first time I noticed one of her front teeth was missing. Another hardship the older K'ekchi' women and men dealt with.

Na'chin's kindness didn't stop there. While she had been making my coffee, her sister had moved to resting on her knees in front of Erlinda's grinding stone that was curved and appeared to be made of cement. It was a foot wide and foot and a half long and rested on the ground. There was some *cua* (or ground corn) and a few kernels of corn already on it. With both hands she picked up the stone used to grind the corn and began smashing the remaining corn in a rhythmic motion back and forth. I had become accustomed to hearing this familiar sound in every K'ekchi' home.

Once the corn was crushed to her satisfaction, making a fine dough-like consistency, she picked up a small portion and rolled it in her hand and formed a ball about the size of a golf ball. She handed it off to Na'chin, who earlier had placed a flat, round griddle made of clay on the fire. The griddle was balanced on three rocks surrounding the fire pit.

Dumbfounded, I sat there observing the meal preparation while thinking how crazy this was. Erlinda was in labor and Na'chin seemed more concerned about feeding her guest. It didn't take us very long once we arrived in the c'alebal to figure out how important sharing food was in showing hospitality. We also learned how delicious the food given so generously was. Beans and tortillas were the staple and I had no idea they could be fixed in so many different ways. *Tzu'uuj* was my favorite. It was a large tortilla with mashed black beans spread inside. If the family had a few chickens and the chickens cooperated, scrambled eggs were served and one used a tortilla as a spoon to eat the eggs. If the chickens didn't cooperate, a soup called *caldo* with boiled chicken pieces (sometimes beef or pork) and lots of spices was prepared. The fat from the chicken formed a nice coating of grease that floated on top with the spices. It made for a unique challenge for someone with a moustache and often we wished we had some Tums® from home.

Na'chin began *xoroc'*ing the dough. This was a clapping motion back and forth as she turned and flattened the round ball in her hand until a perfect seven-inch diameter, flat tortilla was formed. She carefully placed the tortilla on the griddle and it began to sizzle. She quickly made another and it didn't take long for the tortillas to begin to bubble up, as all the best tortillas did. She flipped the tortillas showing the lightly golden side. Next Na'chin took another gourd bowl and spooned out some chicken caldo that was in a pot that had been placed by the fire earlier. She removed a tortilla from the griddle and placed it over the bowl, handing the breakfast meal for me to partake.

How many times had my friends and I complained about the food in the cafeteria in college with all our choices available? And if we didn't like what we had chosen, the gang could always go on a taco run to Taco Tico® that night when we were hungry. So spoiled to think back. Now, I was very appreciative of this gourd of coffee, tortilla and caldo I was being served by my gracious host, but good Lord almighty, her daughter was in the corner of the hut in labor.

On the way over to Erlinda's hut I asked Antonio how long she had been in labor. He said it had started yesterday before the sun went down. Now I was calculating in my head, *So, it has been at least 12 hours!* The minutes ticked by as I drank my coffee and ate my chicken caldo and tortilla. As I ate, I contemplated, *How did I get myself into this situation? I sure wish Randall was here. What the heck am I going to do and how can I help Erlinda?*

Chapter 3
Mennonite Central Committee

"You want to do what?" was the first question out of my mother's mouth on that Sunday afternoon when I came home from college to visit.

"I want to go to Bolivia and work as an agricultural missionary," I nervously repeated. "You know this is something I have always wanted to do. Something like the Peace Corps."

"Yes, I knew you had that interest but really didn't think you would ever do it," she replied.

"Well, I am going to apply and see what happens," I told her. "You know my friend, Randall, he told me about an organization called Mennonite Central Committee and they have a job opening for an animal scientist to work in Bolivia. Randall is going to apply for a position in Bangladesh as an agronomist." I was hoping Bolivia sounded way better than Bangladesh and she'd cut me a little slack.

Randall was a college friend I had met when we both lived in Haymaker Hall my junior year in college at Kansas State University. He and his roommate Dale were from Hesston, Kansas, and both were Mennonites. Up to that point, I had no real knowledge of the Mennonite faith except the idea that they were very conservative people and they all drove horses and buggies. Randall and Dale had explained that there are different types of Mennonite churches from extremely conservative offshoots, such as the Amish who still use horse and buggy, to the more liberal groups that were similar in many ways to my Presbyterian upbringing with only a few belief differences.

Mennonite Central Committee (MCC) is one of the more liberal Mennonite organizations and sends people all over the world to strive to improve lives in Third World nations as well as in the United

17

States. Randall explained they don't go to places to start churches or preach their faith but show their faith through their actions. MCC partners with local churches and organizations with similar values to amplify their impact.

There are three areas MCC focuses on: relief, development and peace. They help with relief during times of disaster, such as hurricanes and wars. They provide support to develop and strengthen people's long-term access to food, water, health care, and education, plus finding ways for people to support their families. Finally, believing in pacifism, they work with partners to teach conflict transformation skills and support peace education, advocating for justice and encouraging people to work together despite their differences. MCC is quite open to allowing non-Mennonite members to join and serve.

"But three years? That's a long time to be away," my mother bemoaned.

"I know, but it is something I really want to do and feel called to do."

My mother and dad looked at one another without saying a word. With a look on their faces that said they knew there was nothing they could do, they gave me their full support and were proud of me.

Though I had grown up on a farm and loved working with livestock, I didn't enjoy the farming part and I definitely had inherited my dad's lack of mechanical skills. I'm not sure he would have made it as a farmer without duct tape and baling wire. Though my parents would have liked for me to farm, they knew it wasn't in the cards for me. I loved working with the livestock but I hated the farming part. I went to college and in the spring of 1979, I had already graduated the previous year with a degree in Animal Science and Industry and was in my second semester of graduate school. From the time I entered college, my plan had been to be a county agricultural and 4-H extension agent. I had loved being in 4-H and it had done so much for me as a young kid. My county extension agent Bob Wareham had been my mentor and hero. However, I decided before I applied for an extension job, I wanted to see what the world had to offer.

Joining the Peace Corps was always one of the things I had thought about doing. I was born in the mid-1950s and grew up in the '60s. I remembered often hearing the words of President Kennedy: "And so, my fellow Americans: Ask not what your country can do for you—ask what you can do for your country."

Being a youth during the Vietnam War, I always feared one day of being drafted and having to fight in that horrible war. So many people expressed with protests and riots how they felt we didn't belong. It divided our country and cost so many American lives. I don't know how many times I prayed that the war would be over before I was old enough to be drafted. I couldn't imagine killing someone. Heck, I felt guilty the time I shot a 'possum and never again used the gun my dad gave me. Thankfully the war was over before I was old enough to have to serve and I felt my prayers had been answered. I never forgot those words Kennedy spoke. I wanted to do something to help others, and I thought the Peace Corps might be my answer so I got an application.

Before I ever was able to apply for the Peace Corps, Randall told me about MCC and that they were very similar to the Peace Corps, trying to help the less fortunate in the United States and around the world. He gave me some information and a list of job openings. I carefully read everything he shared. Randall told me that a recruiter was coming to Kansas State to interview people. It was a little daunting, but I decided to submit my application, sign up for the position in Bolivia, and see what happened.

I was nervous about going to meet Rich, the MCC interviewer. Once entering the interview room in the KSU Student Union, there was no turning back. Rich was a tall, lean man with a black moustache, short, black, curly Afro-style haircut and looked like a skinny

version of Mr. Kot—-teeeerrrrr from the popular late '70s TV show
Welcome Back, Kotter. He was very cordial but asked some very
tough questions. Why was I interested in working for MCC? What
was my understanding of culture shock? Would I be prepared to live
in conditions way different than what I was accustomed? What kind
of things would I expect to experience in a Third World country like
Bolivia? What was my background growing up that would prepare
me for such an experience?

I really had no idea if I answered all the questions to his satisfaction but answered honestly the best I could. I wasn't even sure if I was
satisfied with my answers and definitely didn't fully understand what
I was getting myself into. One question stuck out in my memory after I left. Rich asked, "Would you be open to working in a different
country if we had another opening?"

I remember hesitating a little and stopping to think. I hadn't
even thought about going to Africa or some other country. Bolivia
had been the only position I felt I was qualified to do. I had studied
up on Bangladesh after Randall had said he wanted to go there. That
didn't appeal to me at all. Talk about a Third World country, it was
more like a Fourth World country. I thought he was crazy. I really
wasn't interested in going there. I also had studied a little Spanish in
high school and wanted to take advantage of that rather than learn
a new language. I replied, "I would prefer a Latin American country
but would consider any openings."

After several minutes of chatting and answering his questions,
he asked if I had any questions for him about MCC. My only question was how did MCC feel about taking on people who were not
Mennonite. He replied that MCC volunteers need to have servant
hearts and be followers of Christ. They expected their volunteers to
not drink or smoke and to be a positive representative of the organization. They definitely were open to people of other denominations.

Rich thanked me for my time and said the interview was over. He would be in touch and let me know about the position.

Later that day I met up with Randall and we exchanged information about our interviews. Randall, being Mennonite and also having experienced living in Holland for a year after his freshman year at Hesston College, definitely had more confidence in the whole process. We would just have to wait and see what Rich decided and how our future lives would be touched.

Several days went by with no word. Classes continued and my mother called several times, asking if I had heard anything. I am sure she was wishing the word would be the opposite of what I was hoping. My stomach was tied in uncertain knots and at times appeared to be leaning a little more toward my folks' desired outcome. It was exciting to imagine the experience but also terrifying to think of leaving the comforts of home and how I was used to living.

One afternoon after returning from class I had a letter waiting for me in my mailbox. It had Mennonite Central Committee stamped in the upper left corner. I quickly found a chair, sat and opened the letter. It was from Rich and he thanked me for the time we had spent discussing the opportunity in Bolivia. He said he was sorry but that position was already filled.

My heart sank but the letter continued on. Rich wondered if I might consider another position. MCC was going to be starting a new project in Guatemala in conjunction with a Mennonite church group called Eastern Mennonite Board of Missions and Charities (EMB) who worked starting Mennonite churches around the world. In 1992 they changed the name to Eastern Mennonite Missions (EMM). EMB had been present in Guatemala for many years and were wanting to start a joint venture with MCC to bring in agriculture and appropriate technology to the people they had worked with in rural Guatemala. It was going to be the first joint venture between the two organizations.

As I read on, Rich stated that the position had not been posted yet but he and his wife Martha were going to Guatemala the following February with their daughters, and he would be the Country Director for MCC. Currently there was just one man, whose name was George, in Guatemala who was the country representative. George would become the Country Director until Rich got there. Rich was interested in Randall and me working together to start this program. They wanted us to commit to working there for three years to get the program off the ground and we would start this coming September. With Randall's agronomy background and my animal science background, he thought it would be a good combination, plus we were already friends. This new venture between EMB and MCC was a very important trial to bridge unity between the two groups and he thought we would be a good fit.

What! Did I read that right? My mind was racing. *He wants Randall and me to work together! It sounds awesome to get a chance to work with a friend and not take off to some foreign land alone. And we would get to work with Rich! Is this too good to be true? Will Randall feel the same way? I know he had his heart set on Bangladesh. But Guatemala?*

I have to admit, I had no idea where the heck Guatemala was located. I knew it was a Central American country but had no concept where it was on a map or knew anything about it. I reread the letter to let it soak in some more. Rich wanted me to contact him to let him know if this position would be something I would consider. But first I had to talk to Randall.

I ran to the phone and gave Randall a ring. *Come on, pick up!* There was no answer so I left a message to give me a call when he got home. This was after all 1979, no cell phones or texting available. I was going to have to wait to hear from Randall when he got out of class. The rest of the day was a blur but I know it wasn't spent studying. That afternoon I went to the library and researched Guatemala and discovered it was a small country just south of Mexico. The population spoke Spanish as the national language but there were over twenty different Mayan Indian languages spoken as well. Guatemala City was the capital. Rich's letter stated that we would be located in the city of San Pedro Carchá in Alta Verapaz, Guatemala. There we would be living and working alongside missionaries from EMB.

Randall reached me later that evening and he had gotten his letter. He was a bit disappointed to find out he didn't get to go to Bangladesh, but he was excited about the idea of going to Guatemala. We made plans to meet the following day to discuss the suggestion of working together. *Now to break the news back home!*

Chapter 4
Getting Ready to Leave

It was toward the end of the summer and time had gone by quickly since Randall and I had agreed to accept the opportunity to work with MCC and Rich in Guatemala. Our acknowledgement letters informed us that all new MCC volunteers would gather at the beginning of September for a nine-day orientation training.

Earlier in the summer we attended a week-long Agriculture and Appropriate Technology Seminar that MCC invited us to participate in at Bethel College in North Newton, Kansas. Fremont Regier, who was in charge, was an MCC missionary with a wealth of information to share about what was in store for all of us. The seminar provided hands-on experience, and we learned from others who had been MCC volunteers working in Third World countries. It was great preparation for us before going to Guatemala. It opened my eyes to a whole new way of thinking. The week was a nice introduction to the MCC mission.

There were other newbie MCC volunteers at this seminar like Randall and me who would be leaving at the end of summer for their new work destinations. It was nice to know there would be others we knew at the MCC orientation training. One of them was Dwight and he was a Mennonite friend of Randall's from K-State and a super nice guy. He had volunteered to go to Haiti. I also met Everett who was from Canada. We bonded over the fact he too was not Mennonite and had an agricultural background. He was going to be working in Brazil.

Once back home to our family farm after the seminar, there was a lot to do to get prepared to be away for three years. The days were flying by. We had to get vaccinations for several diseases. *Rich never mentioned that to me in the interview!*

There was one tidbit of information Rich shared in my confirmation letter that caused me to freak out about this adventure. He said we would use motorcycles to get around. *Yike!* I had never driven a motorcycle in my entire life. The only time I had ridden one was behind my college roommate who brought his off-road motorcycle to school. It was a dirt bike and we would go out to the reservoir where bikers would ride up the steep dirt banks of the spillway. It was great fun to watch and ride but I never tried to "drive" one.

Thankfully, Randall had a ton of experience with motorcycles. He had a Honda 550 street bike and had traveled a lot on it. Mr. Adventurous for sure. The summer before he attended KSU he had a serious accident, hitting a pothole and skidding across the highway. He was terribly scraped and banged up. Thankfully his helmet kept him from being seriously injured or even killed. Otherwise, our trek to Guatemala would never have happened. Now my task at hand was to learn to drive a motorcycle since it would be our mode of transportation in Guatemala.

Needless to say, my mother was not excited about me being on a motorcycle, but she thought it better that I learn ahead of time than in the mountains of a foreign country. She had a great idea. Our neighbor's high school son Barry had a motorcycle. Barry helped put up hay for my folks, and they thought the world of him. We asked him to come over and show me the ropes, so to speak. He gave me a few quick lessons and then rode behind me giving me directions. I don't know who was more nervous, him or me.

After a few trips up and down the road, he let me loose in our brome pasture that we had just cut and put up for hay. I did pretty well until I went bouncing over a terrace—my feet flying off the footrests and long legs flying out to the sides in a non-acrobatic move—and came close to wiping out. It scared the living daylights out of me. Barry was laughing his head off as he ran after me and watched my 150-pound skinny body and 6′ 3″ frame trying to steady the motorcycle. I was definitely not a natural. Slowly after several more attempts, I became more comfortable and my fear subsided a little. Barry gave me a reassuring thumbs up that I was ready. One of my first hurdles cleared.

We were told that during the three years we were gone, we would be able to return home once or twice if we wanted, but we would have to pay our own way. However, MCC said we could not come home during the first year since we would be spending a great deal of time in language study and getting accustomed to the new culture. We needed to pack clothes and things we thought we might need for the entire three-year stay.

Packing for three years was quite a challenge to say the least. A letter was mailed to all the new MCC volunteers being sent out across the world. It informed us that we would be going to orientation training in Akron, Pennsylvania, and that we could take two suitcases. We were to bring these two suitcases for our nine-day orientation and then we would be leaving directly from Akron to our new homes. *What! Two suitcases for three years! I had a car full of stuff when I went to college and came home on weekends if I needed something.*

However, tucked in my letter was a second letter. Randall got the same additional letter. "Dear Randall and KelLee, You will not be leaving directly from orientation like the rest of the recruits. We would like for you to drive two pickup trucks from Pennsylvania to Guatemala." *WHAT! Drive two pickups all the way to Guatemala! Did I read that right? Just how far was it to Guatemala, anyway?*

We found out that one of the trucks was going to stay in Guatemala for the Country Director and the other truck was going to the MCC team in Honduras. After orientation, we would drive the trucks back to Kansas, pick up our belongings and head south. This meant we were allowed to take more luggage and even a trunk.

It still limited how much we could take but was way better than two suitcases on an airplane. *What a blessing!*

We also found out in our letter that the Guatemala team was not going to be just the Country Director George, Randall and me. Also joining us were three more people. Carman and Carolyn were a young married couple and Ken was a single guy. We would meet them at orientation training in Akron. There would be five of us driving to Guatemala. *We will have our very own little caravan.*

Chapter 5

First Lesson

The day arrived to go to orientation. I had said my goodbyes to my parents the day before when they dropped me off at Randall's parents, but it wasn't a final goodbye. We would be coming back to the farm with our new MCC pickups in a few weeks. Randall and I were leaving from Wichita, Kansas, to fly to Akron. Dwight, from the summer seminar, met us at the airport.

It was slightly intimidating joining Randall and Dwight heading to Pennsylvania. First, they were both Mennonites versus my Presbyterian background. Both were very athletic with straight blond hair, blue eyes and very good-looking guys. *Is this a Mennonite thing? I'm REALLY not going to fit the mold with my thick, dark, curly hair and hazel eyes.*

I tried to act as calm and collected as the two of them seemed to be. Both had experience as exchange students and had traveled abroad before. My biggest adventure was going to Tijuana for a day with my parents when I was a kid. There was no comparison. If Randall and Dwight were nervous, they didn't show it. We boarded the plane and took off for Chicago.

We arrived with no issues and had a couple hours layover before our plane left for Pennsylvania. Our luggage had been checked in and our only carry-ons were our camera bags. "Why don't we rent an airport locker and leave our camera bags and jackets. We can go explore the airport," Randall suggested.

"Sounds great." I said and we piled all our belongings into the locker, including our passports. The locker had a key we could remove after locking it. Randall turned and pulled out the key. We headed out on the first leg of our new adventure.

We grabbed a quick bite to eat and walked around the airport exploring. O'Hare Airport was huge. I had never been to Chicago before and definitely not to an airport this big. As it got closer to our time of departure, we went back to the locker to retrieve our bags and jackets. Randall pulled out the key from his pocket and attempted to open the locker. "What's wrong with this thing?" he grumbled.

"You sure you have the right locker?" Dwight asked.

"Yes, the number is on the key. It just won't turn the lock," Randall said with a little angst in his voice.

"Here, let me try," Dwight offered. He pulled the key out and tried inserting the key both ways, turned and nothing.

"Oh man, what are we going to do?" Randall asked.

"Here, let me give it a try," I said as I took the key. I had no more luck than either of them. We tried several more times and time was ticking away.

"Flight 233 to Harrisburg, Pennsylvania, is now ready to board," we heard over the loudspeaker.

"Damn, what now?" we all pretty much said at the same time.

Dwight noticed a sign on the lockers that gave a number to call in case of a lost key or emergency. Remember in the '80s, we had no cell phones. We had to either go to a pay phone or ask someone at the information desk for help. Panic was starting to set in. Randall ran and got someone to call the number. The person that answered said they couldn't promise how long it would take for someone to get there to unlock our locker, maybe twenty or thirty minutes. We frantically tried over and over to open the locker but no luck.

"This is the second call for passengers flying to Harrisburg, Pennsylvania, on Flight 233."

Dwight and I had kept our plane tickets in our shirt pockets but Randall had put his ticket in his bag that was now trapped in the locker reluctant to give up its contents. Dwight and I ran up to the departure gate and told the ticket taker our situation and that we didn't know how long before we could get our bags. She apologized for the problem and said, "I'm sorry but we can't delay the flight. You need to board the plane now." We ran back to Randall and he was still working on the lock but nothing. Dwight tried again.

"This is the last call for Flight 233 to Harrisburg, Pennsylvania. All passengers must now be boarding."

Randall said, "You two go ahead and get on the plane since you have your tickets. You can at least be there to get our bags and let them know what happened. I'll try to get there when I can and bring our stuff."

Dwight and I looked at him and said in unison, "Are you sure?"

"Yes, go or you will miss it!"

Dwight and I ran to the door of the air bridge and the ticket taker asked if we had gotten our things.

"No, but our friend is going to bring them once he gets it unlocked," Dwight said.

She gave us a sympathetic smile and handed back our ticket stubs and we hustled down the air bridge to get on the plane. It felt almost like being naked getting on the plane without our carry-on bags and especially our passports. We made it back to our coach seats and settled in, fastening our seatbelts. At the same time, we stopped and took a deep breath, looking at the empty seat between us and a sinking feeling hit us both. *What did we just do? We just left Randall all alone in the Chicago airport.*

"What were we thinking?" Dwight said with this stunned look on his face.

"I don't know. I guess we panicked. We didn't have time to think, only react," I said.

We sat for a few minutes lamenting over what had just happened and feeling guilty for leaving Randall alone in the airport. Over the intercom the pilot welcomed us aboard, asked us to fasten our seatbelts, said we would be leaving soon, and told the flight attendant to secure the door.

Once in the air, the seatbelt sign went off. Guilt continued to plague us as we were chastising ourselves for leaving Randall. To our total surprise, Randall strolled back to greet us. *What the heck!* The grin on his face was priceless and I'm sure the shock on ours was to him also.

"Holy cow! What happened?" I gasped in shock, as if seeing a ghost.

"Well, right after you left I thought to myself, *Dang they just up and left me here all alone, even though I insisted you go.*" He laughed and went on, "I said a little prayer and slammed the locker with my hand and tried the key one more time and heck if it didn't unlock. Guess a guardian angel was looking over my shoulder. I grabbed the bags and took off running for the gate. I was huffing and puffing while carrying our three bags and jackets."

We laughed, teasing him that he must have looked like O.J. Simpson in the Hertz rent-a-car commercial where O.J. was hurdling luggage and dodging people running through the airport.

"When I got to the desk, the lady was smiling and said your friends are on the flight already, I think I can still get you on board. I smiled back at her out of breath and she said 'Come on!' and we ran down the jet bridge. They were just shutting the door when she shouted for them to hold for one more passenger. She smiled at me and said, 'Have a safe flight.' Then she handed me my ticket."

"Man, that's amazing," Dwight said. "We were just talking about how bad we felt leaving you and couldn't believe we had done that."

"It's okay, I told you to go," Randall replied as he handed us our camera bags and jackets. "I still can't believe that locker opened up. The cute ticket taker helped get me on board and even bumped me to first class. It was divine intervention."

We all laughed and enjoyed the rest of the way to Harrisburg, Randall with his well-deserved first-class ticket. Thankfully we had no further incidents. Our first unplanned orientation lesson showed us to have a little faith in the worst of circumstances. To this day, Randall often shares this story as an example of answered prayer.

Chapter 6
Orientation

Orientation training was an interesting experience to say the least. Everett was already there when we arrived and it was great to see a familiar face in the crowd. The gathering of new volunteers was quite an eclectic group from all over the United States and Canada. I discovered to my relief that not all Mennonites were blond, blue-eyed Adonises and I wasn't the only non-Mennonite in the large group of recruits, though there were only a handful of us.

Ken, who was going with us to Guatemala, was also not Mennonite. However, there definitely was a bond amongst the Mennonites and it was easy to see how their faith had led them to this orientation. It was fun watching them play what we called the "Mennonite Game" as they made connections based on last names and locales.

I had learned over the years from knowing Randall and his Mennonite friends that there are, as he would say, "many flavors" of Mennonites with all different beliefs and fascinating history. While most Mennonites are more similar to other protestant groups, others are extremely conservative in their beliefs. Originally the faction that broke off from the Catholic church was known as Anabaptists, which includes Mennonites, Mennonite Brethren, Amish, and many other groups. It was interesting being from outside the Mennonite community to learn of the variations of beliefs. Some of the Mennonite women wear head coverings to go along with scripture while others do not. Other women will only wear dresses while others are okay with pants. Even more conservative are the black bumper Mennonites. They drive cars but paint their chrome bumpers black because the silver chrome is too worldly. The Amish are the most conservative of all, still using horse and buggy.

We met Rich shortly after we arrived in Akron and he welcomed all of us to the orientation. The group was made up of thirty-eight men and women who were going to be spread out in all parts of the world. There were a few couples who had small children as well. Randall and I met the three others traveling to Guatemala with us.

First we met Ken from Arizona via California and British Columbia. He was going to be leaving with us from Pennsylvania. He was a year younger than me, but he seemed older and wiser. He was brilliant and had graduated with an engineering degree by the time he was twenty years old. My first impression of him was he seemed like an extremely nice, intelligent, and quirky guy.

Ken stood about 5′ 6″ and had curly, reddish-brown hair. His mutton chop sideburns almost formed a beard but not quite as he had shaved his chin as a safety measure since beards were then associated with the leftist movement in Central America. It was kind of the Hugh Jackman look in *X-Men* except Ken had a big, bushy, reddish moustache and wore glasses. He often wore a cowboy-style hat with curled up side brims. He looked like he had just left a safari with his vest and pants with many pockets to hold all the necessities to survive in the jungle. Ken had been raised by Wycliffe Missionary parents who were Bible translators. While growing up, he got to experience many different cultures. Even at his younger age, he was way more prepared to be tackling this new environment than I was.

The assignment Ken was given would have him living alone in a totally different part of Guatemala from Randall and me. He seemed to be okay with that and said he was used to being by himself, having been raised a missionary kid. With him as part of our little Guatemalan traveling band of characters, we realized he was a huge asset to our survival.

Ken was already fluent in Spanish and knew some of a couple other languages. None of the other four of us knew much Spanish so his ability would be very helpful traveling through Mexico and once we got to Guatemala. However, while Ken's multilingual ability was amazing, there was one little hitch. He told us he had a slight stuttering problem that seemed to surface when he was nervous or stressed.

Carman and Carolyn, the young married couple, completed our little group. They were a lovely, fun couple from Canada. During orientation, we enjoyed the opportunity to get to know them. They were also just out of college. We were a young group and had no idea what was ahead of us. Randall and I were excited to have them join us on the long drive. We knew they would be fun travel companions. Carman was always cracking jokes and laughing and Carolyn had a witty, dry sense of humor that made us all laugh. They were both very blond-haired like Randall. *More blonds.* Also, Carman's blond hair was an Afro, which was quite popular in the late '70s and made his 6' 3" height appear much taller than mine. The one thing I sort of had going for me was my brown hair, though it was so curly I definitely couldn't pass for a tall Guatemalan ladino. We were all going to stick out like sore thumbs in Guatemala.

We quickly bonded with all the other MCC volunteers and over the week developed strong friendships. When we were finished with our daily classes, we would break into groups to chat, go running, or play games. Several of those I met became pen pals. Over the years we exchanged many letters and compared our experiences of one country to another. These friendships became even more important to share the highs and lows we dealt with that no one else would truly understand. One friendship was with Sandy, a woman going to Haiti with Dwight. She was a nurse and such a happy person. Her laugh was contagious. Others included a woman named Debbie and a man named Rick who were going to Brazil with Everett. We wrote and had hoped to travel to each other's countries one day.

Everett became my closest friend. We hung out together and would go running in the late afternoon after sitting through orientation meetings all day. Over the time we were with MCC, Everett and I stayed in touch and wrote back and forth. It was always a pleasant surprise to get one of the yellow and green airmail envelopes from Brazil. I wrote letters to so many people over the time I was in Guatemala but Everett was the one person I could really open up to and share the good times and emotional struggles because he was going through the same thing.

I never had anything compared to what he wrote in one letter a year and a half after he arrived in Brazil. He, along with three other MCC volunteers, contracted infectious hepatitis. He became really sick and was in bed for ten days and in recovery for almost four weeks. We always wrote about visiting one another, but it was pretty expensive to fly from Recife to Guatemala City. On our MCC salaries, we never made the trip.

One activity that was the highlight of our orientation was going to visit a working Amish farm. The Akron area was a huge Mennonite and Amish community. The leaders of our orientation loaded us into vans and off we went to the Amish farm. I knew there were Amish families in central Kansas but I had never been on one of their farms. The closest I had been to an Amish person was seeing a man and wife in their horse-drawn buggy going down the highway when I went to the Kansas State Fair in Hutchinson.

I learned that similar to Mennonites, the Amish have many different "flavors" as well. Some Amish groups only use hook-and-eye clasps instead of zippers in their clothing. One Amish group might believe it is wrong to use gas engines on farm equipment and use only horses. Ken said, "Actually, the prohibition was on traction. However, it was ok to have a gasoline engine to run equipment but not tractors or other conveyances. That was my understanding from the explanation I was given."

Interestingly enough, the farm we visited during the orientation did not believe in any vehicles using rubber tires. All the farm equipment had iron wheels except the baler. Our host had apologized for that, explaining that he had just purchased the baler and had the steel tires on order but that they were not ready yet. They only used horses to pull their equipment; ironically, on the hay baler there was a gas engine that ran the baler to make the square bales of hay. The bales of hay were pushed onto the trailer connected to the baler and all being pulled by the team of horses. It was quite different from our hay baler pulled by tractor to make big round bales on our farm back in Kansas. We had a great time helping load the hay on the trailer and then stacking the hay in the barn.

The purpose for visiting the farm was to help us understand different belief systems and to be tolerant without pushing off our own beliefs. This would be important working with people in our new countries where they had different beliefs and customs. I liked the fact MCC was emphasizing we were going to help people, not change them.

To some people, the different little idiosyncrasies various groups hold and believe wholeheartedly might seem totally ludicrous. But our lesson was to not judge one man's belief versus our own. It wasn't our place to make fun of or ridicule another just because they might think differently. This was a very valuable lesson and important to follow when heading to a new culture and our future homes, working with such diverse populations. It is something I wish more people would experience and learn.

The rest of our orientation was preparing us for things we would encounter, such as culture shock, when going to a Third World country. The first time I had even heard of culture shock was when Rich asked me in the interview about my understanding and then at the summer training seminar we had attended in Kansas. I was also learning about something called "reverse culture shock" that we most likely would face coming back home after living in a Third World country. In addition, we were told things to do to keep ourselves healthy and things to avoid. For example, we needed to be careful buying food from vendors off the street and avoid drinking unboiled water. Something we might pick up called "amoebas" would not be our friend.

The leaders of MCC shared their policies and how we were to represent the organization. I found the most helpful part when we heard from MCC volunteers who had lived in different corners of the world. They shared about their experiences and all the kinds of things they had done. I was amazed to learn about all the good work MCC did across the United States and the rest of the world. For example, I never knew about the MCC Mobile Meat Canner that travels through the United States and Canada.

MCC Volunteers donate and help prepare cans of turkey, beef, chicken, and pork to be sent around the world. Over 30,000 people a year volunteer to fill, weigh, wash, and label every can. In one year, MCC canned 829,778 pounds of meat. They ship it to countries like Ethiopia, Democratic People's Republic of Korea (North Korea), Haiti, Ukraine, Zambia, and even the United States, including Puerto Rico. Mennonites aren't ones to boast of what they do, so their great works for mankind are seldom heard of by the general public.

The last day we took our group photo and it was time for people to be leaving for their future homes. We exchanged mailing addresses, said our goodbyes to Dwight, Sandy, Debbie, Rick, Everett and all the others in our orientation group. The newest MCCers were leaving directly for the airport with their two suitcases for their new destinations. Earlier in the week everyone discovered that we would be driving to Guatemala, which allowed us to take more than two suitcases. All were quite jealous of the Guatemala crew. Dwight and Sandy were trying to figure out how to drive a pickup to Haiti.

At the end of orientation, Carman and Carolyn flew home to Canada. They would get their belongings and fly to Dallas in a few days to meet up with the three of us after we made the detour through Kansas. Fortunately for them, they were able to bring a few suitcases to Akron to load into the pickups and then went back home and to get more things to bring to Dallas. Ken was stuck with just what he could bring with him to Akron. But it didn't bother him because he was a minimalist anyway and didn't need to have lots of belongings.

After everyone had left for the airport, Rich said to follow him and led us to the parking lot where we saw the two brand-new, identical Ford pickup trucks, except one was green and the other blue. The trucks had just been tagged and had Pennsylvania license plates on the back with long, identical numbers except for the last, which was one number apart. Little did we fathom this might cause a wee problem down the road.

The back of one of the trucks was already loaded with several boxes and large trunks. One of the boxes was wrapped with metal tape to keep it from being opened and had Nicaragua written on the side. The locked trunks belonged to Rich. It worked out for Rich and Martha to take advantage of the fact we would be driving the pickups so they were sending trunks of clothes and other belongings. Martha knew that if they were going to be there for at least three years, they needed clothes for their two girls to grow into. This was a very unusual situation to be able to send extra belongings, but one they were happy to use to their advantage.

Rich handed us the keys to the pickups. Randall and I each took a set of keys and the three of us jumped in and took off pointing west. For the next couple of days, the three of us would be traveling together on our way to Kansas to collect our belongings to take with us to Guatemala. What do they say, the best way to get to know someone is to travel together. That was about to be tested.

Chapter 7
On the Road to Guatemala

Guatemala City, Guatemala, via Delia, Kansas, starting from Akron, Pennsylvania, is approximately 3500 miles. We figured we could get back to Kansas in two days and would spend the first night in Indianapolis. Whenever we would stop for gas or to just stretch our legs, we would rotate who was in each truck so only one had to ride alone for any length of time.

Not too far into the trip we asked Ken if he wanted to drive. He said he liked to drive but not in cities and especially strange cities. That was fine, Randall and I were happy to do the driving. There would be plenty of wide-open spaces and we knew Carman and Carolyn would soon be joining us to take their turns.

We learned quickly Ken was a sweet and personable guy and truly quirky by his admission. He shared a little about his upbringing by his parents who worked for Wycliffe in Arizona and later California and had briefly lived in Mexico City. He shared that he really hadn't spent much time with people his own age. No wonder he came across more like my parents' age than someone just turned twenty. He was very intellectual and he would have fit right in with Sheldon, Leonard, Howard, and Raj on *The Big Bang Theory* sitcom, my favorite TV show. He had a very different dietary habit than us. When we were wanting to stop and get something to eat, McDonald's was not one of his desired stops. He had developed a strong attitude about corporate America, fast-food chains and greedy capitalism.

Our trip to Kansas was pretty uneventful. We finally reached our farm and my parents got to meet Ken. My mom put out a feast that night. It was going to be a long time before I would be able to have another of my mother's home-cooked meals. Ken said he could get used to this. We spent the night and the next day we loaded my things, including my new backpack and sleeping bag, in the pickup.

We were told to bring a large hiking backpack. Randall and I both purchased identical ones, except mine was blue and his was yellow. The backpack had a u-shape metal bar that rested on the back, a large compartment on the top with a flap and tie, a smaller zippered compartment on the bottom and small pockets on the side. Little did we know at the time how much use we would get from these over the next three years.

After saying our tearful goodbyes, we headed south to Hesston, Kansas. It was not quite a three-hour drive to Randall's home. We got to Randall's folks where we were treated to their warm hospitality and spent the night there. Again, we were fed extremely well by Randall's mom. The next day we loaded Randall's things. We kept the trucks going south and started our trek to Dallas to meet Carman and Carolyn.

It just happened that my sister Jan lived in Arlington, Texas, not too far from DFW airport. That would be our last stop to see family before leaving for Guatemala. We picked up Carman and Carolyn at the airport and Jan put us up for the night. My nephew Bo was just a little over a year and a half. It was great to get to see him before we left. I knew it would be a few years before I would see him again and he would change so much. One more night of home-cooked food from Jan. She definitely had learned well from our mother.

It was time to leave bright and early the next day. It was great having Carman and Carolyn join us so someone didn't have to ride alone. The trip south from Dallas to Laredo was long. The five of us new travel companions spent the night in Laredo before crossing the border to Mexico. The following morning, we made our way to the border in our two pickups and easily passed through customs.

This was only my second trip crossing the border into Mexico since I had my one international experience of going to Tijuana when I was nine. Our family made a trip to Disneyland in California and along the way we stopped in Mexicali, California, to visit some old friends who had moved there from back home. They took us across the border to Tijuana. It was a great family experience. We learned about a whole new way of life.

I remember thinking I was glad I didn't live in those conditions. It was loud and bustling with activity and I couldn't understand a word people were saying, but we had a great time shopping. My sisters weren't thrilled to have to ride all the way home to Kansas with my blue and pink donkey piñata that I begged my folks to buy.

My first border crossing we had the comfort of knowing this was just a day trip and we would be crossing back over to U.S. soil. This second crossing into Mexico at Laredo was a passage into a whole new adventure that was going to last for way more than one day.

Looking back many years later at our little adventure trip from Pennsylvania through Mexico to Guatemala, I wonder how in the heck did we do that. Obviously MCC had complete faith in us. I sure wouldn't have the guts to do it today. It helps to be young and naive.

Of the 3500-mile trek, the last 1500 miles were in two countries where Spanish was spoken. With Ken being the only one in our group to speak Spanish, if something happened and our trucks got separated, we were toast. Again, no cell phones. My one year of Spanish in high school with Mrs. Nelson was about as useful as when my classmates Lisa, Gay and I took calculus independent study. We got A's but I can say we learned "nada." I also had a semester of Spanish in college when I was a freshman but I realized quickly my high school Spanish had not prepared me very well for a college course so I took it credit/no credit and passed, picking up a few words and phrases.

Once I knew I was going to Guatemala, I bought a Spanish dictionary and some books to try and learn some essential Spanish phrases. *¿Cómo estás?* (How are you?) *¿Habla usted Inglés?* (Do you speak English?) *¿Dónde está el baño?* (Where is the bathroom?) Needless to say, I was not going to be our translator.

After spending a year in Holland, Randall was fluent in speaking Dutch. He was very good at picking up languages and had learned a little Spanish that would be helpful, though still not conversational by any means. Carman and Carolyn were as useless with Spanish as I was at this point in our adventure. In this 1500-mile journey, Ken was going to be our translator and lifeline to the Spanish language and culture of Mexico. We were so glad he was part of our group.

Before we left Akron, the director of MCC told the five of us to be cautious when we drove through Mexico to Guatemala City. We were to always stay at hotels that had enclosed courtyards and not to drive at night. We should stop early and find a safe place to stay. This was fine by us.

Once in Mexico the trip was honestly pretty boring, driving through the wide-open desert-like countryside. *And people say western Kansas is boring.* I had never seen so much sand, cacti, and skinny Brahman-type cattle—the kind with floppy ears and humps on their necks. We passed through very few towns of any size. A burro was spotted here and there, some sheep, small pony-size horses, plus lots of goats right along the highway. They didn't even flinch when we buzzed by. Lots of small adobe shacks were scattered off the sides of the road. It was pretty eye-opening to see how these Mexican people lived. This was my first experience as an adult to see what poverty was really like. Even my day trip to Tijuana didn't compare to these living conditions.

The first night of our adventure was spent in a small town called Saltillo at a Holiday Inn. It was nice and had an enclosed parking lot. *So far this is a piece of "pastel" (cake).* Since we had a place to stay that was secure from the outside, we decided we didn't need to unload all the luggage stored in the back of the two pickups. It would have been a total bummer to haul into our rooms all the suitcases and trunks from the back of the two trucks. We really didn't want to have to unload and reload all that stuff at every overnight stop if possible. While in Laredo, we picked up enough food to get us through lunch. Even though we were apprehensive about our first meal in Mexico, we were starving. We agreed to meet in the hotel lobby at 6 o'clock to explore the town and find something to eat. We were so thankful to have Ken as our interpreter when he asked the hotel clerk for a suggestion of a place to eat. The clerk recommended a little restaurant just down the block.

The restaurant was a cute little place and smelled even better. The lights were a little dim but one could still tell the colorful red tile floor was coated with a fine layer of dust. The tables were covered with plastic, red checkerboard tablecloths. Each table had four old chrome chairs with red seat cushions that had seen better days. We pulled a chair from another empty table so we could all sit around one table. The place was deserted except for one couple at a corner table. There was Mexican Óchi band music playing over some sound system we couldn't see.

A sweet little lady came out of the kitchen. She had coal black hair pulled back in a ponytail and was dressed in a turquoise skirt and white blouse with hand-stitched colorful designs. Her smile was contagious and she seemed very happy to have gringos frequent her business. She asked what I assumed was, "What would you like to drink?" I recognized a few words but dang she talked fast. Ken helped us by interpreting. We told him we each just wanted a glass of water. He suggested we each get a bottle of pop saying, "It is hard to say if the water is clean and bottled drinks are safer. We shouldn't risk getting 'Montezuma's revenge' so early in our trip."

After the waitress took our drink order, Ken went on to tell us that most likely the pop wouldn't be chilled. We would be lucky to find chilled drinks or ice and probably didn't want to have the ice anyway, unless we were dining at a nice restaurant. "With what

MCC pays us, that won't be happening any time soon," Carman said and we all laughed.

We ordered enchiladas and the aroma of the food was whetting our appetites even more. When the waitress brought our food, we each had a huge enchilada on our plates. *Wow, is this ever tasty. Better than Taco Tico for sure.* There was a little bowl of picante sauce on the table and Carman shared that he loved picante sauce. Ken warned, "You probably are too much of a gringo to handle real Mexican picante."

Carman sneered that he could handle it and dipped his tortilla in the sauce and took a big bite. In just a few seconds I thought Carman was going to go through the roof. It was almost like a Warner Brothers' cartoon where steam starts pouring out the top of the Looney Tunes character's head. We all burst into laughter as poor Carman grabbed the first bottle he could and downed it. He then took Carolyn's and chugged it, while tears rolled down his face and ours too but from laughter. Lesson learned. *Guess we had better listen to ol' Ken when he warns us.*

We enjoyed the rest of our meal and thanked the lady who served us. She was nice and told us to come back. After stuffing ourselves, we strolled around the town square just to stretch our legs after the long ride in the trucks. We made it back to our hotel and were all pretty exhausted.

I have to admit I was feeling a little anxious about being away from the good old U.S. of A. for the first time. It was such a new experience but I couldn't have been with a better group of people. I am not sure how I would have handled being dropped into a Third World country without the support I had from my four companions. I'm pretty sure Carman, Carolyn, and even Randall felt the same way. This trip was sort of a gentle transition into the new culture.

The following day we left early. We had a schedule and really couldn't dawdle. MCC had given us maps and a timeline where we should be each day. We were given a date and place where we were to meet George, the MCC Country Director, in Guatemala City. There wasn't any way to immediately communicate directly with him if something were to happen. He didn't have a phone where he lived. We did have a phone number to leave a message with someone who could contact him if we needed to reach him. It was a very strange feeling of being isolated and on our own.

Our next destination was Mexico City, one of the largest cities by population and square mileage in the world. Since Ken's parents worked for Wycliffe and had taken Ken to the main Mexico City Wycliffe center called the Summer Institute of Linguistics (SIL), he knew that we could stay there that night for a discounted rate. The center was an enclosed compound and would be a very safe place to stay.

Approaching the huge city, Randall suggested we pull over and get gas before hitting the major traffic. One thing we had thought of was the huge issue that if we got separated, we would never be able to find each other. Again, NO cell phones! NO GPS tracking! We had no way to communicate to find each other if we got lost. To make matters worse, because only Ken spoke Spanish, the truck without him would totally be in a world of trouble if we got split up.

I drove the lead truck with Ken as my navigator. Randall, Carman and Carolyn followed behind. We had predetermined the location of the SIL center on our maps in case we got separated. The plan was that Randall would stay as close as possible and I would avoid going through yellow lights. Randall stayed on our bumper and didn't let anyone get between us. Whenever I saw a stoplight ahead, I would slow down a little and then if the light remained green, we would gas it to make sure we both made it through the light.

The trip through the city was what I envisioned driving in NASCAR would be like. However instead of professional race car drivers, here it was crazed drivers of cars, motorcycles, trucks and buses, all needing to get to their destination before anyone else. *What happened to the slow pace of life in Mexico I had always heard about?* Drivers were dodging and swerving out of lanes to take the lead and cut each other off. Blinkers to indicate lane changes didn't seem to work or were unnecessary in Mexico. If one wanted to get in a different lane, just go for the first small opening. It was the wildest driving I had ever experienced—so far.

After about an hour of this zany ride through the city, which felt more like four or five hours, we made it to the Wycliffe mission and drove up to the gates. Ken spoke to someone in the guard house and they opened the massive iron rod gates. Both trucks proceeded into the massive compound and Ken directed us to the main building where we parked. The trucks were still intact, no dents, dings, or fender benders. We were all in one piece and were ready to get our feet on the ground. My whole body ached from being so tense while driving. Carolyn looked like she had just seen a ghost when she crawled out from her center-seat with a full view of all the action. "That was crazy!" she said.

The Wycliffe compound was a beautiful complex. It was well groomed and more upscale than the buildings and housing we had been observing through the city. Ken and Carman went into the building while we waited outside by the trucks. They returned with keys to two little bungalows where we would be spending the night. Ken, Randall, and I had a suite of two rooms with four beds. Again we hauled just the things we needed and left all the rest of the luggage in the back of the trucks.

We were able to find a place to eat on the compound and they served us a sirloin-like steak that was delicious. They even provided water with ice. *Guess we better enjoy!* Ken, having spent a summer in Mexico City just three years before, still knew his way around the city. He suggested we go see the sights. "Sure," Carolyn said, "but we aren't going to drive, are we? I can't handle another trip like we just had."

Ken assured us he knew a better way. He took us to the bus stop right outside the compound and a bus came by very shortly. He said we would ride until we got to the metro or subway then would take it to the downtown market. The market provided another whole new experience. The best word to describe it was chaos. It was like a giant tin Quonset building used back home for storing hay, but this was like ten times larger than any I had seen before. There were vendor booths with all kinds of goods for sale. Fruits, vegetables, meats, clothes, and even piñatas. The market reeked of rotten food and was filthy.

After spending an hour or so at the market, we tried to get back to the mission by bus but we were too late. Our only alternative mode of transportation was a taxi, which Ken hailed. It and the driver were something else. The car needed to be cleaned inside and out. Hanging from the ceiling in the back window were colorful sheets of plastic with shapes cut out. A crucifix hung from the rearview mirror and a Mother Mary figurine stood proudly on the dashboard, both quite necessary and appropriate when driving in Mexico City.

Imagine you are in a roller derby but you are inside a car instead of on roller skates. We were holding on for dear life as we swerved in and out of traffic. *MCC didn't say anything about not taking taxi rides.* I don't know whether a word was spoken the entire trip to the restaurant other than Ken saying, "*¡De-de-despacio!* (Sl-sl-slow!)" Eventually after about 20 minutes we arrived in one piece. Ken paid the man and we all scrambled to get out of the taxi.

The following day we left the mission, continuing to head south. We stopped in a small village that had Aztec ruins. Knowing we didn't have time to see the ruins, we just walked around the open market. The people were very attractive, more so than in any other part of Mexico we had seen so far. They were also very short, obviously from the indigenous influence. The tallest men we saw were no taller than Ken. We also noticed how all the guys were staring at Carolyn and her blonde hair. She really stood out. It was something she was going to have to get used to in the coming days.

We traveled to our next stop, which was the town of Oaxaca. It turned out to be a terribly long day. We had broken the MCC rule of not driving at night because we couldn't find a place to stay before we got to Oaxaca. There had been a mountain range with winding roads we drove through in the dark and we were dead tired. Thankfully, we found a place with a courtyard. The motel restaurant was closed so we all piled into one truck and went looking for a place to eat.

The town was really a challenge to navigate because all the streets were one-way and they had no stop signs. We eventually found a restaurant and of all things it was a pizza place. They had delicious pizza, not like what we were used to but very good. The cheese was not mozzarella but some kind of goat cheese. Well nourished, we made it back to our hotel and fell fast asleep.

At breakfast we met Ken in the dining room and were aghast by the news he had for us. He was reading the local Spanish newspaper and found out there had been heavy rain that night in the mountains we had just traveled through in the darkness. The roads were closed from mud and rock slides. We said a thankful prayer and knew our guardian angel had been with us. *Thank you once again!*

That day we were supposed to arrive at the Guatemalan border but our plans were changed out of our control. There had been a hurricane that went through the southern edge of Mexico, crossing the Isthmus of Tehuantepec a few weeks before. Because of terrible flooding, the roads were awful with potholes and washed-out ruts for about 30 miles of highway. One could see trash three or four feet high up in the bushes, showing how high the flood water had been.

We drove no more than about 30 mph, dodging potholes the entire leg of the trip. It took forever and our trucks were running low on gas. We didn't see a gas station for miles and we were getting quite nervous. Our guardian angel continued to look out for us because one truck ran out of gas just one hundred yards from a gas station. By the time we got to the town of Arraiga, we were so tired we decided not to go on. We found a nice motel and it was still early evening. Before turning in, we spent time talking about our adventure to date and what we might expect when we entered Guatemala.

The next morning we left very early so we could arrive at the border by noon. How did that old Alka-Seltzer* commercial go? "Plop, plop. Fizz, fizz. Oh, what a relief it is!" Well, what a relief it was to finally reach the Mexican/Guatemalan border.

The Mexican customs people dressed in their soldier fatigues were nice, but it was more official, almost an edgy feel, compared to when we had entered the country from the U.S. With the tense climates of the governments of the Central American countries, there was extreme scrutiny of Americans crossing the border. Thankfully they stamped our passports and we were on our way to Guatemala.

Chapter 8

Bienvenidos a Guatemala
(Welcome to Guatemala)

Once cleared by the Mexican customs, we crossed a bridge over to the Guatemalan customs office. Again, the customs guards were soldiers wielding guns. We had to take EVERYTHING out of the trucks. We unloaded our suitcases, sleeping bags, backpacks, trunks and boxes, including all of Rich and Martha's stuff. These were all lined up clear across the floor of the customs office.

The customs official asked to see what we had inside each to make sure we weren't trying to smuggle something into the country. They opened and started going through all of our suitcases one by one. We started to panic because we didn't have keys to Rich's trunks and didn't know what we were going to do.

After methodically going through most of our personal stuff, they came to the box that had the metal tape strips securing it. They asked us what was in the box but we had no idea. MCC had just sent it with us. The bigger problem was the word "Nicaragua" written across the side. The only thing we knew was that the box was to go with the truck to Honduras and be given to missionaries in Nicaragua. This set off a red flag with the customs soldiers and they started talking faster and seemed more serious.

Nicaragua at the time was having the most severe problems of all the Central American countries. The country had just had a revolution that summer and their corrupt government was taken over by Sandinista guerrilla groups. It was in total turmoil. Guatemala had similar problems, too, but hadn't yet escalated like in Nicaragua. The Guatemalan government was wary of the same thing happening so alarms were going off in the custom guards' heads with our securely taped box.

The soldiers motioned for the top customs official. He asked if we were *guerrilleros* (the "terrorist" groups fighting against the government). Of course Ken told him no. The official demanded we open the box, but we didn't have any way to cut the metal tape. One of the soldiers got some heavy scissors and cut the tape on the box. He opened the box and pulled out a book. It was a Spanish Bible. "*¡Ah, misioneros* (missionaries)!*" the official said and started laughing. We nodded, smiling as Ken showed them his Spanish Bible and said, "*Si, somos misioneros* (Yes, we are missionaries)."

The official said they could stop searching and motioned for us to go ahead and reload our belongings onto the trucks. The soldiers were just getting to Rich's trunks at this point, and we collectively let out a huge sigh of relief, not having to explain why the trunks were locked and we couldn't open them. They would have broken the locks just to find children's clothing. *Once again, our angel is looking over our shoulders.*

The customs official stamped our passports. Later we discovered the infatuation Guatemalans had for stamps and how they stamped everything to make things appear official. Once the trucks were reloaded, the soldiers had to fumigate them. *That's a pleasant smell, NOT!* We had to endure the chemical fumes the rest of the trip. The soldiers told us we could leave and to be careful of guerrilleros. In all, it was over an hour before we could get on our way to Guatemala City.

About twenty miles from the border, we noticed cars being pulled over to the side of the road. There were several armed men in military camouflage clothing out in the road, stopping traffic. We were terrified especially after the accusation and warning at the customs office. We had no idea if these were government military men or if they were guerrilleros stopping people. The men all had automatic rifles and pointed at the cars to pull over.

Randall and Carman were driving and maneuvered our trucks over to the side of the road. Randall was in the lead truck with me in the middle and Ken by the passenger window. One of the men came up to Ken's side of the truck and started shouting at him in rapid fire. The man was pointing his rifle at Ken and asking what we *gringos* were doing there. The little problem Ken had getting words out when nervous or upset rose to the surface. This was not a good time. *Stay calm, Ken.*

Ken was trying to explain we were missionaries. He was struggling to get his words out. It must have come across like he was lying and nervous. Two other men were looking at our trucks from the front. One motioned to the man talking to Ken that we didn't have license plates in the front. In Guatemala they had plates on the front and back. Our Pennsylvania trucks only had them in the back. They asked if we had stolen the trucks. Ken tried to explain we were from the United States and we didn't have front plates there.

Then the two men went to the back of the trucks and started shouting to each other the license plate numbers. Because our plates had the very same long numbers except the last digit, they thought we had taken off a front plate from one truck and put it on the back of the second truck. It took some more explanation from Ken saying we were missionaries and showing his Spanish Bible before they believed us. As it turned out, they were government soldiers not guerrilleros. Once they determined we were missionaries, they bid us on our way saying, "*¡Bienvenidos a Guatemala!* (Welcome to Guatemala!)" *Yeah, quite a welcome.*

Chapter 9

Don Jorge

Shaken from our encounter with the armed soldiers, we were ready to get to our destination in Guatemala City. It was a little over 150 miles to the city. Entering Guatemala was like being in a green paradise compared to our path through Mexico. The countryside was beautiful with mountain ranges and lots of trees.

There seemed to be people everywhere. Men were working in the fields on the steep slopes of the mountainsides. People were walking along the side of the road. The women carried huge baskets on their heads while men carried loads of wood or bags of produce on their backs. *Wow! How strong these Guatemalan people are.*

Immediately one of the things we noticed different from the Mexican people was the beautiful dress of the women. The Mayan influence was definitely still present. The colors of the blouses and skirts the women wore were amazing. Some of the men in this part of the country also still wore the traditional Mayan attire but mostly they had on western style clothes.

Upon reaching Guatemala City, we had been told to drive to the Central American Mission (CAM) headquarters located at the Central American Theological Seminary (SETECA) in the heart of the city. It was sort of a safe haven for American missionaries, where the new MCC Country Director George (or *Jorge* as known in Spanish) would meet us.

Seeing Guatemala City, it became apparent just how poor the country was. In 1976 there had been a huge earthquake that totally devastated much of the country and especially Guatemala City. Over 22,000 people were killed. The destruction was still very evident with homeless people on the sidewalks, rumpled shacks and buildings unrepaired.

After having driven some 20 minutes in the city, we decided we had better stop, find a phone, and try to call George. Imagine to our surprise to find out that we had stopped just a few blocks from SETECA! Once we found and entered the SETECA compound it was like going through a portal from a war zone into Shangri-La. The grounds were well manicured and the facility was modern. It was hard to fathom such a dichotomy.

George was waiting for us and it was great to finally get to meet him. He was Canadian and had been with MCC since about 1972. He had lived and worked in Bolivia, Mexico, and Guatemala. He first came to Guatemala in 1976 after the earthquake to help build houses. He had come back to visit about a year before we arrived. The only country representative at that time had to leave suddenly and asked George to stay while he was gone and until his replacement could be found.

Besides all the paperwork for MCC and helping to find us places to live and work, a big part of what George did was to collect loan money from those who MCC had helped build houses. The money was to go back to the community cooperative to help others build houses and for community development. He spent a lot of time traveling the country and had a good understanding of the people.

George was a unique individual to say the least. First he was extremely tall, at about six-foot-eight, and a gangly fellow. He was three or four inches taller than Carman and me. He had a great smile and it was obvious he had no fashion sense and cared not. He shared he liked to have his clothes made by local tailors, who stitched out their meager living with their trade.

Most of the *campesino* (Spanish term used for the farmers or poorer people) men's clothing was made by tailors in the country, not store bought. Denim was too costly so no blue jeans. The material was mostly an inexpensive cotton polyester blend and could make a nice pair of pants or a shirt at a low cost. George, being such a tall guy, obviously didn't spend much time with the tailor getting fitted. Let's just say he often would have done okay in high water. Add the plaid fabric (probably the cheapest) he sometimes chose for his pants, he made quite a sight. Though I can't say much, thinking back to my college days and my plaid bell bottom pants.

We had a meal at the mission and stayed up late talking with George about our trip and our future work. After our long drive and unsettling encounter earlier in the day, we were exhausted and our beds were quite welcome.

For our first morning in Guatemala, George had our day planned. He started by taking us around the city to see the sights. The *Palacio Nacional de la Cultura*—also known as the *"Palacio Verde* (Green Palace due to its green color)—was beautiful and the President's headquarters. We saw a large Catholic church that was nearly destroyed by the earthquake and was being rebuilt. One of the coolest things was a giant relief map of the country. It was a 3-D map almost 20,000 square feet and originally built in 1904–1905 and showed the topography of the land with mountains, volcanoes and rivers. When it rained, the water ran down the map where it would in reality.

There were beautiful skyscrapers that hadn't been affected by the quake. Not even a window broken. Obviously, they had some great engineers in the country. It was quite an unexpected sight to see Pizza Huts, McDonalds and Kentucky Fried Chickens in the downtown area. After our trip from the border through the backcountry to Guatemala City, it seemed so out of place to see these "American" restaurants.

There were hotel chains, movie theater billboards, Chinese restaurants, and clothing stores. It was like any American city's downtown in many ways. The *Teatro Nacional* (National Theatre) was breathtaking with its incredible architecture and green and blue striped walls.

George wanted to show us the "wealthy" side of the city as well as the poor to illustrate the disparity. Sections of the city had mansions behind protective walls where the rich enjoyed the best that life had to offer. It was quite a contrast to the mass of people living in squalor in the rest of the city and outlying areas. George emphasized how the vast majority of the people were extremely poor and a very small minority of rich people controlled the country and wealth. There wasn't much of a middle class.

In the early evening we headed to George's house, which was in a small town outside Guatemala City called Chimaltenango. It was about twenty miles, as a crow flies, but the winding mountainous road was just over thirty miles long. We couldn't fit into the one pickup that was remaining in Guatemala. The other truck was left at the mission for a person from MCC Honduras to arrive to retrieve it. George said Carolyn and Ken would ride with him in the truck and he asked Carman, Randall, and me to take the bus. Another new experience. It was like a regular school bus back in the states but painted all kinds of colors.

The bus driver looked about eighteen. Being so small in stature, it seemed he could barely reach the accelerator, clutch and brake without standing. Later we noticed some of the drivers had a wooden block attached with a string to the accelerator so they could reach it. *Now that is scary!*

The driver's helper, who looked even younger, hung out the door watching for people flagging the bus to stop and taking their money as the passengers got on board. As we moved down the road, the bus would often swerve off to the side of the road (our knuckles white from holding on so tight to the back of the seat in front) and make a quick stop to pick up passengers or for those who shouted out when they wanted to be dropped off.

We were packed in and the three gringos were definitely the center of attention. For the most part, the people were polite. We noticed the ladinos would look at us then just ignore us while the indigenous people were more inclined to stare at these strange people. The little kids were pointing fingers and smiling at us. It was a strange, uncomfortable experience and brought a reality to what it felt like to be in the minority for once.

Since none of us spoke but a few words of Spanish, George had given us exact directions and told us to keep our eyes open for a gas station where we were to get off. We definitely had kept our eyes peeled. When we saw our landmark, we shouted "¡Alto!" like the others had shouted when wanting off. Were we ever elated to get our feet on solid ground! With all the "stop and go," it had taken us about an hour-and-half to get to our destination. The pickup gang made it in about 45 minutes. I'm not sure who was happier, Carman or Carolyn, to see the other after the rides each had taken.

The house in Chimaltenango where George lived had been rented by the previous MCC worker. It was a nice, simple two-bedroom house but still more modern than where George wanted to live. He had put in solar panels to have hot water so as not to use as much electricity. He was very conscientious about living a simple life and seemed embarrassed to be living in this *casa de lujo* (house of luxury) as he put it. He preferred to live with the people but MCC rented this house for the time being.

MCC owned a little yellow Toyota car that was way too small for George's long body, or any of us taller gringos as far as that goes. When he climbed out with his long legs and arms, it appeared he had to unfold himself. At one point he had the five of us join him on a short trip and we were packed in the car. It reminded me of one of the clown acts at the circus when a gaggle of clowns emerged from a tiny car.

However, George's preferred mode of travel was by motorcycle because it consumed less gas. Picture a near seven-foot-tall skinny man getting on a little Yamaha dirt bike motorcycle. He lifted his extremely long leg over the bike and pulled down the round goggles off his helmet. He'd kick start the bike and put his size fourteen shoes on the little pedals. Knees and elbows were sticking way out to the side and his brown or plaid pants rode up to mid-calf. He just needed a round red nose. It was quite a spectacle to see.

It didn't take us long to figure out that George was a talker. Maybe it was the fact he hadn't had anyone to speak English with in a long time. He was fluent in German, which accounted for his slight accent. He was also fluent in Spanish but he would never be truly accepted as Guatemalan even after years living there. Having us there to talk to, he made up for lost time. One bit of news George shared was that right after Christmas, we would all get together for a retreat at an ocean resort in southern Guatemala. *Now that's exciting! I can't wait to see the ocean!*

Mennonite Central Committee and Eastern Mennonite Board were going to hold a joint retreat with all Central American workers. George billed it as a way for the two groups to build unity and work together. There would be a guest spiritual speaker and time to meet workers from the other countries of Honduras, El Salvador, and Nicaragua. This was definitely something for us to look forward to after four months of language training.

George had fascinating stories to tell. However, it wasn't long before we were exhausted physically from the travel during our sightseeing tour and mentally from his prolific sharing. We just wanted to go to bed. He was quite an imposing figure and our new leader, so none of us felt we could interject that we just wanted to get some sleep. It wasn't until Carolyn fell asleep from total exhaustion that she and Carman were able to go to bed because they fortunately had one of the bedrooms.

Ken, Randall, and I would sleep on the wooden sofas with foam cushions George covered with blankets. These "beds" were out in the main room of the house so there was no escaping George and his stories until he decided to call it a night. We were up into the wee hours. The following day continued with George's version of MCC orientation. He took us to a small village and to a farm to see some of his projects. Everywhere we stopped the people would run to say. "¡Hola, Don Jorge!" A man of respect was referred to as *Don* in Spanish. The children adored him and would grab onto his long legs. It was amazing to see the warmth they showed toward him and realize the impact he was having on lives.

One proud man wanted to show us the solar shower with hot water that Don Jorge had helped him to build. The shower stall was a four-sided, wooden frame with plastic for curtains on each side, just big enough for one person. For the shower mechanism, it was amazing what one could do with a large tin can, some rubber tubing, a clamp, and a wooden box lined with black plastic.

These parts were all assembled and placed at the top of the shower stall. Water was added to the wooden box overhead. The black plastic not only held the water but also caused the sun's rays to quickly heat the water. A rubber tube inserted in a hole at the bottom of the plastic was taped to make it watertight. The warm water flowed through the rubber tube into the tin can with holes in the bottom. A clamp on the rubber tube served as the means to start and stop the flow of water. *Quite ingenious!*

The temp of the shower was directly related to how much sunshine there was that day. On extremely sunny days, cool water had to be added to the box because the water was so hot.

We also saw large cement storage containers used for water or grain. We had been told about these at the appropriate technology seminar at Bethel College that summer. It was fun to see one in use. This was on our list of things to try and hopefully teach others about in our future home.

George took us to a rug maker that made beautifully hand-sewn woolen Mayan rugs. Guatemalan rugmakers dyed the material themselves and created incredible printed patterns on their rugs. They were made from burlap and then cut yarn hooked into beautiful Mayan figures and designs. The rug maker sold these in the markets and a small one about 2 ft. by 5 ft. cost $14.

To help provide more income for the Guatemalan people, MCC was trying to get handmade products like these to the United States to be sold. When there was a demand, MCC would pay the craftsman for their wares then ship the goods to the States to be sold in stores. All profit went to the craftsmen.

The following day George wanted to take us back to the city to run some errands. He decided we should take the pickup and had three of us pile into the back end. Not a good decision. We were stopped by a policeman on a motorcycle just as we got close to the city. Pulling over, George said, "This isn't good because I don't have an important document I need." *Oh, great!*

After our previous experience with the military stopping us, we were definitely nervous. But in perfect Don Jorge style, he just went through his billfold—it was about an inch thick—and proceeded to show the officer every paper and card he had. After a while the guy got tired of Don Jorge's rambling and told us to get on down the road. *Disaster averted. New lesson learned.*

Chapter 10
Heading to Our New Home

Our third full day in Guatemala was a travel day. The six of us were going to San Pedro Carchá, where Randall and I would be working, to meet the American missionaries with Eastern Mennonite Board. This part of the country was called *Alta Verapaz,* which loosely translated means "Mountains of True Peace." There were over a quarter of a million people living in this remote mountain region.

The indigenous people in this area were the K'ekchi' and just one of twenty-one different Mayan indigenous tribes. Each tribe spoke its own language though there were similarities and common words. Cross over a mountain and there was a good chance one wouldn't be able to communicate because of the language difference. We would be learning the K'ekchi' language.

Heading to our new home, we followed our leader George to take the bus from Chimaltenango to Guatemala City. Since Randall and I would be staying, we had lugged all our suitcases, backpacks and other belongings, including large pieces of foam for mattresses George had bought for us. These were rolled up and wrapped in plastic in case of rain, always a possibility.

Once in the city, our bus meandered through the crowded streets until George shouted "Alto." We departed the bus, unloaded all of our stuff, and carried it a short distance to our next stop. This was the bus station to catch the bus going to the city of Cobán, the capital of *Departamento de* (department or state of) *Alta Verapaz.*

George bought our tickets and we chuckled at the precision and authority the person selling the tickets had in stamping our tickets with his official stamp. Again, everything had to be stamped in Guatemala to be official. We had a little wait for the bus since everything ran on Guatemalan time. The bus arrived and it was similar to the other colorful bus we rode earlier but this one was painted solid green with the word "Cobán" written above the windshield.

Randall and I joined everyone else in loading our things on top of the bus with all the other cargo, including crates of chickens and produce. Once we had our belongings loaded, the driver ordered Randall and me to get on the bus. We thought we would save seats for the other four while they stood outside waiting to get on.

The driver's helper came on board and removed two rows of seats. The driver boarded the bus—and to our panic—took off, leaving the others back at the bus station. *What the hell! What's happening?* Randall and I moved together in one seat since we figured the others had missed their chance.

After about thirty minutes driving through the back streets of the city, we pulled up to *El Mercado Central* (The Central Market). This was the largest city market in Guatemala City. Talk about a zoo. People. Buses. Animals. Produce. Noise. Smells. Pandemonium. Travelers had to pay close attention to find the right bus amongst the deluge and there didn't seem to really be any kind of schedule. Just take off when the bus was full. We weren't about to get off our bus.

The driver and helper began loading more passengers on the bus and it was getting pretty full. The owners of the buses had devised a pretty slick trick to get more people on board. They pulled the bench seats in toward the center aisle, leaving a gap between the seats and another by the walls. This allowed one more passenger in each row. Depending on the size of the people, three, four or five would be on each side and there was someone standing between the two seats, the space being just wide enough for one leg. The passenger standing had to face to the side to be able to get both legs between the seats.

Once the driver's helper had the bus full to his satisfaction, he pushed back the ones still trying to get on the bus and the driver shut the door. Off we went, wild eyed and wondering where we were going next. The answer was back to the bus station where we had started. Once there, the driver and helper replaced the two rows of seats removed earlier and loaded the other passengers still at the station. George, Ken, Carman, and Carolyn got on board—finding seats in the front seats earlier removed—and we just shrugged, knowing our attempt to save seats had been futile. The bus was filled to capacity. I imagine we were a little over the manufacturer-posted capacity by at least twenty people.

The trip to Cobán took about nine hours (ten hours for Randall and me with our little detour), winding up and around the mountain sides. We thought the taxi ride in Mexico City was wild. The roads were two-lane highways with blind spots around every winding turn on the mountain. The buses just honked their horns and pulled out to pass whenever a slower truck or bus was in front. There was no such thing as a slow lane and I guess there was a shortage of yellow paint to show no passing zones. There wasn't anything like a guardrail on the curves to keep people from driving off the side of the mountain. But the Department of Transportation did put large rocks about the size of pumpkins along the shoulder of the road overlooking the steep canyon below. *Now that's reassuring!*

We stopped at every little town along the way to drop off passengers and pick up new ones. Each stop would have vendors, usually women and children, running up to the bus with their goods to sell. People would reach out the windows to buy tortillas, mangos, or *helados*—which translates to ice cream but in this case were homemade popsicles of frozen juice or fruit drink on a stick. Another popular item to our amazement was Coca-Cola·. The vendors would offer the parched travelers a Coke. I was expecting a chorus of singers from the TV commercial to pop out at any time from behind the huts at the bus pitstop and start singing—*I want to buy the world a Coke and keep it company.*

Interestingly though, the buyers didn't get the iconic bottle with a red and white Coke label. The vendors opened the bottle, poured the warm brown liquid into a plastic bag, put a colorful plastic straw in it, and held the bag up for the thirsty buyer to grab. The bottles had too much value for the vendors that could be returned for cash.

A couple hours into the trip there was a region where we went down in altitude and it was more arid with the landscape not as green. It looked more like parts of Mexico. The temperature in the bus climbed and we began to sweat and were uncomfortable. Needless to say, the bus was more odiferous. It didn't take long though and we began another ascent up the mountain.

Once we made it past the drier region, the mountains were breathtaking. Never back in Kansas was it ever this green. Along the route were valleys with fincas with pastures and cattle grazing. Waterfalls and rivers were everywhere. This part of Guatemala certainly lived up to its name "The Land of Eternal Spring." Other areas had thick forests and vegetation. We passed a sign that read *Biotopo del Quetzal.* George informed us that this was a national park reserve for the preservation of the Guatemalan national bird, the resplendent quetzal.

This quetzal is mostly green in color with a very long tail. The tips of the bird's wings are black and the breast is deep red in color. It is a magnificent bird and rarely seen in nature. We were told the bird would not thrive in captivity and there are only two zoos where they can be seen, ZooMAT in Chiapas, Mexico, and Zoo Ave in Costa Rica.

The currency in Guatemala is also called the quetzal, named after the beautiful bird. Every paper denomination of money has the bird's image shown in flight. It is said that in ancient Mayan culture, the tail feathers of the quetzal birds were used as currency.

After hours of sitting, we finally arrived in Cobán, a city with a population of about 45,000. It was a beautiful Spanish colonial style city with cobblestone streets; stucco walls lined the streets with homes behind colorful doors. The bus went around a large municipal building located in the center of the town square and pulled up beside a green building that matched our bus. The red lettering told us we had reached the bus station. The Cobánites disembarked, a whole new slew piled on the bus, and we took off for our final destination, arriving in about twenty minutes in San Pedro Carchá.

Chapter 11
San Pedro Carchá

Once we reached San Pedro Carchá, we were never so happy to get off that bus and stretch our legs. Later to our dismay and our sore bottoms, we learned that there was a bus company called Guatemala Escobar with air-conditioned buses called Pullmans These were old Greyhound buses that ran from Guatemala City to Carchá. The price was a little more (something like $5 versus $2) and most compesinos didn't have the extra money for the Pullman. These buses traveled directly without all the stops and took about three and a half hours in comparison to what we had just endured.

George refused to take the luxurious mode of transportation since the compesinos couldn't afford it, thus we had taken the "chicken bus"—as this mode of transportation was affectionately called in reference to all the chickens carried on board and loaded in crates on top of the buses.

San Pedro Carchá was a quaint city but much smaller than Cobán with about 10,000 people. One of the first landmarks to see was the beautiful cement bridge painted white that crossed the river, which ran through the city. Once over the bridge, buses and cars had to go up a steep hill where the road changed from asphalt to intricately shaped cement blocks placed closely together.

After climbing the hill, we reached the city square filled with shops and Spanish style buildings. The pink color of the stucco administration buildings and *Banco de Guatemala* was quite different from buildings one would see in the States. Adding to the uniqueness was the soldiers with machine guns in hand stationed in front of the buildings. Something we definitely weren't used to back home.

It must have been quite a spectacle at the town square when the six gringos exited the bus. Our stuff was unloaded from the top of the bus and dumped into a pile. Collecting all of our belongings, including the foam mattresses, the six of us looked like packrats loaded down to the max. I believe with George being such a minimalist, he was a little embarrassed at all of the possessions we had. We started for one of the EMB missionaries' houses with George in the lead and the rest of us looking like his five ducklings following behind in a line. There is no doubt we were the talk of the town.

A great feast was prepared that first night as the EMB missionaries welcomed the MCC team and invited us to stay in their homes. We learned there were three couples living in Carchá. The EMB director was Bob and his wife, Sandy. They had two young children, a boy and a girl. Two other couples were Millard and Priscilla and Larry and Helen. Millard and Priscilla had two daughters. Larry and Helen had a boy and two girls. Each couple lived in a nice Spanish-style home that would be considered a low middle-class home in U.S. terms.

The couples had all lived in Guatemala for several years and had established many churches and were in the midst of building a Bible Institute to provide training for K'ekchi' pastors.

A fourth couple, Daryl and Rhoda, had two very young children. They lived in an area north of Carchá called Cahabón. This was a new outreach in a remote area. They had not been in Cahabón very long. They only came back to Carchá about once a month when supplies were needed. The people there raised the best peanuts in that area and Daryl always brought us huge bags of peanuts to eat.

In addition to the couples, there were three single EMB missionary ladies living in Carchá. Debbie and Linda were nurses and held clinics providing medicine and checkups for the indigenous people while also training locals to be health promoters in the remote c'alebals. The third roommate was Ruth who was a literacy worker. She taught reading to adults. Ruth was home on leave but would be returning soon.

The EMB K'ekchi' work started with agriculture and literacy. Larry worked with chicken projects. There were Volunteer Service (VS) personnel who worked in agriculture. Unfortunately, the VS program closed. The missionaries wanted to have a holistic ministry from the beginning. Prior to going to Alta Verapaz, they approached the Guatemalan government and the government officials very much encouraged EMB to work in agriculture and later in health. Sandy was the first nurse who set up a clinic in the c'alebal *Cojaj*.

Debbie and Linda felt that MCC had more resources to offer. Due to lack of volunteer service people and MCC's experience in development, it was decided that it would be a stronger ministry if both agencies (with their strengths) would work together. Thus, EMB contacted MCC and we were added to their team.

It was difficult for George to be on board 100% with the EMB living arrangements because his belief was to be able to minister to people, one had to live with the people. He didn't want us to live in a house in the city but to live in a remote area with the K'ekchi'. Part of the negotiations when MCC signed on board to work with EMB was that Randall and I would eventually live with the people in a c'alebal and not in Carchá. But first we had to learn the language.

Before we arrived in Guatemala, George and Bob had made arrangements with two local K'ekchi' families to have Randall and me live with them during the time we were in language study. We were not going to be working in Spanish but solely in K'ekchi'. What better way to learn the language than to live with a K'ekchi' family and be submerged in daily life. George had paid the families to build rooms for us onto their homes and we would pay them a monthly rent for room and board.

George and Bob went with us to check out the rooms and families where we would be living. I can't say I was totally prepared for this phase in our adventure. After staying with George and the missionaries in their nice homes, it was a little shocking to see our new residences for the next few months.

The patriarch of the first family we went to see was named Antonio Ca'al. To show respect, we called him Don Antonio. He and his wife had seven children. All the kids were as cute as could be and so shy. He was a delightful and intelligent man. He had a small *tienda* (variety store) and they sold almost anything one needed to survive. It turned out though he was a bit of a procrastinator. The room for one of us to live in was not ready.

At that time, the "room" had a couple cement block walls and the cement floor had yet to be poured. Since the family didn't have the room ready, they had reserved a place for their new guest from someone else. We went to see this alternative room. It had a dirt floor, no electricity, no lock on the door and a window with slide-in boards. Needless to say, it was a little scary, depressing, and an inauspicious start to our new Carchá adventure.

We went over to meet the other family. Bob introduced us to Don Chepe (Spanish nickname for José or Joseph) Xol, the father of the family. I later learned that the last name Xol translated as "fox." We all shook hands and he welcomed us. Don Chepe was forty-five and had a sewing business. The top of his head was about three inches below my shoulders. His wife Matilde was thirty-eight and they had five children.

Don Chepe's two older boys (Óscar 10 years old and Rolando 8 years old) stood at attention and saluted like little military men, while the other three children (Fidelina age 6, Esperanza age 4, and Rigoberto age 2) were hiding behind their mother's skirt. All the kids were barefoot. Matilde kept one hand in front of the lower part of her face and would barely look up.

To our delight, Don Chepe told us the room was ready and would show it to us, but first he gave a tour of his entire house. The house had one portion that was stucco cement block walls that included two rooms. One was the bedroom where all the family slept. It had the common red and white tile floor similar to the missionaries' houses.

In the large main room where we had entered was Don Chepe's sewing business. There were three sewing machines right there in what was also their living room. Two large wooden windows along with the door opened to the street and gave total exposure to the room.

Don Chepe made men's clothes and George had commissioned a pair of pants, extra-long inseam. His pants sold for $6 and his shirts for $8. Most of his work, though, was making and repairing tarps that truck drivers used to cover the beds of their trucks. With all the rain, it was essential to have tarps to keep their goods from being ruined. He also reupholstered seats for buses. Don Chepe's little sewing room was filled with old tarps to repair. I thought, *Looks like Don Chepe does a good business.*

We went through a side doorway and into what seemed like a step back in time. We entered what was the dining room, storage room, clothesline, and play area for the children. It had a dirt floor and tin roof. The walls were rough-cut wood boards nailed overlapping with a few gaps. One side of the room was completely open and showed there was about a four-foot drop-off from the dining area to the ground with a steep hillside that went down to the river.

The backyard hill had some banana trees, a couple of coffee plants and a few other plants but was mostly dirt. Tied with ropes in the sloped backyard were their livestock. Don Chepe had two pigs and a nanny goat that was quite pregnant. There were also a few chickens and a couple ducks running around loose.

Wooden steps led to the lower level where Matilde's kitchen was located. The walls of the kitchen were soot-covered, wood posts that ran to the ceiling, which was thatched with cornstalks. For cooking she had a cement block-like table where the embers of the fire built earlier to cook lunch remained.

Matilde stored her dishes, cooking utensils and produce on plank shelves attached to the walls. Just outside the door was a large, cement *pila* or sink with running water, which was used for washing clothes, dishes and bathing the little one.

A few yards away from the kitchen on the sloping hillside was an outhouse. Leading to it were wooden planks to walk on when the ground was muddy from the rain, which was most of the time. The outhouse had colored sheets of plastic for walls and was situated so the waste would go down the hill into the river that ran behind the house. They did have an outdoor open shower but the floor was mud. Most of the time though Don Chepe and the boys bathed in the river. *Definitely not going to do that!*

Matilde and the girls washed off at the pila. (The nurses earlier had offered for us to come to their house to shower, which we were overjoyed to accept.) George told us that when he came back, he would show us how to build a solar shower for our families. My anxiety level was skyrocketing but I was trying to remain calm, cool, and collected and not appear to be in total culture shock.

It was now time to see either Randall or my room. Making up one wall of the dining room was the new addition to the house. This room had freshly cut, planed-wood boards for walls and a new tin roof. Don Chepe opened the door and pulled the cord to the single light hanging down in the middle of the room. He proudly pointed out the freshly poured cement floor. The two boys ran ahead of us and spun around in the spacious room as we joined them.

Don Chepe had made a wooden bed. The bed was like seven feet long. I am guessing when he and George met to make the arrangement for one of us to live there, Don Chepe figured he better make the bed extra long. There was a little unfinished desk and chair made from pine that he had purchased.

Óscar opened another door showing that it opened out to the street, giving the room a private entrance. There was a window that swung into the room and would allow in fresh air. Though it also allowed anyone walking by on the narrow street to look right in the room or stop and talk unannounced.

During the tour of both homes, Bob spoke to the families in K'ekchi' and then would translate for us. He said he emphasized to both that even though the families did speak Spanish, they needed to only communicate in K'ekchi' to help the new caxlan cuinks learn the language. After Bob told Don Chepe, he grinned and said, "*Hehe'* (Yes)."

After we finished the tour at the second home, Bob said to Don Chepe one of us would be moving in on Monday. Reality and culture shock were setting in. *What the heck did I sign up for?*

After we saw the two rooms, we went back to Bob's and had to decide who was staying with which family. There was no comparison in the two rooms. The second room was The Ritz-Carlton compared to the first not even being a Motel 6. The only fair way to decide was if we drew for rooms. Luck was on my side as I drew the room that was finished. I felt very guilty that I was getting the "nice" room but thought, *I am so relieved!*

It truly wasn't safe for Randall to stay in the alternative room that Don Antonio suggested. Bob and George decided he would stay in the *pensión* (hotel) until his room was completed, but he would eat all his meals with his family. That resulted in Randall getting lots of exercise because Don Antonio's house was on the other side of the river and a good ten-to-fifteen-minute walk from the pensión. In true K'ekchi' fashion, the progress was very slow on Randall's room and it took a couple months for it to be finished.

Chapter 12

Campat

It was our first Sunday in San Pedro Carchá, and our MCC companions left early that morning to go back to Chimaltenango. Bob invited Randall and me to go with him to one of the remote c'alebals to attend church. EMB missionaries had been starting churches throughout the region for several years before our arrival.

The EMB and MCC joint venture experiment that brought Randall and me to Guatemala to start an agricultural program would hopefully help improve life in the K'ekchi' c'alebals. We were excited to be a part of this new idea and thought we would impart our wonderful agricultural knowledge from college. Wow, did we have a lesson or two to learn.

The plan was set for us to start with one c'alebal and live there rather than reside in the city of Carchá where the EMB missionaries were based. Campat was the c'alebal chosen for us by the missionaries and where Bob wanted to take us that Sunday.

Bob told us this c'alebal was one of the poorest, being so isolated in the mountains. The missionaries had built a great rapport with these people and thought they would be receptive to having caxlan cuinks living there. It wasn't until months later that Millard told us the story of how years earlier missionaries initially were chased out of Campat by a man with a machete. We might have had a few more trepidations about this plan had we known.

While waiting to move in with our new families, we had been staying with Larry and Helen. Helen fixed us a great breakfast saying we would need the energy for the hike. Was she ever right! Bob picked us up bright and early before the sun even had risen. We loaded into his Land Rover and headed out of town. It was a little misty but hardly enough to need to use the windshield wipers.

He shared that we would first be going through a small city called San Juan Chamelco. *The saints certainly have a lot of towns in these parts.* It was about a fifteen-minute drive on a gravel/dirt road from Carchá to Chamelco. One could get there on a paved road going through Cobán in about thirty minutes, and during inclement weather was the way to go.

Entering San Juan Chamelco we noticed the city was not as large, with a population of just over 6,000, or as prosperous as Carchá. The first thing we observed was the beautiful Catholic church standing proud and tall in the center of town. As we drove by, there were already people gathering for Mass. We had learned early on that every town had a large Catholic church. Catholicism had been the primary religion in Guatemala for centuries.

The Mayan people were conquered in the early 1500s by the Spaniards. After conquering the Aztecs in Mexico, the conquistadors moved south to try and capture the Mayans. Several of the indigenous tribes were defeated but two tribes located in the highland regions of Alta and Baja Verapaz were fierce warriors and could not be conquered. One of these tribes was the K'ekchi'.

The Spaniards eventually gained control but it was through religion. *Fray* (Friar) *Bartolomé de Las Casas* came to Guatemala in 1537 in an attempt to get the locals to accept Catholicism and the Spaniards. Ken noted, "He also advocated for the rights of the indigenous. My understanding was that he made a deal that the Spaniards would not try to force the K'ekchi's to convert but would allow him to try to convert them peacefully—thus the name *Las Verapaces* (True Peace)."

Incredibly, by 1540 the friar was successful and the Spaniards gained control over the highland regions. It was interesting that there were a lot of similarities in the Mayan and Catholic practices. To put it in rather simplistic terms, the Mayan people sort of just added the Catholic saints along with their Mayan gods and beliefs or just started referring to their gods with names of the saints instead. Double the coverage so to speak.

The missionaries explained to us when we first got to Carchá that those who went to the non-Catholic churches—*Evangélicos* (Pentecostals in Guatemala), Baptists, Evangelicals, Ecumenical, Presbyterian, Mennonite, The Church of Jesus Christ of Latter-day Saints (Mormons), Eastern Orthodox, Oriental Orthodox—which was basically any church but Catholic. These church members called themselves believers

Believers had given up their Catholic faith and Mayan idols. Those who didn't were referred to as non-believers. This was an interesting description to me because many of the Guatemalan Catholics I met had incredible faith in God. Today the number of Catholic church members is just slightly larger than that of Protestants.

Just past the Catholic church, we turned onto a street that led out of town and soon became a potholed dirt road. We bounced along and the car tossed us around like rag dolls as we held on for dear life. The road was lined with banana trees, sugar cane, coffee plants, and lots of vegetation. We passed a few small huts along the way with lots of kids running out to see this uncommon event of a vehicle passing by.

About thirty minutes had passed since we had left Carchá when we came to a small cement bridge. It was wide enough for our vehicle but there was no road on the other side of the bridge, just a dirt trail that went up a mountain. It obviously was just a foot bridge but ironic that the government had spent so much money on building a nice cement bridge that no car would ever pass over.

Bob stopped the car and said we were hoofing it from there. As we were getting out of the car and locking it, a man stepped out of a small wooden house not far from the bridge. Bob told us this man's name was Marcos. Marcos waved and we waved back. Bob went over and greeted the man in K'ekchi' and asked if it was okay to park and leave our car there by his house. The man smiled and nodded his head giving his permission. He told Bob he would keep an eye on it, not that Bob was worried anything would happen to it.

Before we left, Bob had told us to bring the bolsas that Helen had given to us as presents when we arrived. They were great for carrying our passports and the K'ekchi' Bibles and hymnals we had been given. We also had our rain gear Bob had brought for us.

The rain gear was a piece of colorful plastic about four feet by five feet that could be placed over one's shoulders and tied in front below the chin, making a slick rain cape. One could even pull a section up over the head like a hood. When not being used, it folded up nicely into a little square and was a perfect fit for one's bolsa. It was an ideal solution used by the K'ekchi'.

Right after we parked the car and started our hike, it started to drizzle. Something Bob said we would come to expect, especially in the late afternoon. We tied on our rain gear and Bob had an umbrella as well.

We were excited to start our first hike up over the mountain to where we hoped would be our future home. The path was worn by the people using it to get to town to buy and sell goods. The trail started off gradually but quickly turned to a steeper incline. Some of the trail was quite rocky and other parts were covered with soil that seemed to be pure clay and super slippery. *Now I know why Rich said to bring hiking boots.* Even with our hiking boots it was hard to get traction on the trail.

The higher we climbed the more the trail was cut out along the side of the mountain and at times there were steep cliffs where one certainly didn't want to slip. The wet path was hard to navigate, especially on a mountainside. With all the rain, sometimes the sides of the exposed mountain and the trail had green moss growing. That made it even more dangerous for walking.

These novice caxlan cuinks were slipping and sliding. Linda always said that the Campat people didn't have to go to the movies, they just went outside and watched the gringos come down the mountain. It was their comedy show. I chuckled to myself as I thought of what my dad would always say when something was slippery at the farm. *Slick as snot on a doorknob.*

The trail climbed at a good forty-five-degree angle most of the time. Certainly not like the Kansas Flint Hills that I walked to check for newborn calves in our pastures. We were huffing and puffing. Bob was obviously in much better shape and used to this terrain and altitude.

The landscape was lush and green but we really couldn't look around at the scenery. With the heavy mist, visibility wasn't very good and we were keeping our eyes on the slippery path. We pretty much kept our heads down and focused on our footing. Probably was a good thing for our nerves to not be looking around, eyeing the deep crevices hundreds of feet below the trail. One misstep could have been deadly. Up, up, up we went until eventually we reached the summit and Bob told us the valley below was Campat.

Where is it? We literally were in the clouds that settled over the valley below us. It was amazing. One could barely make out a few of the little huts scattered sporadically amongst all the green on both sides of the mountain. The bottom of the valley wasn't even visible. *How far down does it go?*

We could make out that there was smoke billowing through the thatch roofs. Bob said the families' open fires inside their homes served to keep them warm and to cook their meals. As the clouds separated a little, he pointed out a little patch of silver way down at the very bottom of the valley. It appeared to be a larger building with a tin roof. He said, "That is the Mennonite church where we are going." I thought to myself, *How does the saying go? What goes up must come down.*

If going up the mountain was tricky, try going down a slippery mountain slope. The trail wrapped around the side of the mountain with a slight decline when possible but sometimes was a steep drop. We were holding onto the side of the mountain with one hand as we descended. The grooves in our hiking boots designed to provide better traction were pretty much useless since they were filled with clay. It reminded me of a kid at prom trying to dance while wearing new dress shoes on the slick gym floor.

Eventually we reached the bottom of the mountain where it was flat and headed to the church. We were wet and the bottoms of our pant legs were muddy. Exhausted, we were tired and ready to sit.

The Campat men had built the little Mennonite church a few years earlier. The missionaries had supplied the nails, paint, and tin for the roof. Bob said the tin sheets were carried up over the mountain into the c'alebal on the men's backs. The strength of these people was truly staggering. Randall and I were exhausted after hiking a good hour and a half over the steep mountain trail, and we weren't carrying anything but our bolsas. Try carrying an eight-foot piece of corrugated tin on your back on flat ground let alone up a mountain.

The church members provided the rough-cut boards for the walls of the church and labor to build it. Bob told us the congregation was very proud of their little church and held services on Wednesday nights, Sunday mornings, and special occasions.

The church was painted a robin's egg blue color, the only building in the c'alebal we noticed that was painted. Heck, because of the fog it was the only building other than a few huts we saw. On the front of the church above the wooden door were the Spanish words in red lettering *Iglesia Menonita* (Mennonite Church).

Singing was resonating from the church. The pastor waved for us to come in as we entered the doorway. First thing that stood out was the colorful plastic square cut-out decorations hanging from the bare rafters at the front of the church. It was the same plastic we used for our rain gear and kind of reminded me of the taxi cab in Mexico City. It was their interpretation of stained glass I suppose.

Seven or eight rows of short wooden benches (short poles in the ground with a plank on top) lined either side of an aisle that went to the front of the church. There was a dirt floor all except at the front of the church where the floor was covered with wood planks raised about a foot to make a little stage.

Pastor José Mariá (how appropriate was that, Joseph Mary) stood at a little wooden podium on the stage where he was leading the song. A couple of men played old, beat-up guitars. Later we learned the men's names were Luis and Santiago. They would become two of our best friends.

Just like most churches back home, the front "pews" were empty. José Mariá motioned for us to sit there as if they had been reserved for us and we made our way to the front. There must have been twenty-five to thirty people standing and singing their hearts out and smiling at us as we passed by to our seats. One thing that immediately jumped out at me was that all the women were on one side of the aisle and the men on the other. The children were scattered on both sides with either their mothers or fathers.

After the song was over, José Mariá made sure to welcome us and asked everyone to sit. The bench was only about a foot off the ground so with our long legs our chins were basically resting on our knees. The pastor invited Bob to speak and he went to the front to the homemade wooden podium. Bob introduced us and shared we were new missionaries. It was amazing to listen to him speak so fluently in K'ekchi'. I could hardly imagine ever being able to speak so eloquently, though we really had no idea what he was saying or if it was correct. *The people aren't laughing at him and they seem to totally understand him, so I guess he's doing well.*

Bob shared with us later that he talked about what a great pastor they had and they were a very special congregation of strong believers. He read a couple of verses and planted a few seeds without letting on that we hoped to move to Campat. He shared Matthew 25: 31–40. "I was hungry and you gave me food, I was thirsty and you gave me drink, I was a stranger and you welcomed me." *Very sly, our new friend.*

Once Bob sat back down, José Mariá began his sermon. Talk about fire and brimstone. He put the most charismatic American TV preachers to shame. Bob helped us follow along best he could. When the congregation started repeating after José Mariá, we learned he was teaching them the Lord's Prayer. Few of the people could read so he was having them memorize the passage.

The whole service was quite mesmerizing even though I didn't understand a word. They sang a few more hymns and Bob showed us which ones in our hymnals. We were familiar with the tunes and could almost read the words and try to sing along.

After the service, the men came up to us to shake hands and the women would say hello. It was a very warm welcome. José Mariá insisted we go to his house to share lunch with his family and we followed him on the muddy path. His hut was very small. Smaller than the size of my family's living room back home.

From the few huts we saw, this was not one of the better ones in the c'alebal. It was obvious he was very poor in money but he was wealthy in spirit and compassion. He had a beautiful family that he loved dearly. He and his wife had five children who were excited to see us. The seven of them shared this little space they called home.

Though in ragged clothes, the older two boys (about seven- and eight-years old) stood proud and tall, shaking our hands. The younger three, two girls and a little boy, were extremely shy and hid behind their mother's skirt. José Mariá's children appeared to have some health and possibly genetic issues. The children all seemed to be normal sized for their ages but the two oldest boys and the youngest boy appeared to have arms that were very short. There weren't any parts missing but the limbs looked about four inches too short for their build and were held awkwardly against their bodies. Their arms seemed to work just fine but it was very sad to see the deformity. We wondered how it would affect their lives as they got older and needed to work in the fields.

José Mariá invited us into his home to sit on the little plank benches against the back wall across from the door we had entered. The room had two small wooden beds (for all seven of the family), a tiny table, and a little cabinet. The stove was a pile of wood burning on the ground with a metal stand to set pots and kettles on. The house didn't have much ventilation so the roof (which was thatched grass and corn stalk leaves) was black with soot. As I tried to avoid coughing, I thought, *How they stand this smoke is beyond me.*

His wife served us *poch*. Poch was corn masa (or ground-up corn) wrapped in a banana leaf and boiled. You would peel back the banana leaf and use it as a napkin holding the poch. It was about the size of a baked potato but more rectangular shaped. It was kind of rubbery in texture and very bland tasting. For a drink, she served us a liquid corn mixture called *uk'un* (or *atol* in Spanish). It was cornmeal mixed in water. It sort of made me think of what it might taste like to drink runny wallpaper paste.

Bob told us later that when a family was extremely poor, they often didn't have coffee to serve and served uk'un. Usually the drink was sweet but obviously José Mariá's wife didn't have sugar to put in the drink. It was humbling to experience how these people treated us with such hospitality when they had so little.

We enjoyed our lunch and Bob shared it was time for us to start our hike back up the mountain. After handshakes and much appreciation for the hospitality, we bid adieu in K'ekchi', saying the words Bob taught us on the trail, "*Bantiox. Chaquil aquib* (Thanks. May we see you again)."

The steep ascent awaited us with our spirits high and tummies full. The rain had subsided but it was still very slippery. With only one or two falls, we eventually made it to the top and began the descent. It was not nearly as steep with a longer decline and much easier than going down into Campat.

We asked Bob tons of questions about everything we saw and heard. Making much better time coming down the mountain, we reached the waiting Land Rover. We bounced our way back to Carchá. Bob returned us to Larry and Helen's, where we couldn't wait to get out of our muddy clothes and take warm showers. All in all, our first trip to Campat was a big success and we looked forward to many more.

Chapter 13
Happy Birthday

It was move-in day and what a way to start my twenty-third birthday. Bob helped us load our suitcases and other things in his Land Rover. We had learned going to Campat that the four-wheel drive Land Rover was an essential mode of transportation when going out to the remote c'alebals. The off roads were horrible, mostly just clay soil with lots of chuckholes. We were to have many bumpy rides in our future. Each of the missionaries had their own vehicle. The nurses had a small yellow Suzuki Jimny.

Taking us to our new homes, Bob shared that though this was not the way EMB did things, George had insisted that his new volunteers live as much like the people as possible. Bob wanted us to know that he and the other EMB missionaries were there for us and wanted us to be safe and comfortable. We could come to him anytime we needed, which was really reassuring to know.

After MCC paid to have the rooms built, George worked out an agreement that for six months MCC would pay rent for us during language training. Afterward, the families could use the room as they pleased to rent out, use for a tienda, or provide another bedroom for the children.

Don Chepe's house was closest so they dropped me off first before taking Randall to the pensión. Don Chepe, Matilde and the Xol children were all there waiting to welcome me. The kids ran out in the street with excitement after we pulled up. Óscar and Rolando were in regular ladino-style clothes, but Fidelina and Esperanza wore the typical K'ekchi' blouses and skirts as did Matilde.

The skirt material was made on a large wooden loom. White thread was tied in knots and dyed black. When the knots were removed, a white and black tie-dyed pattern remained. These long threads, eight yards in length, are placed on the loom. A pattern using multicolored threads was woven back and forth on the loom to create the beautiful material.

Similar to how the embroidered blouses could help distinguish the locale of the Mayan people, the way the skirt was worn could as well. For example, the K'ekchi' women wore their skirts cinched around the waist with the material gathered to make pleats and stopped about mid-calf. Another indigenous group wrapped the material around the waist and it hung straight down almost to the ground with no pleats.

The littlest one, Rigoberto, had on a dirty t-shirt that was about two sizes too small (with his big belly sticking out) and no pants. No need for diapers. This was his normal attire unless it was Sunday church day or the family was going to the market. Then he was cleaned up, jet black hair slicked back, and wearing a clean shirt and britches.

Once we moved my suitcases and belongings into my room, Bob and Randall took off for the other side of town. Don Chepe scooted the kids out of my room to give me some privacy and I began getting things arranged. The wooden bed was amazing because it was long enough for my body. *Thank you, Don Chepe!*

The foam mattress fit perfectly. MCC had sent a whole box of sheets for us and plenty of covers. For a pillow I had a rectangular piece of foam that I put into a pillowcase. I made my bed to be ready for my first night in my new abode.

Not having a chest of drawers or closet, I would be living out of my suitcases. It didn't take too long to realize that I needed to keep my suitcases and belongings up off the cement floor. The rainy weather tended to make the cement damp and things got moldy very quickly. Don Chepe had knowingly placed a couple of small wooden stools in my room. The stools protected my suitcases from the condensation on the cement floor. I also learned to be sure to keep the suitcases closed at all times. Little critters hoped they might find a new place to call home.

Around noon, Óscar lightly tapped on my door that led to the house. Upon opening the door, all five children stood smiling at me. Fidelina was carrying her little brother Rigoberto and Esperanza wiped his runny nose with the sleeve of his shirt. Óscar said, "*Tocau'ak anakcuan.*"

My face must have said it all as I shook my head not understanding. Óscar began the game of charades that we became pretty good at over time. He used his hand to motion eating and I smiled, realizing that he must have said, "It's time to eat now."

I nodded saying the words I remembered Bob had taught us, "*Us*" (pronounced "Ew-s" and means good or okay) and "Bantiox acue (thank you)."

Óscar and Rolando each grabbed one of my hands and led me to the dining area where Don Chepe was sitting at the head of the table. Fidelina handed Rigoberto over to his papa's lap where he would be fed while Don Chepe and the boys joined me for lunch. The girls headed down the steps to the kitchen to join their mother.

Don Chepe pointed to Rigoberto and said "Rigo" stating this was his nickname and what I called him from then on. Rigo's face with his chubby cheeks broke out in a huge smile knowing we were talking about him. Don Chepe then motioned it was time to say a prayer and we bowed our heads while he led us in prayer.

The girls never ate with us but helped their mother in the kitchen and brought food to the table. I found out later that after the men finished their meal, the women would then eat. Sometimes I would go back to the table after the "men" had eaten and sit and talk to Matilde. She always seemed pleased when I did.

Matlide had prepared what seemed like a feast for my first meal but turned out to be a typical meal she served. She fixed roast beef (fried in a pan), tortillas, fried cauliflower (dipped in egg), black beans and of course coffee (my first cup in Guatemala but definitely not last). It was a delicious meal. *This just might be okay.*

After lunch I once again thanked my hosts but I said, "*Gracias*" in Spanish. Don Chepe smiled and shook his finger at me and said, "Bantiox," informing me that I needed to stick with K'ekchi'. We all laughed and I said, "Bantiox acue, Don Chepe." He patted his chest and said "Chepe," meaning no need to call him Don Chepe, just Chepe. Going back to my room, I felt like I was now accepted into the family.

Our first language study class was to be held that afternoon. EMB nurse Debbie had agreed to be our language teacher. Randall and I had made plans to meet at the town plaza before going over to the nurses' house after he had checked into the pensión and visited his family for his first meal. Randall was waiting when I got there. He said, "I bet you are the only person to ever start learning K'ekchi' on his birthday." I grinned and he said, "Let's celebrate with some ice cream, my treat."

During our tour with Bob the day before, he had pointed out there was a vendor with a little store on the plaza called Copo's that sold helados. This was the real thing, not frozen fruit drink on a stick. It was very good ice cream, not quite Blue Bunny* but close. It had a strong vanilla flavor.

Vanilla extract was made and sold in Guatemala that seemed twice as strong as what my mom had used in her baking back home. The vanilla was made from vanilla beans or pods from vanilla orchids and was native to Alta Verapaz and Baja Verapaz in Guatemala.

There were several flavors of ice cream to choose from and I tried the pineapple. It was very creamy and tasty. We headed to the nurses' house for class while licking our helados served in something similar to waffle cones. *So far this is turning out to be a pretty good birthday.*

Chapter 14
Culture Shock

Our goal was to spend a few months studying the K'ekchi' language before eventually moving out to Campat to live and work with the people and start our agricultural program. We would spend many days studying with Debbie at the nurses' house.

Debbie, Linda and Ruth had lived several years in Carchá. They were fluent in K'ekchi' and it was fun to hear them speak this strange language. It was so different from English. Debbie said she was excited to try her hand at teaching us. Not only did she teach vocabulary and pronunciation, but she taught the K'ekchi' grammar structure.

During all of my studies from grade school through college to now learning K'ekchi', sadly I never had any phonics training or real understanding of English grammar. Studying K'ekchi' with Debbie really gave me a better grasp of English sentence structure, even though the two languages were very different. My thoughts were, *Why didn't I have this training before I tried to learn K'ekchi'? It would have made learning so much easier.* Later in my teaching career, I made it a point to emphasize teaching phonics and grammar to my third-grade students.

K'ekchi' was a guttural language with many of the letter and syllable sounds formed at the back of the throat. It was very choppy and staccato language. Every other syllable was like someone hacking up a hairball. K'ekchi' wasn't a language that rolls off one's tongue the way Spanish did.

The written language was filled with apostrophes after syllables, showing breaks and sounds being cut off when spoken. For example, the K' at the beginning of K'ekchi' was barely audible when pronounced. Leave off the accented glottal stop in a word though, it could become a different word or meaning. For example, *sa* meant "happy or good" and *sa'* meant "in."

It was daunting to think we could ever master K'ekchi' like the nurses and the missionaries. Debbie patiently helped us to slowly learn this strange language. Randall was much better at picking it up than I was. He always encouraged me though, saying I was doing great. He emphasized that having already learned Dutch in Holland as a cultural exchange student was a huge help in his learning another language. Linda always urged me not to be discouraged because I was having a harder time. She told me it had been the same for Debbie and her. Debbie had been a whiz at picking up K'ekchi' while she had struggled.

Debbie gave us lessons using instructional materials written by two Wycliffe Bible translators named Fran and Ruth who had lived in Cobán for years. Their teaching manuals had helped dozens of English-speaking missionaries to learn K'ekchi'. Debbie also had a couple of K'ekchi' men work with us. She called them our language informants or helpers. Mine was named Santiago and Randall's was Julián.

Santiago was from Campat, and was one of the guitar players we met at our first church service. Julián was from a nearby c'alebal outside of Carchá. Both were young guys with families. Julián was a pastor and both he and Santiago were health promoters the nurses had trained. They were delightful to work with and had great spirits. They would help us to learn new words and especially with pronunciation of words.

Santiago used to laugh and joke about my ineptitude in trying to get words out correctly, but he was very patient with me. He in return wanted to know what the English word was for everything he was teaching me in K'ekchi'. Hearing him try to pronounce something in English made me realize how silly I must have sounded in his language.

After our first day of study, the nurses had invited us to stay for supper and play games. We had told our families earlier in the day we wouldn't be back for supper, at least I hoped that was what I had conveyed. Chepe seemed to understand my gestures and the few words in Spanish I did know, saying that I would not be there for supper. Debbie and Linda had made a cake for me for my birthday and we had ice cream again. The nurses taught us to play their favorite board game called *Acquire*. I had played games all my life growing up but had never heard of this one. It quickly became one of my favorites, too.

This turned out to be a great birthday and certainly staved off the homesickness and culture shock I had felt creeping in once we had reached Guatemala several days before. Linda did warn, however, not to get used to the ice cream. Once we were living in Campat there wouldn't be a Copo's, or electricity for that matter, and we all laughed.

Once the birthday celebration was over, it was time to spend my first night at my new family's house. Randall stopped at the pensión, which was not too far from the nurses. I had several blocks to go and it was a little creepy out at night. It was dead silent except for a random dog sometimes barking in the distance.

There were street lights every so often along the way, giving off eerie shadows in the still night. I finally reached Larry's house and turned to go down the street for Chepe's. No lights on our street. It was totally dark and a long block to my room. Bob had given both Randall and me flashlights, saying we would be needing them. He was sure right, but I still felt very uneasy walking down the street at night in the dark. Let's just say I didn't dawdle.

When I reached Chepe's part of the cement block part of the house, it was dark and boarded up tight. I was glad to have my flashlight to light the keyhole to unlock my room's door that faced the street. Once open, I flashed the light around until I found the little string that dangled from the lonely lightbulb that hung down in the center of my room. I pulled the string and the light lit up the room. I quickly shut the door and some of my anxiety vanished, feeling much better behind the closed door.

Giving my room a quick once over, it was quite depressing. It made my barren dorm room in college seem like a five-star motel. *What did I get myself into?*

My little shell of a room was a stark contrast to the nurses' home I had just left with all the modern conveniences of the day—refrigerator, stove, washing machine, hot running water, comfortable furniture and beds with mattresses. They even had a phone that we could use to call back home directly.

I had called home to my parents from the nurses to let them know we had arrived in Carchá safely. It was ironic that if our parents wanted to call us at the nurses' house, they had to go through the international operator and it could take some time to get connected. In comparison I just dialed my parents' number from the nurses' phone and they would answer. It was expensive to call but worth every minute to hear their voices. Just having the knowledge that we could call them at a drop of a hat was very comforting and made it feel they were closer.

It was getting late but before I went to bed, I sat at my new table and wrote a letter home to share about my birthday events. I made a journal entry as well. A very good college friend gave me a journal as a going-away present. She told me to document my adventure and I took her advice. I made my first entry the night before leaving for orientation in Akron.

I tried to write letters as often as possible and an entry in my journal every day. My letters home were always more upbeat and quite detailed about daily events. The entries in my journal covered more of the bad experiences or events, such as the bombing in the capital city, that my parents didn't need to fret over. In addition, I shared more in my journal about the emotional ups and downs and daily struggles that I went through. Writing became a daily habit since there wasn't any other activity to do at night, just sitting alone in my room with no television or radio.

In one of my first letters, I asked my mother if she would save my letters for me to read one day to reminisce. She kept every single letter (over one hundred), placing each one in a plastic sleeve. She then put them in chronological order in a huge binder to preserve for me to have to recall my experience. My sister Jane did the same thing. I am forever grateful to this day they did this for me.

Besides letters, we made and received taped messages. Randall brought a little cassette player/tape recorder. He said he would much rather make a tape than write, though he wrote many letters, too. He would lend me his recorder and the nurses also had tape recorders that I could borrow to listen to the tapes my family and friends sent to me. It was always the best day when a tape arrived.

After a full birthday of activities, I was exhausted and ready for some shut-eye. The missionaries gave me a beautiful Guatemalan woolen blanket with blue and black stripes woven into it with a pattern of a large quetzal bird. My little room was pretty cool from the night air and I spread the blanket over my covers, turned off my light, and crawled into my new bed. It was toasty warm and I fell right to sleep.

The next morning I woke up at about 4:30 a.m. and had a pulsing, slightly painful sensation right between my eyes and above my nose. *Damn! Something bit me in the night.*

My face felt swollen. I found the light string and was blinded by the sudden bright light. I dug in my suitcase, looking for a small hand mirror, one of the things on our MCC list of supplies to bring. I couldn't find the mirror and panic was starting to set in. I didn't have a sink or running water to wash my face. *Note to self, get a pan with some water to keep in the room.*

Eventually I found the mirror and there was just a little swelling between my eyes. It felt much worse than it looked. I crawled back in bed to stay warm, but I remained wide awake with the light on for the rest of the morning.

At about 5:30, I heard some rustling going on in the Xol house. I began to smell the smoke from the fire in the kitchen so Matilde was up early fixing breakfast. I got up and got dressed, still a little anxious over the bug bite. Around 6:30 there was a tap on my door. Óscar said in Spanish, "*Buenos días.*"

I think he was feeling sorry for me not understanding anything they said. Opening my door, I replied back, "Buenos días."

It was so early it was still pitch-black outside. Óscar was standing there with a giant glass of freshly hand-squeezed orange juice for me. My panic attack had pretty much subsided by now and this kind boy was bringing me juice. I asked him to come in and he handed me the glass. He was trying to tell me breakfast would be ready soon and to join them. "Drink up," he said in K'ekchi' as he motioned for me to drink.

I looked down at the juice and was about to take a big drink when I noticed floating on the top of the orange juice a raw egg. My eyes looked up at Óscar and Rolando, who had joined us, and I gave a little laugh. *Is this a joke?* But I could tell from their proud faces this was no joke.

There was no way I couldn't bring myself to drink the slimy, raw egg, no matter what MCC training had told us about eating anything given to us with humility and appreciation. I thanked Óscar the best I could. I am sure my face was scrunched up showing I didn't like raw egg.

My instincts kicked in and I began to demonstrate breaking an egg into a pan and cooking over a fire. He was confused at first but then he began to smile. He patted my arm as if to say he understood that I wasn't too excited about the drink, and he said something, tugged on my shirt sleeve, and motioned for me to follow him.

We made our way through the dining room and climbed down the rickety wooden stairs, me holding my glass of juice with a floating egg. Matilde was making tortillas and had a perplexed look as to why this caxlan cuink was in her kitchen. Óscar said something to her and she covered her mouth and chuckled, trying to not let on how silly this seemed.

Matilde had a skillet beside the fire and I pointed to it, asking if I could use it. She nodded yes and I—with all my vast wisdom—proceeded to take a spoon and try to scoop the slimy egg out of the juice and into the pan. That alone had to have been a sight for Matilde but she kept her composure.

Once I had most of the egg removed, I pointed to the fire. She poured a little oil into the skillet and moved it onto the fire. I scrambled the egg as it cooked and was very proud of myself. Matilde was so polite and kind, smiling at me as she dished up the egg and put it on a plate for me once it was cooked.

With my remaining juice and scrambled egg in hand, I climbed back up the stairs and joined Chepe and the boys, waiting for me at the dining room table. There were smirks and comments back and forth between the boys and their father. I couldn't understand but figured I knew what they were saying. I just smiled and shrugged my shoulders. *Hey, I'm a foreigner in your world.*

Matilde brought up the rest of breakfast to the table—tortillas, black beans, fried plantains, AND scrambled eggs (which Matilde had obviously made before my little demonstration). Talk about feeling foolish. They just laughed at my reaction and I knew they weren't upset with me.

Chepe had a glass of orange juice and showed me the egg floating on top. He broke the rule of not speaking in Spanish and said "*Mírame* (Watch me)," which I understood as he motioned for me to watch. He demonstrated, tipping up the glass to his mouth, and with one big gulp swallowed the egg and some juice. I gave him a thumbs up and big smile, but I never did try it nor did they offer it to me again. We didn't have *mosh* that day but we often did. Mosh was a very sticky oatmeal (something I never ever liked as a kid). Matilde would sprinkle cinnamon and sugar on top making it tolerable. To my amazement, one day Chepe had a huge smile on his face and placed a box on the table. I recognized it immediately with the red and green rooster on the front. It was a box of Kellogg's Corn Flakes® cereal. He poured a little of the flakes on his mosh and handed me the box to mimic. *I guess Chepe doesn't like mosh that much either.* The crunch totally helped to get the mosh down.

After telling the nurses about my orange juice experience, they laughed and informed me that it was a delicacy to have the raw egg in orange juice and an honor to be served by someone. Talk about humble "egg" pie. They also told me, chuckling, that they couldn't drink it either. That was the only thing they had ever politely turned down. Knowing that made me feel better. Weeks later when I could communicate better with my family, I apologized in K'ekchi' saying "*Chacuy inmac* (May you forgive my sin)." We often had a good laugh at my little cooking demonstration.

I was so thankful for the patience the Xols had for me. It was also nice to know that my stay with them provided some much-needed financial support as well as comic relief. After surviving the initial culture shock, Chepe's family became a very special part of my family.

Chapter 15
Settling In

Language study was going well, though it was quite exhausting. We had classes on Monday, Tuesday, Thursday, and Friday with Debbie. Our informants came to study about three times a week. They were a tremendous help with pronunciation.

One day Randall and his language informant Julián joined Santiago and me hiking to the top of Carchá hill. This was a little mound projecting up on the outskirts of town. The word "Carchá" was painted in large letters for all to see. What a gorgeous view of the town square. The sun was shining bright on the Catholic church. It was a great place to study with the informants pointing out things and teaching us the words for them.

When I was in my room studying on sunny days, the tin roof could make my room quite toasty. I usually would have my window open to get some airflow. Chepe often stopped by and looked in my window to check on me. He always asked if I needed anything. Sometimes he'd go over lessons with me when he had time. One day to my surprise, he bought another table for me. He noticed I needed more space to put all my books and for Santiago to use. He treated me so well and I know he appreciated the extra income that was benefitting his family.

The three oldest Xol children went to school. Óscar went to school in Cobán because Chepe said the teachers were better there. He said if the Carchá teachers didn't like you, they wouldn't pass you. Rolando and Fidelina were both in first grade in Carchá, but Rolando should have been in second grade. Soon I discovered Rolando was called Rollie for short so that is what I called him from then on.

From interacting with the boys, I discerned Óscar was a pleaser and more serious. I was sure he was a good student. Rollie was more energetic and a little ornery, liking to tease and not take things as seriously. I had no doubt Rollie was just as intelligent and he read his books to me in Spanish. I assumed Rollie might have been more of a daydreamer in class and got into trouble. Chepe said it was quite frustrating that Rollie was not progressing in school and he would go to Cobán the following year, even though it was quite expensive. *Another good reason I am staying here.*

The kids would come home from school and make a beeline to my window to say hi. Óscar would hoist up Fidelina to see in, while Rollie pulled himself up with eyes peering over the ledge because he wasn't quite tall enough either. The two boys seemed to love to play soldiers. The first time they would see me each day they would stand at attention and salute like I was their general.

All the children enjoyed helping me with my language study from the get-go. Fidelina and Esperanza were more reserved but eventually warmed up and would come into my room and chatter away with me. The day Rigo toddled into my room and crawled up on my lap, I figured I had completely been accepted into the family.

Since we didn't have class on Wednesdays, Randall and I took advantage of the day each week to explore. The first free Wednesday, we jumped on a bus and rode over to Cobán to check it out. Much to our surprise, we found we could buy about anything available back home. There was a store that reminded me of what an old general store must have been back like in the good ol' days.

There were things way more expensive but also the opposite, which was quite fascinating. An item that was very expensive was peanut butter. One had to love the brand name, *Gato Gordo*, or Fat Cat peanut butter. I bought the two important papers that brought me sanity and comfort—thin airmail paper for writing letters and toilet paper. My big purchase that day, and probably the most important item I ever bought in Guatemala, was a fold-up umbrella.

After just one week living with Chepe, George wanted us to come back to Chimaltenango over the weekend to report how things were going. For this trip, the nurses were going to the city as well. Linda and Debbie were going on to Honduras to get visas to stay in Guatemala. So strange how things worked in Central America. Linda drove us to Cobán the day before to buy tickets at Guatemala Escobar for the Pullman bus to take to the capital. *Thank goodness no chicken bus this trip and hopefully never again, no matter what George says.*

The morning we left, Matilde got up at 4:30 to make sure I had breakfast before leaving. She had a heart of gold. Our trip was supposed to be a quick three-and-a-half-hour ride, but the bus broke down about halfway there. We had reached the much lower area of the country and it was hot. We were sweating like crazy, not being used to this much heat. The driver worked and worked trying to fix it but to no avail.

Another Pullman came by about two hours later and it was already almost full. Everyone who was on our bus piled onto this bus. Randall and I ended up standing in the aisle (much of the time with weight on only one foot) for the rest of the trip. After a couple hours of standing on a swaying bus, we had a good laugh about the luxurious air-conditioned Pullman. *Karma?*

Once we got to Guatemala City, we said our goodbyes to Linda and Debbie. They were lucky because the Pullman to Honduras was right there at the same bus depot. Randall and I went to where we had been dropped off the week before to catch a bus to Chimaltenango and George's house. Traveling in Guatemala was starting to come second nature and we weren't nearly as anxious over it.

We were excited to see our three travel colleagues and hear about their adventures, even if it had only been a week. They were at George's when we arrived. They had all been studying Spanish in Antigua, Guatemala, since they would solely be speaking in Spanish where they would work. Ken was going to be studying for a shorter period of time as it was more of a refresher course for him. They loved language study and Antigua.

Since Ken would be finished with his Spanish studies soon, George had already arranged temporary lodging with a family in the nearby town of Santa María Cauqué where Ken would be working. We went over to see where he would live. His room (one of three adjacent rooms) was part of one of the *Casas Suizas* (Swiss Houses built by a Swiss NGO after the 1976 earthquake). The room was in the backyard of the house of one of the community leaders, Don Buenaventura. It was part concrete block and part (well-sealed) wooden planks with a fiber cement roof. Ken seemed to be excited about his new home and neighbors.

As part of our orientation, George piled us in the car (with Carolyn literally laying across our laps in the backseat) and took us on the highway about 35 kilometers (about 20 miles) west of Chimaltenango to visit *Chirijuyú*. Here MCC and the community built some beautiful *bajareque* (which means mud wall enclosed by sticks) houses. They used wooden posts for walls, nailed slats on, filled between the slats with mud, and plastered them with lime and sand. It kept the houses quite airtight and warm compared to my wooden plankboard room.

On our way back to George's we stopped at a market. It was really a clean market in comparison to Guatemala City Central Market. The people were sitting at their stands selling fruits, vegetables, clothes, or whatever. The food was very inexpensive. A banana or an orange was a penny. Tomatoes were four cents each. A skinny little pig was ten dollars. I sent my dad a photo of a pig and shared I could buy him one for ten dollars. He wrote back, "Thanks, but no thanks."

George shared he had something we could look forward to doing in a few weeks after being swallowed up in language study. He planned a three-week orientation for the five of us to participate in some courses. It was billed as a chance to reconnect, discuss our first month in Guatemala, learn more about the country, and prepare for our future missions. We really had no idea what we were getting ourselves into. It was at this time that George informed us at some point, Randall and I would also be sent to Antigua to study Spanish for eight weeks. *We are going to learn two languages!*

It really was necessary for us to know at least some Spanish for traveling and for when we were in Guatemala City. Even in San Pedro Carchá, many of the ladino people only spoke Spanish, and those who did know K'ekchi' only wanted to talk to us in Spanish. It was kind of like it was below them to speak K'ekchi'. I was looking forward to being able to learn more Spanish but talk about a formidable task. My reaction was, *How the heck am I going to learn another language? My mind is so confused now.*

A hot topic for discussion with George was the plan for Randall and me after we finished our language study and started working in the c'alebal. His idea was for us to find a little piece of land in Campat, build a house similar to the indigenous people, and live there for the remainder of our three years.

The EMB missionaries suggested we stay in the c'alebal during the week and on weekends be in San Pedro Carchá. There was no store for supplies in the c'alebal and we would need to replenish our food supply. Also, the missionaries had Bible study on Friday nights and thought we should be there. We preferred this idea and George was okay with it, too.

Then the question was, where would we live while in Carchá? The missionaries wanted us to live in one of their houses while they rotated being on furlough. George did not like the idea of us living in such luxury. He preferred on weekends we have a little room in Carchá, like at Chepe's. Talk about being between a rock and a hard place. Thankfully we had some time to figure it out and Rich would be coming in February to take over as Country Director. It would be his decision. We couldn't worry about it now because we had plenty of language study to deal with first. After our weekend stay at George's, we hopped on the bus back to Carchá.

We survived the first few weeks of study. Every so often Debbie would give us a test. After the first one, she said we were doing great. Knowing we had a break on the horizon and would be going back to Guatemala City for George's surprise, it helped us to stay focused. We also were getting to know the missionaries better and they were so much fun. We were invited to their houses for meals and to play games, *Uno!* ™ and Canasta being the card games of choice.

One night after having supper with Millard and Priscilla, I mentioned my thick, curly hair was getting pretty long and wild, no thanks to the humid climate. *Oh, I wish I had Randall's straight hair in this humidity but my mop is still better than George's thinning hair,* I chuckled to myself. Priscilla said it was time for a trim. She pulled out her clippers, put a towel around my neck, and had at it, giving me my first Guatemala haircut. She did a great job and became Randall's and my barber.

We enjoyed the Friday night Bible studies and had prayer partners. We also got together once a month with missionaries in the area from other denominations. One couple we met was Royce and Linda, who were with Mission Aviation Fellowship and lived in Cobán. We hit it off quickly because they were from Kansas City. Royce was a pilot and his organization provided aviation, technology, and communications services to Christian and humanitarian agencies, isolated missionaries, and indigenous villagers in the world's most remote areas.

We spent the most time with the nurses. They often had us over for supper and played *Acquire* or cards. The nurses always had some kind of treat they had baked for us after our study sessions. One day Randall and I decided to go to the market and bought food to make supper for the nurses.

It was fun shopping in the market and being able to put our newly learned K'ekchi' to use. We always seemed to shock a few of the little market ladies when we spoke to them in K'ekchi' instead of Spanish. Randall and I were pretty good cooks and I think we surprised the nurses with our culinary skills.

Life at Chepe's was always an adventure with something new every day. One morning when Óscar knocked on my door for breakfast, I found the children all excited. There had been a couple of hens roosting on some eggs for days in one corner of the dining area. One hen's chicks had hatched. There were about a dozen little chicks roaming around everywhere, including under the table. Each of the girls had picked up one of the little brown chicks and was holding it to show me.

Chepe's farm continued to grow. Rollie jumped up on my window one day and couldn't wait to tell me the news. He was talking so fast I couldn't understand him. I opened the door to the street and let him in. He didn't even hesitate, grabbed my hand and took me through the other door to the dining area. He pointed at the nanny goat tied out in the yard. She had delivered her twin baby kids. They were adorable and Chepe's human kids loved the new kids on the block. *Oh joy, triple the bleating goats.*

The missionaries often invited us to go with them to make visits out in the rural areas. These little expeditions provided an escape from language study and the "animal farm," at least for a little bit. Bob invited us one day to go with him to visit a man named Mateo who lived in the c'alebal *Chirrubiquim.* Mateo had built an adobe brick oven to bake bread.

We traveled by Land Rover for an hour over bumpy, muddy roads. At the end of the road, we hiked another hour up and down a muddy, rocky path. Our hiking boots, socks and pants were soaked by the time we reached the man's home. It was amazing to see how isolated some of the areas were where people lived and the poor living conditions.

Mateo had built his oven with the help of one of George's friends. It was made from bricks formed from clay and straw. All the bricks had been carried in over the same trail we had just traveled. Amazing what these people could carry and their will power.

The oven was working well as he experimented making *pan* (bread) to sell. Mateo mixed the flour and ingredients into dough on a flat table. He meticulously rolled the dough into identical little balls and placed them on a flat metal sheet and put a little dollop of a sugar and flour mix on top. It amazed me at how slow the man moved. Just another example of how nobody in Guatemala appeared to be in a hurry and time was of least concern. I kept thinking, *You could be making twice the amount of bread. Hurry up!*

Mateo made one hundred and fifty rolls with this batch. He would slide a full tray in his adobe brick oven that was heated with a wood fire. Then it was time to sit and wait for the bread to bake.

We met Mateo's wife, who gave us coffee and some pan they had made earlier. The pan was delicious and the coffee helped warm us. His wife was about twenty years old and had given birth to three children already. The oldest had died from diarrhea, which was a common cause of death for infants and young children. Her newborn was in a cloth sling. The sling was tied around the mother's neck and rested on her back. It was muddy, damp and cold, but the two-year-old was running around barefoot in only a shirt. I was freezing and was bundled up. *These are very tough people.*

Mateo sold the rolls for two cents apiece and made about $10 from a ten-pound bag of flour. He sold to his neighbors but also hiked over the long path to Chirrubiquim, carrying the pan in the empty flour sacks to sell in the market. We bought a couple dozen to take home, putting them in our bolsas, and thanked them for their hospitality.

The hike back to the car was just as sloppy as before. We were simultaneously sweaty from the hike and cold from the dampness and wet clothes. The heater in the Land Rover felt pretty good. We were ready to get home after the hour drive. Once back to my room, I had to change out of muddy clothes and crawl into bed under the blankets to get warm. For the land of Eternal Spring, we had way too many cold, damp days during our language study.

Chapter 16
Friends World College

The weeks flew by and it was time to go back to George's and to find out what he had planned for his new MCC volunteers. We discovered a new frustration traveling back to Guatemala City. The little bit of Spanish we had known before seemed to have evaporated out of our brains, being replaced with K'ekchi'. It was difficult to communicate because we kept trying to use K'ekchi' words.

To make matters worse, Debbie told us when there wasn't a word in K'ekchi' that translated from a Spanish word, the K'ekchi' just used the Spanish word. The only kicker was that most Spanish words ended with a vowel. In K'ekchi', they didn't have words ending with vowels so they just dropped the vowels off of the Spanish words. For example, *camioneta* is the Spanish word for bus. The K'ekchi' didn't have buses all those many years ago so didn't have a word for it in their language. They just adapted and would say *camionet*. This would be the way we would learn the word. Spanish speaking people gave us some very strange looks when we said words without the final vowels. *Like our American accents aren't enough.*

Our travel gang met up at MCC headquarters in Chimaltenango. It was time for what we later called our "Let's Learn about Guatemala" crash course. The first event George planned was to go to a small village close by where most of the houses had been destroyed by the earthquake. He had helped build the homes now standing. They were 10 ft. by 20 ft. wooden homes with tin roofs. He also showed us a solar shower he built at one of the homes.

Then George took us to meet a family he was friends with that had five small bajareque houses with thatched roofs. The wife's kitchen was in one of these where we were invited in. Immediately the smoke choked us up. *How do they survive living in this smoke? I can hardly breathe.*

The wife fixed atol for us. Her version of atol was quite different from the uk'un we had received from José Maria's wife. This was a sweet, thick corn drink. It slowly poured out of the glass when not stuck on the sides. We had to use our fingers to scoop the last bit of the thick corn mixture into our mouths. It sort of reminded me of a creamed corn casserole my mom made back home but this was very sweet. We all smiled and showed our appreciation even though it was kind of gross. Carman and Carolyn had to choke it down. It was hard to not make the "yuck" face and avoid offending our gracious hostess.

On Sunday we went to church with George. It was strange to attend church with indigenous people and have everyone speak Spanish rather than a Mayan language. George and Ken were the only ones in our group who had a clue as to what was being said. It started with Sunday School class at 9:30. The people were divided by sex and age. That meant poor Carolyn was in a class all by herself. The five of us guys were in a class together. It was kind of cool because the Guatemalan men were dressed in their indigenous attire, all except one man. The lone wolf was kind of hilarious because his attire was a gray tuxedo with a blue collar and cuffs.

Sunday school lasted until noon. Then it was time for church. The people sang, gave testimonials, and the preacher gave a VERY long sermon. We finally finished around 1:30. *What a day! I don't know when I have ever been so bored.*

After a couple of days at Chimaltenango and listening to George share for hours on end, it was time for us to partake in a class he signed us up for given by an organization called Friends World College. We thought it was going to be learning about the history of Guatemala. That was not what it started out to be. We discovered it was a university course and day one was a lecture defining culture, nature, economics, politics and social class. Nothing to do with Guatemala.

The best description of those in attendance comes from a letter I wrote home after the first class. "The students are something else. They are very free spirited and don't hesitate to let you know what they are thinking. One guy can't do anything without a cigarette in his hand and his nerves seem to be getting the best of him, making us all nervous. Most students are from the United States, but there is a student from Norway, one from Germany and one from Japan. It is going to be a long two weeks. Hopefully tomorrow we will start to learn about Guatemalan history."

The man in charge was a Guatemalan man named Julio. Interestingly enough, we discovered that Julio had gotten his Master's Degree at the University of Kansas and was familiar with our home state—even though he had gone to our archrival university. By the end of the first week, he inundated us with the political history of Guatemala. The information we gained was very eye opening.

I really had no background knowledge of Guatemalan or Central American history. None of my high school or college history classes covered the United States involvement in Central America. One startling piece of information provided insight into why there was so much turmoil in Guatemala.

We learned about the United States Central Intelligence Agency (CIA) involvement with a coup in 1954 that overthrew the democratically elected president. The coup centered around The United Fruit Company—now the Chiquita Brands International—which owned all of Guatemala's banana production and monopolized the exports. In addition, it owned the country's telephone and telegraph system and almost all of the railroad track.

Julio shared that in the 1950s, the company's revenue was over $65 million, more than twice that of the Guatemalan government.

They owned over 550,000 acres of land with less than 15% cultivated. It was like a country within a country with its power and control.

The first democratic government in Guatemala was elected in the 1940s, and a second democratically elected president, Jacobo Árbenz, in 1951. Julio said this new government wanted to help the poor people so they began land reform. Thousands of unused acres of land owned by the United Fruit Company were partitioned out to landless peasants. Agricultural production actually began to increase.

The United Fruit Company was unhappy with losing this unused land, and more importantly, control within the country. They lobbied the United States with money and influence, to intervene and overthrow the Guatemalan government. They spread misinformation and wrongfully portrayed the elected officials as Communists.

President Harry S. Truman authorized a plan to topple the Árbenz regime but it was cancelled. In 1952, President Eisenhower had run for president on a hard stance against communism. His U.S. Secretary of State John Foster Dulles advocated the Guatemalan coup d'état in 1954. He and his brother Allen Dulles, director of the CIA, were known to have connections to the United Fruit Company. The United States CIA deposed the democratically elected government and Árbenz resigned June 27, 1954. In its place was installed a pro-United Fruit Company military dictatorship. The military officer Carlos Castillo Armas was placed in power.

Julio explained that the right-wing political organization with which he was affiliated was a strong ally to the United States. Armas assumed dictatorial powers and banned all opposition parties. Political opponents were imprisoned and tortured. All of the social reforms of the previous revolution were reversed. Julio stressed that this had resulted in decades of civil war.

Leftist guerrilleros were fighting the authoritarian regimes backed by the United States. These regimes had dehumanized the campesinos and resulted in the genocide of the Maya peoples. It was disheartening to learn how the ruling dictator government, anti-government terrorist groups, mass murders of the poor, and the horrific living conditions of the majority of the people could all be traced back to U.S. involvement years ago.

The civil war Julio told us about began in 1960 and lasted until 1996 when a peace agreement was made. More than 200,000 people were killed during the 36-year-long skirmish. It is estimated over 83 percent of those killed were Mayan descendants.

All these years later after the civil war ended, violence and intimidation continue to be a major problem in the political and civilian life of the Guatemalans. Organized crime groups operate openly and factor heavily in political circles. Kidnappings for ransom and murders to intimidate people are a daily occurrence. Today as immigrant refugees are coming to America to try and escape to a better life, it should make Americans stop and look in the mirror before casting stones at immigrants trying to flee their beautiful country because of the danger and poverty.

We went to the city each day for class and then returned to George's to spend the night, where we would debrief and discuss what we learned that day. After a week of classes, the students were split up into pairs to travel to different parts of the country. Each pair was to travel to somewhere they had not been before.

For being such a small country, the type of climate and the topography were quite diverse. There were hot deserts, hot and humid tropical rain forests, year-round spring-like highlands, rainy mountainous regions, and sticky coastal areas, not to mention the beautiful volcanoes, black sand beaches, and natural lakes.

Each pair was given a list of things to research about their area and bring back to share with the group. Since we weren't actually a part of the class, George paired us up. He chose for Ken to go off by himself since he was fluent in Spanish. Ken shared, "I went to *Nue-*

va Concepción and (I believe, *Tiquisate*) in the south coast area where there are a lot of plantations and the labor force is mostly from the highlands. I also experienced the 7.6 earthquake while there plus the aftershock almost as intense. The epicenter was in the Pacific off the coast of Guatemala so it felt really strong."

Carman and Carolyn, with their few weeks of Spanish study, had a little advantage over us and were sent to the western part of the country. Randall and I were to go to the eastern side of the country in a low-lying, more desert-like area. It was way different from our mountainous green oasis.

Chapter 17
San Pedro Pinula

The town of *San Pedro Pinula* was our selected location with a stop in *Jalapa* along the way. Randall and I left early on Saturday morning for the Guatemala City Central Market where we were able to find a Pullman-type bus going to Jalapa. However, a few things were different on this Pullman.

First, it wasn't air conditioned. The second thing was, unlike the bus to Cobán where everyone had a seat, they piled the people on and a few stood in the aisle. Lastly, another difference was that the Cobán bus never stopped to pick up people. This bus stopped in every little town and more people got on board, filling up the aisle. After about an hour, two ladies got on board. We gave them our seats and stood the rest of the trip. We were getting accustomed to this being the modus operandi for transportation.

Upon arriving in Jalapa, my first thought was, *Thank goodness we get to live in Carchá.* The experience of staying in Jalapa was very depressing. The streets were terribly dirty and crowded with people in every direction. These were some of the poorest people I had seen so far. They were even poorer than the people in places devastated by earthquakes that George had taken us to see. There were crippled men and children on the side of the road begging for handouts. It was upsetting to see people living in these horrible conditions.

We discovered there wasn't a bus until the next morning for San Pedro Pinula so we found a little pensión (no Best Western but still nice) to spend the night. It was much better than the one Randall stayed in at Carchá. It cost us $2.00 apiece. They also served supper for $1.00 and we had scrambled eggs, refried beans, tortillas with cream-like butter, a sweet little baked pastry, and excellent lemonade. Not bad on the $60 budget we were allotted for six days.

After restless night due to noise outside, the next morning we found the bus to our final destination of San Pedro Pinula, which was just fifteen miles down a dirt road. As crowded as the chicken bus had been going to San Pedro Carchá on our first trip, that was nothing compared to this trip. Easily there were eight or nine people across each row of seats. We counted there were seventy-two people on the bus. The back of the bus had a sign that showed the capacity was forty-eight. *Just a tad over.*

I was sitting beside two drunk men that smelled to high heaven. It was early morning and already drunk? Maybe they were the ones making noise all night. Being the novelty of two gringos, they were fascinated by us. Every time we hit a bump their heads would bounce like bobblehead dolls or their bodies would bump into me due to their inebriated state.

When we weren't playing bumper cars and they weren't dozing, they were trying to get us to talk to them. They were so drunk and slurring their words, making it even more difficult to understand them with our little knowledge of Spanish. We kept looking forward and tried to ignore them the best we could, hoping they didn't get sick and throw up on us. Eventually the guy next to me fell asleep, leaned against me and drooled on my backpack. *Please, Lord, let us reach Pinula soon!*

To make matters even worse, it was like an oven inside the bus. The hot sun beat down on the bus and the packed, sweaty riders just increased the temperature inside. Anyone whoever rode on a school bus would know how hard it was to get the windows to go up and down. They stuck all the time. The few bus windows that worked were down but that didn't seem to let much air in. When air did come in, the dust was swirling in the windows as we bumped along the pothole-filled dirt road.

At one point we were stopped by a herd of skinny Brahman-type cattle walking down the middle of the road. Even being an animal scientist, I hadn't seen many of this breed of cattle back home except in rodeos for bull riding. These with their exposed ribs and backbones would have been laughed out of the arena by the cowboys. Herding the cattle down the road were two men on horseback following behind. I probably should say "pony" back because these were the scrawniest horses the men were riding. The men had on cowboy hats and dressed the part. But with their legs not far off the ground, it reminded me of the time when the Harlem Globetrotters came to town. They played a charity game of donkey basketball with their long legs dragging the court.

The road had a steep hill on one side and a cliff-like drop off to a deep valley on the other. There was no place for the cattle to move out of our way. We had to wait for the herd to spread apart and cattle passed on each side of the bus as we slowly crept past. I thought, *It's like Moses parting the Red Sea. Well, maybe not exactly.*

The bus driver waved at the ranchers and they waved their cowboy hats back, like this must have been a common occurrence. Once past, we left them in our dust and bounced along to our destination. It was probably the longest hour of our lives to go just fifteen miles. Thankfully we finally arrived at Pinula, finishing that ghastly trip and departing the bus.

San Pedro Pinula was no fantasy vacation paradise but still way better than Jalapa. It too had a huge Catholic church in the center of town, just like all the other Guatemalan towns. Pinula was a little less crowded and a lot cleaner. To our amazement as we got off the bus, a group of Cub Scouts in uniform were meeting in the town center and greeted us. Who would have thought we'd find a pack of Cub Scouts in this locale? They were as surprised to see two gringos get off the bus as we were to see them.

All talking at once, they asked us where we were from and what we were doing in Pinula. We said *Estados Unidos* and with our limited Spanish tried to explain that we were just visiting. We asked where a pensión was located. They motioned for us to follow and the whole pack led us in the right direction.

Our home for the next three days was behind one of the doors in the stucco walls that lined all the sidewalks. The pensión definitely wasn't a Waldorf but would be just fine. We were able to get a room and went to check it out before we went to explore the town. The room was pretty plain with the typical red and white tile floor we were now accustomed to seeing. There was a little window to the courtyard, a table and two beds. Each bed sunk in the middle, forming a deep valley. It was like sleeping in a bowl. Randall put a chair under his to see if it would provide any support. Didn't help much.

There was a little restaurant in the pensión and we ate our meals there the first day. When we left to do our exploration, we took our backpacks rather than leave them in the room because it didn't seem too secure. Reaching the market, old and young ladies with lots of children were everywhere selling most anything imaginable. We bought oranges, bananas, and some bread to take back to our room.

There was a lovely woman selling pottery she had made. The pottery was made from a yellowish clay and glazed. Her little daughter was selling miniature pottery just like her mother's that she had made herself. I bought two little pieces to remember the visit. Each cost five cents. The other big purchase was some coconut, molasses and sugar candy for later.

Leaving the market, we strolled around town to see what all was going on. Being Sunday, there was a lot of activity near the Catholic church. At the entrance were musicians. Three were playing a huge marimba, another man was on drums and the last one played an electric guitar of all things. They were amazing.

We saw people parading toward us down the cobblestone street, carrying banners, pots smoking with incense, and colorful pennants. They walked past the musicians and into the church. Simultaneously, people started shooting off firecrackers and huge bottle rockets exploded with loud bangs overhead. Everyone was just milling around and taking it all in. We never did know exactly what they were celebrating or if this was just an every Sunday occurrence. All the people were very friendly and we decided this wasn't such a bad place to spend a few days.

I'll never forget one event that had us laughing until we were crying and we couldn't wait to tell Ken, Carman, and Carolyn. Shortly after arriving in Pinula, we saw a man and a boy with two ropes (each about twenty feet long) lassoed around a big healthy Brahman heifer's neck. She was way healthier than any of the cattle on the road. This cow was running down the street and the two were running behind, hanging on to the ropes for dear life. They were shouting for people to get out of the way.

The heifer slowed just enough as she ran by a tree that the man was able to run around the tree, hop over the rope, and make a loop. This stopped the heifer dead in her tracks, jerking her head around as she snorted and bawled loudly. Everyone was laughing and pointing at the poor guys trying to control the cow that obviously had a mind of her own and knew where she wanted to go.

A few minutes later as we were going down the street to continue our exploration of the town, out of nowhere the heifer came running by us again with her owners frantically trying to keep up. Laughing, I thought, *That's one wild cow. Reminds me of when one of my steers got away at the Delia Fair.*

There was a small hill that overlooked the town so we went to check it out. It was a great spot to get a view of the entire town and we took some amazing photos. People were wrapping up their trading day in the market and starting to head home. We were getting thirsty so we jogged down the hill and found a little tienda to get a bottle of pop.

A young man about our age was working in the tienda so we struck up a conversation with him best we could. He was very patient

with our Spanish and knew a few English words. The young man's
name was Carlos Enrique Granillo. We found out that the tienda belonged to his parents. The store faced the street and the family lived
in a house connected in the back. Carlos was home from school after
finishing his studies in bookkeeping. He had ten brothers and sisters.
On the wall were six diplomas for college. Two of his sisters were in
the States. One lived in Los Angeles and the other lived in Boston.

Carlos was most congenial and wanted to practice his English
with us. We figured he was a great resource to help with our Friends
World College assignment. With his help, we were able to get answers to check off several of the questions we were given to research.
We enjoyed chatting with him and it was interesting learning about
his family and more about Guatemala.

All of a sudden Carlos jumped up and motioned for us to join
him in the room adjacent to the store. It was their living room and
he wanted to show us their new television. The room had the same
red and white tile floor, faded pink walls, a bench, chairs and the TV.
He was so proud of the TV and said they were one of the few in the
pueblo (town) to have one. He turned it on and unbelievably Game 2
of the World Series between Pittsburgh and Baltimore was playing.
Holy cow! And here I thought I was getting away from Howard Cosell.

We were excited even though it was a rerun of the game. None of
the missionaries had TVs so this was the first time we had seen one
since leaving the States. It was the ninth inning and we watched the
end of the game.

A *fútbol* (soccer) game came on next that was being broadcast
from Germany. However, the announcer was speaking in Spanish extremely fast. We couldn't make out one word. Then someone kicked
the ball into the net. The announcer went wild and without taking a
breath screamed, "GOOOAAALLLL!" We wondered how he could
do that without passing out. Carlos shared that fútbol was the national sport in Guatemala and was played everywhere. Later that

night he was going to play and invited us to come watch. *Sounds like fun.*

Before going to the soccer match, we figured we'd better grab something to eat. We went back to the pensión restaurant and sat next to a window facing the street. Out of the blue the heifer from earlier in the day went running by the window. The same two guys were running along behind her again. We couldn't stop laughing. We wondered just how long this little game of chase had been going on.

Right after the cow and chasers disappeared, two guys rode up on their horses. They got off and walked into the restaurant with spurs on their boots jangling. They had on holsters with pistols dangling off their hips. They each had a long rope in hand that was being drug in from outside.

They found a table and sat down, dropping the rope by the table. We realized the ropes were attached to the horses' bridles outside so they wouldn't run off while the cowboys ate their supper. We had to refrain ourselves from chuckling out loud. We felt like we had just stepped onto the set of *Gunsmoke* in Dodge City. *Festus, where's Miss Kitty?*

After supper we went to the soccer field Carlos had told us about. I think every kid in town turned out to watch the match. However, Randall and I were more of a spectacle than the game. While the teenagers and young adults were playing, the younger ones were pestering us asking us how to say this or that in English. Needless to say, we didn't get to see much of the game. One thing we didn't have to teach the kids was "Goodbye." They probably knew that just like back home we all learned *hola* and *adios* as kids. They got a kick out of saying, "Goodbye my love" as we left to go back to the pensión.

That night I began to feel ill and had my first experience of Montezuma's revenge. I decided the coconut candy I had purchased in the market was the culprit since Randall hadn't tried it and was okay. (To this day I'm not a coconut fan.) The nurses had given us some precautionary medicine to take with us for amoebas and I was so grateful. With horrible stomach cramps and several trips to the bathroom, it was a long and scary night. I think I slept about two hours. Thankfully I survived and felt a little better by morning. *Thank you, nurses!*

In the long run (bad pun intended), being sick turned out to be a small blessing. We had seen a *farmacia* (pharmacy) the day before and we went there to see if we could get some kind of antidiarrheal medicine. The pharmacist was a woman who spoke excellent English. She helped us get some more medicine similar to what the nurses had shared plus Pepto Bismol®. I was never so happy to see that pink bottle and it never tasted so good.

The pharmacist told us that she had lived in Boston for six years. She had come home to take care of her sick mother and one day would return to Boston. Thanks to her, we were able to get answers to all of the rest of our assigned questions to bring back to the Friends' class.

We took it easy the rest of the day since I was pretty wiped out (literally). I had only eaten a banana and a piece of bread all day and was getting hungry by evening and feeling much better. The nurses' medicine was working. That night we went for supper at a little restaurant we had passed the day before. We figured it might be good to eat somewhere besides the pensión. Typical to most small restaurants, there was no menu. One's meal was whatever the cook made for that day. It made things easier for us not speaking Spanish.

Our food was brought to us and it looked delicious but for one odd thing. The meat was not familiar to us and had tiny little bones. Randall and I looked at one another wondering *What in the world is this?* It was covered with some kind of picante sauce and smelled pretty good. Randall said, "Look at those tiny bones. Do you think it's a cat?"

"Or maybe a rat?" I added with my face scrunched up. After those comments, we both refused to eat it and just had beans and tortillas.

After the sleepless night before, I was ready for a good night's rest. I hoped not to hear the church bells ring again like the night before at 1, 2, 3, 6 and 7 a.m. Thankfully, I slept well and felt much better the next day, as the K'ekchi' would say, "*Bantiox re li Dios* (Thanks be to God)!"

The previous day, our new pharmacist friend asked if we had been to *San Luis Jilotepeque*, a little town about an hour over the mountain. She said their market was on Tuesday and they had all kinds of pottery and hand-woven materials there. We decided to go and grabbed the bus. The bus to San Luis was the same bus we had ridden from Jalapa to Pinula days before. *Oh joy!*

It was about an hour's ride over a bumpy mountain pass. It was like riding the tractor at home over a plowed field. The countryside was gorgeous with deep valleys between the mountains. It wasn't as green as Carchá but it was still beautiful.

Arriving in the town it was quite picturesque but very dirty. We strolled through the market and saw indigenous women selling colored yarn and material. It was interesting that in Pinula and Jalapa we noticed almost all of the women were dressed in ladina clothing, not indigenous attire. *Make a mental note for Friend's class.*

Pottery was made in this area from their red clay, not glazed and had hand-painted black designs. It was quite different from the pottery in Pinula. I purchased three pieces of miniature pottery to take home. My favorite was a little replica of a pitcher. I paid a whopping sixteen cents for all three. It truly was a nice experience and the people were warm toward us, even though we could tell they weren't used to having gringos there. Eventually we become accustomed to stares.

We had seen all there was to see in the little pueblo. As soon as the bus returned, we got on board and went back to Pinula. We had noticed that the buses usually stayed about thirty minutes once they arrived in a town before going on to the next stop. Since our class questions were all answered (thanks to our new friends), we decided we might as well head on back a day early. When the bus pulled to a stop in Pinula, we jumped off and ran to the pensión. We packed our belongings and ran to catch the bus before it left for Jalapa.

As we were jogging to the bus, we were given a cheerful send-off by Carlos in the tienda and the woman in the farmacia, both smiling and waving at us. It felt like we were in a Hallmark movie. The people in Pinula had been incredibly nice. We made some wonderful friends and realized how with a smile, communication barriers can be broken. The people still on the bus laughed and cheered seeing us run and jump back on. Crazy gringos!

Chapter 18
Día de los Muertos
(Day of the Dead)

After spending another night in Jalapa at the same pensión, we arrived back at Chimaltenango to recover from our long trip. It was great to see our three amigos. George wasn't there but arrived shortly after we did. George had gone to Pinula to check up on us, but we had already left and missed him. *Oops!*

Ken, Carman and Carolyn asked us if we had felt the earthquake and the few aftershocks. We hadn't felt it in San Pedro Pinula. They had felt two or three other earthquakes since arriving in Antigua where they were studying Spanish. They were a little shaken up from the experiences. Bad joke. But we hadn't noticed anything and felt a little left out. Guatemalans seemed to be pretty used to them. I guess it was like us with tornadoes back home. You just learn to live with them.

As nice as it was to get back to George's house, unfortunately Randall got sick after we returned. He was suffering from what I had experienced in Pinula. I was almost recovered and still a little tired, but he got hit hard. It took him a couple days to recover but he was a trooper and never missed any of the activities George had planned for us.

It was a beautiful warm, sunny day on our first day back. We sat outside on the grass and soaked up the sun while reading and relaxing. It was good medicine for us after both feeling puny. There were four Holstein milk cows owned by a neighbor out in the yard. George allowed the cows to roam freely to mow the grass.

The scene outside of George's house could have made the most gorgeous landscape painting. There were beautiful yellow flowering trees called *tecomasuche* (in some places known as buttercup trees) that are native to Guatemala and huge blue hydrangea bushes. He had a garden with corn, beans, and a few other vegetables. There were small orange trees loaded with fruit. Surrounding the property were pine trees that blocked the view of the mountains. But if we walked just one hundred yards down the road, we could see the majestic mountains and volcanoes in the distance. It was breathtaking.

After a week on the road, we needed to do our laundry. George's washing machine was a large, cement pila similar to Matilde's back in Carchá. Part of the arrangement for my room and board at Chepe's included doing my laundry. I always felt bad when Matilde had to wash my muddy clothes after our treks in the rain. She even ironed my clothes. *Never have I ever had my underwear ironed before.*

Poorer families who didn't have pilas with running water took their clothes to the river. To carry and wash the family's clothes, some women used a plastic laundry basket but most used a giant, oblong, platter-like object made from one solid piece of wood. It was about a foot and half wide and two feet long with a shallow bowl-like indention.

Imagine a woman loading this large wooden platter with dirty clothes, placing it on her head, and balancing it while walking to the river. The wooden platter would be placed in the water. She would put a piece of clothing on the board and begin scrubbing with a brush or her hands. Sometimes the women would beat the clothes against the rocks in the river. If there was no place to lay the clothes out on larger rocks or shrubs to dry, the women would load the wet clothes back on the platter (way heavier than before) and carry them home to dry.

George's pila had a faucet in the middle that spilled into a deep sink with a plug. We filled the sink with water. Very cold water! On each side of the sink were two flat shallow surfaces with lips to keep the water from spilling out or back into the middle sink. This shallow area also had a drain in the back. One would dip a small bowl in the sink of water and douse the clothes.

George showed us the laundry soap. It definitely wasn't Cheer® in a box like we used back home. Enclosed in a plastic wrapper, it was a cylindrical bar of soap that was about three inches long and two inches in diameter with blue and yellow stripes. The coloration kind of reminded me of toothpaste that was white and green striped when it was squeezed out of the tube. We asked George why the two colors. He honestly didn't know, but my best guess was maybe one color was detergent and the other was some sort of stain remover.

Once wet, we rubbed the clothes with the wet bar of soap and then used a brush to work the soap into the material. Added more water. Scrubbed some more. Rinsed. Repeated the process until the clothes looked clean. Needless to say, it wasn't the best treatment for clothes to last a long time. It took many rinses to get all the soap out of the clothes.

Next was wringing out the clothes by hand as best possible to help the clothes dry faster. My arms were aching by the time the clothes were ready to be hung to dry. It reminded me of helping my grandma wash clothes when I was a little boy. Back then, my arms ached from cranking the handle to the wringer to wring out the clothes. This was way more work. My respect for Matilde and all Guatemalan women grew exponentially after my first experience of washing my own clothes by hand.

On sunny days, like the day we did our laundry, the clothes were hung on a wire or rope strung between two trees for a clothesline. But on rainy days, like the majority of the days in Carchá, the clothes were hung on a clothesline strung under the veranda. It was so humid on rainy days it took forever for the clothes to dry. I learned quickly to plan ahead because it might be a week or two before my clothes were dry.

Shortly after arriving back to Chimaltenango, we got to experience *Día de los Muertos* (Day of the Dead). This is a two-day holiday Guatemalans celebrate on November 1 and 2. *Día de Todos los Santos* (All Saints' Day) is November 1 and *Día de Difuntos (*All Soul's Day) is November 2. It was quite different from anything I had experienced back home with only trick-or-treating on Halloween.

These holidays are huge celebrations in Guatemala, other Latin American countries, and Latino communities in the U.S. We were told that people decorate their loved one's graves by covering them with pine needles and placing beautiful flowers and wreaths. The relatives prepare their lost loved one's favorite food and use only the best ingredients because one wouldn't want to insult the dead relative. They leave the food and favorite alcoholic drink on the graves to entice the spirits of the loved ones to return.

People often light candles that burn all night. This is to help the spirits find their way back in the dark. The following morning, they replace the day-old food with plates of fresh goodies.

We went by a cemetery in Chimaltenango and there were little vendor booths set up around the outside where people were selling food, candles, and trinkets. There was a guy selling cotton candy and made me think of football games and the county fairs back home. But what really made me chuckle, next to the cotton candy was a lady frying *chicharrones* (pork rinds) and spooning beans inside them. *I've never seen that at a football game.*

The graves were beautifully decorated and reminded me of our past celebrations on Memorial Day. Except ours were more somber and reflective, while theirs were more joyful and festive. They see it as a return of their friends' and loved ones' spirits. From another vantage point, the scroungy stray dogs on the street seemed to be the happiest and winners of this event. They made out like bandits, stealing food from the graves.

Chapter 19
Getting More Education

It was time for our course to wrap up with Friends World College. We were quite ready for it to be completed. We gathered at Friends to report about our expeditions and share the knowledge we had learned about different areas in Guatemala.

Julio talked about the diversity of the people. For a small country about the size of the state of Tennessee, there were twenty-one different Mayan languages with twenty-eight different dialects and two non-Mayan Amerindian languages. Spanish, of course, was the national language but all twenty-one Mayan languages were still spoken. Today K'ekchi' (or Q'eqchi') is the second most prevalent with over 555,000 who speak the language.

At the end of the class, we attended what was called the Interfair (International Fair). This event was for big corporations from many countries to display their industrial goods and new technology. The countries represented included the Netherlands, West Germany, Israel, Guatemala, Mexico, El Salvador, United States, Spain, France, Czechoslovakia, Pacific Islands and many more.

The large buildings downtown where the event was held were new and beautiful. It was quite interesting all the fancy displays with new technology and goods most Guatemalans couldn't afford. It was such a contrast to the poorer side of Guatemala we had seen. The best part of the event was seeing Guatemalans working in some display booths and wearing their typical native dress, compared to the people in other booths dressed in business suits and ties.

While at the Interfair, we saw a man with no legs. He was along the sidewalk, begging for money. Many people were stopping and giving him money. At first I didn't know what to do. *Give him money? Avoid him? Not stare? What?*

We each gave him some money and went on. George shared that thousands of people lost everything in the earthquake that hit only a few years earlier and many lost limbs. They had no alternative but to beg. It was gut wrenching and so obvious how difficult a life this man had. It made me count my blessings even more and hope we could help the people.

For the final week with George, he signed Randall and me up for a five-day class sponsored by an organization called World Neighbors. There was only room for two students and the other three of our colleagues went back to language study.

The class was located about thirty minutes from Chimaltenango in a town called *San Martín Jilotepeque*. George made arrangements for us to ride with the instructor who was named Don Marcos. He was a native Guatemalan about 65 or 70 years old. Don Marcos was an agronomist and quite a learned, intelligent man. He instructed us in very well-spoken English.

Soon after departing Chimaltenango, Don Marcos steered off the paved road onto a gravel road. If his vehicle had shock absorbers, they certainly didn't have the Midas˙ touch. It made for a horrible ride. The gravel, pothole-filled road back home that ran by our farm seemed like a super highway in comparison.

Finally reaching our destination and still in one piece, we were surprised to see a busy little park. In addition to Randall and me, there were eight Peace Corps forester volunteers taking the class. They were a pretty rowdy bunch, prone to cursing, and didn't seem to take things too seriously. Quite the change from the EMB missionaries. But basically they were a good group of guys. They definitely had a different philosophy about life and their reason for being in Guatemala compared to ours.

Our purpose for the class was to learn about soil conservation by using simple techniques, but more importantly, how to successfully teach what we learned to the campesinos in their villages. The main emphasis Don Marcos stressed was to be very slow in the teaching process and make sure our students understood each point discussed before moving on. If not, they would give up and think they were dumb, which was not the case. They were just not educated. He said many of the campesinos only had a third-grade education at the most. *Very important lesson to remember.*

Don Marcos shared that World Neighbors started working there in 1972, and after six years, the program was entirely run by the campesinos. The organization taught the poor farmers the importance of soil conservation. The loss of good topsoil was a major problem in the mountainous country.

Deforestation (campesinos cutting down trees for firewood) and all the rain was washing all the good topsoil down the mountains. It resulted in poorer and poorer crop production. Don Marcos showed us some miniature hillside examples set up with different terracing and contour farming procedures. These techniques helped save the topsoil from washing away and improve the land for more abundant crops.

During one of our trips to class, Don Marcos shared about his experience during the 1976 earthquake. Hearing how horrific it was from someone who lived through it was way different than reading about it secondhand. He shared he had survived after the ceiling of his house came crashing down on him, suffering through the long, cold night buried under the rubble. He heard people crying and screaming for help throughout the night. He eventually was rescued, and he believed he was saved to help his fellow Guatemalans live a better life. He devoted his life to doing just that.

The World Neighbors had incredible displays to showcase their work for visitors. These displays sort of reminded me of 4-H booths back home that we used to make at the Jackson County 4-H Fair but way better than anything we ever created. The displays showing how the land could be contoured to improve farming were fascinating. In addition, they had earthquake-proof housing, health, and nutrition demonstrations set up.

There was a lot of construction going on since they were adding on to their facility. A fun part was a little fair-like amusement area with a merry-go-round and Ferris wheel. But the hot-ticket items were the foosball tables set up in the center. It was hilarious watching the Peace Corps workers and campesinos competing against each other.

After finishing our tour of the facility, we went to where our class was held. It was located about thirty minutes away at one of the local World Neighbors instructor's farms. If we had thought the first road was bad, this road was even worse. The best way I could describe it was a dry creek bottom with lots of rocks jutting up. It was the roughest ride yet. I thought to myself, *I think my stomach and kidneys just swapped places.*

Don Marcos described the land as hilly. The Flint Hills back home was hilly. This was straight up mountainous. The first two days at the farm were very cold. The wind was blowing and it was miserable. To top it off, mosquitos were quite prevalent. *Here I always thought cold and wind didn't go with mosquitos. Little do I know.* However, the class was excellent and made up for the negative conditions.

The instructor had contoured his land, planted trees, sown pasture, and planted different types of crops. Most farmers just planted corn year after year. The instructor said he used to have time to just plant two-thirds of his land to corn and still did not have enough corn or money to last the whole year. He would have to leave his family and go to the coast to work on the huge cotton finca for a few months.

He shared this was what most all campesinos did. and they received very little money for working on the fincas. The living conditions were horrible. But he said, "One has to do what one has to do to survive." It was a very sad situation and vicious cycle for the people.

After learning from World Neighbors how to improve his land and farming techniques, he was then able to plant only one third of his land to corn. The new techniques and improved soil helped increase corn production enough to last his family all year plus have surplus to sell.

On the remaining land that he had used for corn before, he now planted and sold different crops at the markets. He didn't have to go to the coast to work, or even have the time, because he was continually working to improve his land and was financially successful. It was truly amazing to see the work he had done and how it had helped improve his life.

The corn plants we saw that day brought back some wonderful memories from home. Rossville, the town where I grew up, had the Annual Tall Corn Festival, which always turned out to be held on the hottest August day of the year.

Saturday morning was the Tall Corn Festival Parade, including homemade floats with people tossing candy, kids on bikes with streamers, and old antique cars honking. One couldn't forget the Rossville Palomino Horse Club (of which I was a member), riding golden-colored quarter horses and wearing yellow shirts, black pants, white cowboy hats and black Roy Rogers neckties. We were quite the sight and won many trophies for best saddle club in area parades. My sisters and I took turns over the years riding our palomino horse Queen, who loved to prance down the street showing off. After the parade we had barrel and pole bending races on the ball diamond in front of the grandstand.

The biggest parade attraction was the convertibles with the Tall Corn Princess candidates, waving to the crowd down Main Street. You voted for your favorite princess to be Tall Corn Festival Queen by putting money in jars around town and it was a penny a vote. My sister always says she got robbed the year she was a princess because the grandpa of one of her competitors put a hundred-dollar bill in his granddaughter's jar.

The main stage event was the Tall Corn Contest. The farmers searched their fields to find their tallest stalks and the biggest ears of corn. Entries were brought to the high school baseball diamond packed with people waiting in anticipation. The measurements were carefully made and each farmer hoped to win bragging rights for the year.

Having grown up my entire life on a farm where we grew corn and entered a few of those contests, I was shocked at the Guatemalan corn we saw at our World Neighbor's class. The corn stalks were easily fifteen feet tall. The ears were so high I couldn't reach them. They had to cut down the plants to reach the ears of corn. This corn would easily knock my dad and his farmer friends out of the running for the Tall Corn Festival grand prize.

The rest of the week we learned how to build terraces. I thought back to our farm and the terraces I had bounced over during my motorcycle training session. Our terraces had been made by machines. This was back-breaking work, digging the soil by hand to make the small hills along the contour of the steep land. The weather turned colder and it was misty but all the workers kept digging and building up the terrace we were creating. Terraces would provide much better crops for years and keep the good topsoil from being washed down the hillside.

The last day we were tired and sore but felt a sense of accomplishment. We said our goodbyes and Don Marcos jostled us back over the bumpy roads to George's warm house. It was humbling to imagine our new campesino friends we had toiled with going back to their homes with cornstalk roofs, open wood fires, and being barefoot on the cold, clay-soil floors.

Chapter 20
Back to Carchá

Our classes were finally over and our heads were reeling with all the information we had learned. It was going to be nice to get back to Chepe's, see the missionaries, and just focus on studying K'ekchi' again. Six weeks prior, I never imagined I would have thought this.

We had one last excursion before going "home" to Carchá. George took Randall and me to a small town called *San Antonio Aguas Calientes* (Saint Anthony Hot Water) close to Antigua to see how they wove their beautiful material. The technique, dating back to the reign of the Maya, is still in place today. The textiles are woven from cotton yarns that are dyed first. They used plants, such as carrots (orange), hibiscus flowers (pink), avocado trees (beige) and herbs (green) to make the vibrant colors.

The women used backstrap looms just like their ancestors. A weaver would attach one end of her loom to a tree or post and the other end around her back with a leather strap. She would lean back and use her body to stretch the string material attached to the loom. This would provide the necessary tension for weaving colorful threads back and forth through the strings, creating strong and sturdy, beautiful fabric. Their artistry was amazing.

At last, it was time to get back to Carchá. We weren't able to take the Pullman bus this time because we had two sleeping mattresses for the missionaries that wouldn't fit on the Pullmans. It was back to the chicken bus. We left at 10 a.m. and didn't arrive until 5:00 p.m. *Long day!*

It was pouring down rain when we got to Carchá. Thankfully the mattresses were wrapped in plastic. Randall ran over to Bob's house so Bob could bring the Land Rover to haul the mattresses to his house.

When I got to Chepe's house, was I ever shocked. With the monthly rent we paid Chepe for my room and board, he had bought a television with an antenna for better reception. It seemed to me it might have been better to improve the thatched roof, smoky kitchen and put a cement floor in the dining area.

The kids were excited to show me the fuzzy, black and white *telenovela* (Spanish soap opera) they were watching. Once in a while I would watch TV with the kids and it was a good way to learn some Spanish. Imagine watching *Hawaii Cinco-Cero (Hawaii Five-O)* with Steve McGarrett dubbed in a not-so-suave voice saying "*Reservale, Danno.*" It didn't have quite the effect as "Book'em, Danno."

But my all-time favorite was when I heard the music from *Gunsmoke* start playing. I ran in to see Matt Dillon and Miss Kitty speaking rapidly in Spanish. *There's Miss Kitty from Pinula!*

However for me, there was even more exciting news. Chepe was building a *baño!* In English that is BATHROOM! It had a toilet and a shower. *No hot water but I can't complain about that.* This made up for the TV. I was glad that staying with our families was allowing them to have some improvements to their lives.

I was in my room writing a letter when Óscar knocked on my door to tell me it was time for supper. He saw me and asked who I was writing to. I told him I was writing to my sister and he asked if he could write a message. He wrote, "*José Óscar Xol. Chan xacquil. Ma sa sa' la ch'ol? Lain sa. Bantiox re li Dios. Nintakla sahil ach'ol.*" This loosely translates to "How are you? Are you happy in your heart? I am happy, thanks be to God. I send happiness to your heart." Later Jane wrote back how special that was and she couldn't wait to come visit and meet Óscar and my K'ekchi' family.

Randall checked with his family to see if his room was finished. In the true Guatemalan timeline, it wasn't ready but coming along. Don Antonio's family was much poorer than Chepe's and they were running out of money to finish the room. MCC gave them a cash advance to help finish it.

Rather than stay at the cheap pensión, we borrowed a cot from the missionaries so Randall could camp out in my room for a "week" until he was able to move to his finished space. It rained hard the entire first night we were back. In the morning part of the floor was wet on Randall's side of the room. Obviously, the walls weren't water tight. *Glad we have our things up off the floor!*

We resumed our K'ekchi' study and it felt good to get back into it. Debbie was happy with how much we remembered after our hiatus. Randall's informant Julián was unable to keep working so Santiago began helping us both. He hiked in from Campat through the rain and stayed over for the days he tutored us. The nurses had a little room beside their house where he would sleep.

Santiago hadn't had the easiest life. Not only did he have his young family but he also cared for his ailing mother, who lived with them. The nurses said she had some kind of respiratory problem (possibly even tuberculosis) from years of breathing in the smoke from the fire. Linda and Debbie were proud of his work as a health promoter and said he was very smart and always dependable. The money we paid him for language training was helpful for his family. He was a fun-loving guy and always smiling and laughing at the caxlan cuinks botching up words.

It continued to rain for three solid days after we got back. Chepe told me that during the weeks we were gone it had been beautiful and sunny. It hadn't started raining until we got back and he teased, blaming me for bringing it back from the city.

At times, it was the hardest I had ever seen it rain. Were we ever very glad we had bought our umbrellas because we needed them to go to Debbie's for class or when Randall walked to his family's house for meals. When the wind was blowing though, umbrellas weren't much help. It was getting depressing trying to stay dry and warm while living in my damp room. After about the second day of rain, the entire floor was pretty much wet all over, with parts having almost an inch of standing water. It just never had a chance to dry out.

The third night we were exhausted from our studies and tired and cold from walking in the rain. The rain was beating so hard on the tin roof of our room that Randall and I could barely hear each other talk. We were shouting and started laughing at how futile it was. We decided to just go to bed, get under our warm covers and read until we fell asleep, hoping for a better day tomorrow.

That night it continued to rain hard and the wind rattled the tin on the roof of my room. During the night I heard some commotion from the family in the dining area, but that wasn't uncommon because they could be up, rustling around at all hours. I didn't even consider getting out of my warm bed.

At about 4:00 a.m. I was awakened when I heard more noise than just the rain pounding on the tin. My bed was beside the wall of the dining area so I could hear the ruckus going on. There was a little bit of light shining through the cracks of the walls, which was really unusual to have the lights on this early in the morning. I figured something was up and decided to check it out. Grabbing my flashlight, I found and slipped on my clothes, being careful not to let my jeans touch the wet floor. I slid my feet in my shoes and I quietly got up without turning on the light so as not to wake Randall.

Entering the dining area, I found Chepe and family all awake and looking quite worried. They had been up all night, keeping an eye on the river that was beginning to flood and making preparations in case the water got too high. I was shocked to see the shallow river that ran behind the house was now a huge river and had climbed up the 25-foot slope. In the backyard, water was covering everything but the roof of the little shed where the goats stayed. The pig pen was completely underwater. The rushing water had washed away the poles, plastic curtains, and wooden stool to the "one-holer" outhouse.

Chepe had moved their two pigs from the backyard across the road onto higher ground. He kept them tied to trees to keep them from running off. The boys had helped catch the chickens and ducks, moving them up to the dining area outside my room. They had moved everything out of the kitchen up to the dining area. They had moved the mother goat and her babies into the kitchen. Everyone was soaking wet and the children were running around barefoot. I never understood how they could survive but they were tough.

The water was getting close to reaching Matilde's kitchen. Thankfully the kitchen was about four feet lower than the house so the water had a ways to go to get in the house. During the short time I had been up, the water continued to rise rapidly and was inching closer and closer to entering the kitchen. We had to move the goats across the road, too. I also helped carry Chepe's firewood and the pieces of tin for the new baño that were stored behind the house to higher ground.

Chepe's sister Media and her little boy Edgar, who was about five or six, lived next door. They were extremely poor and I never knew if her husband had died or left her. Their house was lower and closer to the river. The house had just a dirt floor with rough wood walls and a tin roof. During the night they had moved all of her belongings to Chepe's, praying Chepe's house was safe. They had even removed the tin roof from her house in case it washed away.

Matilde went ahead and made breakfast somehow. She made coffee, mosh, beans, and tortillas. Chepe was shivering, he was so cold. His sweater was soaking wet so I went and grabbed one of mine for Chepe, which woke Randall. He was shocked to see the river. He was worried about his family

With his umbrella in hand and homemade plastic poncho, Randall trudged into the windy, drenching rain to see if Antonio and his family were okay. They lived on the other side of the river so he had to cross a bridge. It was covered by two feet of water so he couldn't get there and returned back to Chepe's. Thankfully, he found out later that Don Antonio's family was safe. Their house was on the high side of the river and all was okay.

Shortly after we had eaten, the river crested and began to recede. It dropped about two inches in the first half hour. It never reached inside Matilde's kitchen and she said, "Bantiox re li Dios!" Unfortunately, Chepe's sister's house had gotten about three or four feet of water in it and left several inches of silty mud, but at least the water didn't wash away the walls of the house.

The water receded quickly but the backyard was just mud, too muddy for the animals. The next morning we awoke to Old McDonald's (Chepe's) Farm with all the animals (two pigs, nanny goat and two kids, two ducks, one rooster, two hens with sixteen chicks, three laying hens, and about a half dozen half-grown chickens) serenading us. Add in Chepe's kids and Edgar singing, screaming, and crying, it was more like a zoo than a farm. But we all survived. That was the important thing.

The dynamics changed for the few days that Media and Edgar lived with us until their hut could be rebuilt. They weren't used to being around caxlan cuinks so it was a new experience for them. Edgar was such a lonely, poor little boy. He didn't go to school like Chepe's kids. His clothes were just rag hand-me-downs from Óscar and Rollie. He followed Randall and me like a little shadow and would not leave us alone. It was hard to not lose patience with him, but we would sit down and try to talk. I never saw much of him again after they moved back to their rebuilt hut.

Chapter 21
Church in Carchá

Settling back into language study, it was nice to have a routine. The rain finally stopped. Well, it actually seemed to never stop in Guatemala in the highlands. The joke was that it rained thirteen months out of the year. Though Guatemala is called the Land of Eternal Spring, they do technically have two seasons compared to our four seasons back home.

In Alta Verapaz their seasons are described as dry season (November through April with February being the driest month) and rainy season (May through October with June being the wettest month). I might prefer to describe it as wet and wetter seasons. I believe their classification is based on the amount of precipitation. We actually thought it should be the reverse because there were more cloudy, misty, or rainy days in the winter months. But during the summer months, one could almost set a watch by the timing of the afternoon rains, but they were short downpours and then the sun would come back out.

Being November, the heavy rains we had experienced were quite a strange occurrence. After the flood, we wondered if there had been some kind of tropical storm or hurricane blowing through. Later we discovered Tropical Storm Jimena had traveled up Central America from Panama, but the eye took a turn out to the Pacific before getting to Guatemala. It was still devastating even without a direct hit. Wonder what it would have been like if it had traveled farther up north. Angels must have been watching over us again.

The weather was pretty depressing during the months of language study. We were told it was a very unusual year. *Just our luck.* I thought we might develop webbed feet. It was a very healthy environment for mold and fungus to grow. With the dampness and cool temperatures that could dip into the upper 40s and low 50s and warming into 60s or low 70s (if the sun came out), we found ourselves often quite chilled to the bone.

In Spanish, the fine misty rain we experienced almost daily was called *chipi chipi* (pronounced chee pee chee pee). The nurses best described it as if one were walking in a cloud and could see and feel the water droplets. The K'ekchi' would use the name chipi chipi as well, but in their language the term was *mutz' mutz' hab*, which was almost as funny sounding.

Chipi chipi seemed to occur mostly during the "dry" season but could be any time of the year. We were in the midst of it and went twenty-one days without seeing the sun. The streets were always wet. In the beginning we thought chipi chipi was fun to say. It quickly became one of our least favorite words.

On the weekends we often went with the missionaries to one of the remote churches for services. One of my most memorable services though was going with Chepe and his family to church. The children were bathed and faces gleaming. The boys each had their hair slicked back with some sort of gel. Matilde and the girls were dressed in their best uks and beautifully stitched huipils. I had never seen Matilde so beautiful, wearing silver chain necklaces and having her coal black hair slicked down and pulled back in her usual ponytail. Chepe was dressed in a nice blue suit he had made. He was very proud of his family.

Earlier on in my stay, Chepe had shared with me what a rough life he had lived. Through my limited language skills and lots of pantomime, he told me how poor he had been growing up. When he was in his twenties, he had gotten married to another woman. I never did know exactly what happened or if this wife had children, but he mimed tipping up a bottle and staggering like an alcoholic. His first wife left him because of his drinking.

For several years he said he did odd jobs, including repairing tarps, and drank *boj*, the sugarcane juice alcohol. He told me he became a Christian believer with the missionaries' help and quit drinking cold turkey. Once sober, he started his own sewing business. Then he met Matilde and they started their family. Because he had gotten married to his first wife in the Catholic church, they never got divorced. He and Matilde weren't legally married and that bothered him a great deal but nothing he could do about it.

The Sunday I went to church with Chepe's family, it was a sunny, beautiful morning with no rain. *Ch'ina' us li sak'e!* (The sunshine is pretty!) I even left my umbrella in my room but had my bolsa with my K'ekchi' Bible, hymnal and plastic rain gear, just in case. Chepe had his bolsa too but he carried a Spanish Bible, which was a little more prestigious, plus the Carchá Mennonite Church was mostly conducted in Spanish. Each of the girls took one of my hands as we walked the five or six blocks to the Mennonite church.

The church was a cinderblock building with a dirt floor and tin roof. There were wooden pews for seating and a little wooden stage at the front where the pastor gave his sermon. A couple of the missionary families were already sitting in the pews and waved when we got there.

The pastor leading the services was a ladino man named Francisco (Paco), who was about my age. The service started with a lot of singing in both languages but no musical instruments in this church.

Óscar would help me to turn to the correct page in my hymnal when we sang in K'ekchi'. Since I knew most of the tunes of the songs they chose, he was surprised I could read the words and sing along. A few people got up and read scripture. It appeared that some got up and gave emotional testimonies about their lives, but I really couldn't understand anything but a few words here and there.

Paco gave the sermon in Spanish because he didn't speak K'ekchi'. Paco actually could understand K'ekchi' but refused to speak it. Rubén, the music leader and also a pastor, was K'ekchi'. He was bilingual and used both languages. The services lasted from 9:30 a.m. until 12:00. That was a lot of sitting.

The thing that amazed me most was watching the children. They all sat perfectly still with their best behavior. There was no whining or complaining about this long, boring service.

Toward the end of the sermon, the three oldest Xol children and the rest of the elementary-age children left with a woman escorting them outside. Right after the sermon was over, the children marched back in single file, singing a song and pretended to each be playing musical instruments while they circled the pews several times. *How cute is this!*

After church we returned home where Matilde fixed lunch. We had some kind of beef that was boiled in a soup with tomatoes and onions. It wasn't the typical caldo, more like the roast beef my mother made for Sunday dinner after church. We also had rice and sliced cucumbers. Since the water had to be boiled to drink, coffee was the only choice. I was getting quite used to it and surprisingly, starting to like it. I was amazed at what an incredible meal she could prepare over that open fire.

Chapter 22

Thanksgiving in Guatemala

When I signed up to go to Guatemala, I don't think I had any idea that we would be fed so well. We learned the native food was delicious. However, who would have guessed we would be fed so well by the missionaries. They were awesome cooks. The markets and the store in Cobán had most everything needed to make great meals similar to back home.

We shared many meals with Debbie and Linda (the nurses) and Ruth, the literacy worker who arrived back from her furlough shortly before Thanksgiving. Ruth brought back lots of treats from home that were either too expensive or unavailable in Guatemala. For Linda's birthday, Randall and I even made pizza. Quite happily we figured out early that we weren't going to starve.

Being away from home and family for Thanksgiving was the first holiday that really made me homesick. Thankfully we were able to spend it with the missionaries. In addition, we were very happy that Ken came and spent the weekend with us. The other three MCC volunteers were Canadian so didn't celebrate Thanksgiving in November but had Thanksgiving Day on October 11.

It was fun to spend time with Ken in our setting. Randall continued bunking with me (now going on two weeks) since his room was still not finished. Borrowing another cot, Ken joined us and our little room was a tad crowded but we had a great time. It was interesting to hear his perspective on George and how it lined up with ours. Ken said with the two of them working more closely together, he felt George looking over his shoulder. It was good for him to get away for a little bit.

The missionaries put out quite a feast for our celebration. Our meal included chicken stuffed with dressing, mashed potatoes, giblet gravy, fresh peas and carrots, home-baked bread and apple butter, cranberry salad, lemon meringue pie and shoofly pie. Shoofly pie was a new thing for me. Many of the missionaries were from Pennsylvania and they told me shoofly pie was a Pennsylvania Dutch tradition. In Pennsylvania Dutch it is called Melassichriwwelkuche. *Oh my gosh, it sounds crazy enough, it could be a K'ekchi' word.*

Shoofly pie is made from molasses. Eggs and brown sugar are about the only other ingredients. The molasses mixture is poured into a pie shell and brown sugar crumb topping sprinkled over the top. *Wow, is Priscilla's shoofly pie ever delicious.*

After our Thanksgiving meal, we were stuffed and spent the rest of the day talking and singing. It was a Thanksgiving to remember. That evening we went to the nurses' house and played games before heading back to my little room at Chepe's. Ken was quite impressed with the missionaries and I think a little sad to not have the camaraderie we were able to share. He lived alone in his town but he had made many ladino and campesino friends. It would be nice to have Carman and Carolyn joining him in Santa María Cauqué after language study.

After walking back to our room late that night, Ken said he could never walk at night like that where he lived and he shared his struggles. While the village he lived in was relatively safe, the surrounding area was increasingly a hotbed of turmoil and guerrillero activity. He had to be very cautious and not be out of the village at night because it wasn't safe. Often campesinos disappeared off the streets of nearby towns, never knowing if they had been grabbed by the military to be "in the army now" or killed by either the guerrilleros or government death squads. It was not uncommon for him to hear or read in the paper that one of the wealthier families had a family member kidnapped to be held for ransom.

For being in the same country, his was a totally different world than Carchá. Thankfully Randall and I didn't experience anything close to what he dealt with in Santa María Cauqué. We never felt nervous or in danger in Carchá. After hearing Ken share how it was often difficult being alone with no one to talk to about what he was going through, I was even more thankful to have Randall and the missionaries to share this experience and didn't take them for granted.

At times, Randall and I felt like we were attached at the hip because we did almost everything together. We had lots of great times but also plenty of struggles learning to communicate even though we had been friends for several years. It was hard dealing with this strange new environment, culture shock, and figuring out our roles working with the K'ekchi'.

One of my biggest issues was insecurity and self confidence in myself. Often Randall and I would need to work through ordinary issues that arise when two people work and live together so closely. There were many days when we had long talks and then days we didn't want to talk at all. We would try to encourage each other when things were depressing (like chipi chipi for days on end with no sunshine) or we were struggling with some ailment, most often an upset stomach.

Randall once sent a letter to my sister and wrote, "I've found through my experience in Holland that when it's all said and done, we were able to laugh at the bad experiences. And those difficult experiences are the ones we laughed about the most." That certainly came to fruition. Randall was a great friend and I wouldn't have wanted to have had the experience with anyone else.

Probably the most important thing we shared was helping each other deal with being homesick. Being away from family was hard, especially on special occasions. About eight months after our arrival, I got a call from George that my grandma had passed away.

My grandma had devastatingly suffered from Alzheimer's disease for nearly thirteen years and didn't know us at all the last few. This horrible disease had taken her from us much earlier than her death. It still was sad to know she had passed and difficult knowing I couldn't be there for the funeral and with family. I appreciated Randall and the missionaries' support in tough times like that.

Randall had an additional reason for being homesick. He began dating a college friend of ours named Cindy at the end of our last semester. Things got pretty serious over the summer and here he was leaving for three years. Cindy had a couple years of college left but for Randall to leave, knowing they would be apart for so long, was extremely difficult. They did the long-distance relationship thing, writing letters and making tapes. Cindy was able to come visit a couple times over the three years. It was a challenging situation, but they made it work.

The second day of Ken's visit we took him to Copo's to get ice cream. The nurses joined us and we bought a container of pineapple ice cream and took it back to the nurses' house. One of the great things about living in Guatemala, we were close enough to the States that lots of visitors came. It was also easy and not too expensive to fly back to the States on furlough.

We were often being sent, or people brought to us, American products we craved. Chocolate was too expensive to buy in Guatemala and not really that good. When asked what to bring us when people came to visit from the States, top of our list was chocolate. The nurses stored their valuable chocolate stash in the freezer and indulged just on special occasions and two Hershey Kisses every Sunday.

The nurses had someone bring them a can of Nestle's Quik*. On this occasion with Ken present, Linda made a pan of hot chocolate syrup with the Quik. We added bananas to our pineapple ice cream and drizzled chocolate syrup over it. *Delicious!*

On Sunday, the three of us joined Bob and his family to attend church. We told Ken it was in the c'alebal (or *aldea* in Spanish) called

Chima' che'. Ken was fascinated by the language. I figured he would have picked it up very quickly had he lived Carchá.

The church service included the typically long sermon. The K'ekchi' pastor was a super nice guy and been through biblical training at the Bible Institute where Bob and the other missionaries provided instruction to pastors. This day's sermon was about Samson and Delilah from Judges 16:4–20.

Since most of the church members couldn't read, often a pastor would choose a Bible verse that went with his sermon and have the congregation memorize it by repeating it many times after him. In K'ekchi', the verse the pastor chose this day was, *"Laj Samson quixra ru jun li ixk lix Dalila x'caba. Rajlal cutan naxic chi rilbal li ixk a'an."* Translated it was, "Samson loved one woman named Delilah. Every day he went to see her."

Over and over we repeated this verse. Once someone thought they had the verse memorized, they would stand and repeat it. Even Bob stood and repeated the verse. Needless to say, Samson loving Delilah and going to see her every day was probably not the most inspirational verse for one to memorize. We had a good chuckle on the way back, hiking over the mountain as we repeated the verse. Bob said he had more work to do at the next Bible Institute.

What was even crazier was that Ken seemed to be picking up the language just from this little exposure. He could repeat the verse as well as we could. *What a gift!*

Ken said, "During the afternoons in Antigua when in language study (mornings only), I would often work on learning a little *Cakchiquel* (another Mayan language) from the vendors there. Thus, I already had some background with cognates." Cognates are words in two languages that share a similar meaning, spelling, and pronunciation—e.g., *bantiox* (K'ekchi' for thanks) and *matiox* (Cakchiquel for thanks), *us* (okay) and *utz* (okay).

That afternoon Ken caught a bus for home. He seemed to have enjoyed himself. We were really glad he came and spent time with us. It wouldn't be too long before we would see him again around Christmas. Now it was full steam ahead with language study.

The day Ken left was also the long-awaited day for Randall to be able to move to his room with the Ca'al family. After fifteen days living in my cramped quarters and two months since we had arrived, he was finally going to get his own place.

Randall's room was just a little larger than mine and had the same problem with having a damp floor. After weeks without seeing sunshine, it took time for things to dry out. He was excited and anxious to spend more time with the and get to know them even better. He said in a letter to my mother, "It should be quite a change from never having a younger brother or sister to having seven of them. Guess I'll finally get my wish of having a younger brother or sister."

Randall was able to build Don Antonio's family a solar shower and it turned out really well. Even with just a few days of sunshine, he was able to take some warm showers. It took his family quite a while to decide to use it. He didn't know if Don Antonio ever used it and seemed to be kind of rebellious and stubborn about it.

Chapter 23
Shopping in Guatemala City

Three months had passed by so quickly since arriving in Guatemala. We were deep into language study. Debbie was working us hard and Santiago continued to provide tremendous help. Slowly I felt as if I was getting at least a little grasp of K'ekchi' and could communicate without playing charades.

Óscar and Rollie were my little helpers. They never made me feel like an idiot when I goofed or said something wrong. That's the beauty of little kids. I felt comfortable asking them how to say things and they loved to learn words in English. They were like little sponges soaking up English phrases. Every morning the ritual began with them asking in English, "How are you today?" and I would reply back in K'ekchi', "Us, bantiox acue."

As Randall and I settled into our routine, there were a few things we never got accustomed to being around or seeing. Incessant rain, mangy dogs, dirty children, no public restrooms and most of all, alcoholics.

The World Health Organization in 2010 reported that of the seven million men in Guatemala, eight percent had an alcohol problem. It was not uncommon to see drunk men on the streets of Carchá. The drink of choice was either rum or beer but the poorest campesinos drank the fermented sugarcane juice boj. It smelled disgusting. It wasn't uncommon to see women drunk as well.

The saddest day was when Randall and I saw a woman who was drunk and had fallen face first on the cement pavers in the street. Some men were helping the bloody-faced woman get up and trying to move her out of the street. Around this same time, Chepe told me there was a woman who had drowned in the river. He didn't know if she had been drunk or just fallen into the river and couldn't swim.

Many believers in the churches had been alcoholics like Chepe. I found it interesting that some of the K'ekchi' churches had musical instruments and others didn't. I asked Larry why and he explained some of the church members had been alcoholics before they became believers. They equated the musical instruments and the music with getting drunk with friends while partying. The instruments brought back temptations and longing for the drink. Thus, some churches didn't include instruments, especially those whose pastor had been an alcoholic.

The nurses and Ruth needed to go to Guatemala City for a few days and they invited Randall and me to join them. They drove a Land Rover, leaving on a Thursday to shop and get some medical supplies. Then on Saturday, Debbie and Linda took the GRE exam for entrance to graduate school. They were leaving to go back home the coming summer and submitting applications for colleges to get their Master's degrees. Randall and I jumped at the chance to join them in the city, but we couldn't leave until Friday because Santiago was planning on tutoring us.

Friday afternoon we took the Pullman. It was a great trip with no breakdowns. All along the route we noticed there were little fires started alongside the highway and in the towns we passed. We found out that at exactly 6:00 p.m. on December 7, all the Catholic believers participated in *La Quema del Diablo* (Burning the Devil) and set off firecrackers to chase him out. Upon reaching the city at about 7:00 p.m., the place was hazy with smoke. We met the nurses and Ruth at the Central American Mission. They said firecrackers had been exploding all over the city and it looked like the city had gone up in smoke.

Since the three of them had lived in Guatemala for so many years, they knew all the best places to eat in the city. That night they took us to a Bavarian restaurant and we had sauerkraut. *YUM!* It was so good and made me think of all my Czech friends back home where I grew up. This definitely made me homesick.

Walking back to the nurses' car afterward, we heard what sounded like a band coming down the street. It sounded like polka music. Maybe it was having just eaten Czech food. I was taken right back to the Bohemian Hall and polka dances I went to as a kid. Coming toward us were three statues on large wooden planks that looked a little like floats in the Tall Corn Festival Parade back home. They were, however, missing a trailer with wheels and something pulling it. There were several people on each side of the "floats" carrying the statues and a large group following behind.

First was a statue of Mary and women carried her. The other two (who we thought were supposed to be Peter and Joseph) were carried by men. The nurses told us that the people participating in these processions paid the church to join in carrying the statues. It was a way to make atonement for their sins. The people following would swap out periodically, taking turns to have their sins wiped clean.

The next morning I woke up with my eye swollen almost shut from a mosquito bite. It was a relief to have nurses there to give me medicine for the bite. Thankfully the swollen eye didn't last long but felt weird.

The nurses left to take their exams, and Ruth was our guide to downtown Guatemala City to check out the sights and to shop. It was great to have our own personal interpreter since she was fluent in Spanish as well as K'ekchi'. I wondered, *Will I ever be able to switch back and forth between languages like Ruth?*

Downtown was just like any big city in the States with all kinds of stores, banks, businesses, nice restaurants, and even movie theaters. One place we wanted to check out was an agricultural store where they sold garden seeds. We bought several types of seed and rubber boots, a necessity we discovered with all the rain. Our hiking boots were starting to get moldy because we could never get them dried out.

Though I never was much of a shopper, we enjoyed checking out all the different stores. We also bought stamps, Christmas cards, and gifts for our families. Because we couldn't cut down pine trees for Christmas because of the shortage of firewood, we bought a little fake greenery for the nurses and Ruth to decorate their house for Christmas. The big item for Randall was a cheap guitar and we also got one for Priscilla. She had asked us to get her one and wanted Randall to teach her to play.

The nurses met up with us after finishing their exams. They wanted to celebrate so we went to a movie. We ended up seeing *Lo Que El Viento Se Llevó* (*Gone With the Wind*). Randall had never seen it. Linda loved the movie and had seen it four times. Deb, Ruth and I had each seen it twice, but we were happy to see it again.

Thankfully the movie was in English with Spanish subtitles. I'm not sure I could have sat through that long a movie in Spanish. Could you imagine Scarlett with a Spanish accent instead of her southern drawl? I think if it had been in Spanish, I would have had to tell Linda about seeing the movie, "*Francamente querida, no me importa un bledo.*" Just doesn't have the same ring as "Frankly my dear, I don't give a damn," does it?

After the movie the ladies took us to their favorite restaurant in the city. They had been telling us about this place ever since we had arrived in Carchá. It was called Giovanni's and was an Italian restaurant. It was everything they billed it to be. We left there stuffed.

With Randall's and my salary of $39 per month from MCC, this trip was a huge splurge but totally worth it. We had spent very little on personal things the first two months and I still had about $20 left in my account even after this trip and buying gifts for Christmas. Things were so inexpensive but it did take some getting used to bartering for prices of things in the market. You were expected to dicker over the price like at a flea market back home and it was almost an insult to not barter for a lower price.

The nurses' car was too full with medical supplies for us to ride back to Carchá with them on Sunday. We waited about three hours for a Pullman to come to the bus depot. Obviously, it had broken down again. The wonderful time we had in the city made up for the long wait. When something was delayed, my dad used to joke saying "Hurry up and wait." This took on a new meaning for me in Guatemala. Eventually a bus arrived and we made it back to Carchá without it breaking down.

Óscar turned eleven on December 9. What a celebration for his birthday. It was my first experience with a Guatemalan birthday. On special events or holidays (such as weddings, birthdays, and Christmas), Guatemalans made tamales. Matilde started very early that morning and had five women helping to make birthday tamales. I asked if I could watch, and with her shy grin she said "Us."

They started by making the dough out of grease and the masa (or ground-up corn) used to make tortillas. It was a greasy dough that looked like very thick mashed potatoes. They made tomato sauce from fresh tomatoes, culantro (a cousin to cilantro or coriander) and a few spices. Next, they cut up pieces of meat. It was usually chicken but if they had a little extra money, they purchased pork or duck at the market. Matlide was using chicken and pork in her tamales. Finally, they had raisins and pieces of red peppers to include. They were ready to assemble the tamales.

To start, they cut banana tree leaves into rectangles about seven inches by ten inches. I found out it took two kinds of banana tree leaves. The women steamed the leaves to make them flexible and so wouldn't tear. They stacked one of each of the two kinds of leaves and put a little of the tomato sauce on the top leaf. They added a spoonful of the greasy corn masa dough and spread it out on the leaf. Then a piece of chicken and a piece of pork, a few pieces of red pepper, and one raisin (because they were expensive) were placed in the center of the greasy dough. Sometimes they would add vegetables, dates, and more raisins but it was very costly to add too many ingredients. Once these goodies were added, they spooned on more tomato sauce and topped with a little more of the greasy corn dough. Then they folded the leaves around the tamale into a nice tight rectangular, almost square, shape. Using string made from sisal or some other kind of plant stem, they tied the tamale tight to keep the ingredients from leaking out. The bundles were placed in a big black kettle of boiling water and cooked over the fire for four hours. In all, Matilde said she had made seventy-five tamales.

Chepe invited Pastor Paco plus a bunch of their friends. He also asked me to invite the missionaries. There were about thirty of us altogether. The kids were all dressed to the nines. Paco gave a sermon in Spanish and there was a lot of praying and singing.

Chepe called Óscar to the front and everyone prayed for him on his special day. We sang *"Feliz Cumpleaños"* (Happy Birthday) to Óscar. He was beaming from ear to ear, being the center of attention. Earlier in the day I gave him a book for his birthday that I had bought during our trip to the city. He loved it, giving me a big hug.

After the hour-long service, Matilde served the tamales and *pasteles* (pieces of cake). Chepe bought the cake from a bakery that made bread and desserts. We ate the tamales right out of the banana leaves by using tortillas to scoop up the gooey insides. They were delicious. All of Matlida's hard work had paid off. We had enough left over that we even had tamales for breakfast and several meals to follow. I have to say, tamales weren't nearly as enticing for breakfast.

Chapter 24
'Tis the Season

Our first Christmas was fast approaching. Ruth directed a Christmas music program at the same Carchá Mennonite church Chepe's family attended. She formed a choir and asked Randall and me to join. The lyrics were in Spanish but we knew all the music. At practice we just sang right along as if we knew what we were singing.

Things were starting to look a lot like Christmas at the Xol's. Chepe purchased a string of Christmas lights and strung them over the new television. The kids were excited and he was pleased to bring the Christmas spirit to their lives. One night after supper I sang Christmas carols in K'ekchi' with the kids and Matilde. She had a beautiful voice and I often heard her singing in her kitchen.

The next day Chepe made another big purchase, a refrigerator. It was a tall, upright fridge that they put in the dining area. I don't think I had ever seen Matilde with such a huge smile. The plan was to freeze helados (the popsicle kind) and sell them in the town square. I was sure they would do quite well.

We kept trudging along with language study and each day we felt we were making a little more progress. Debbie gave us our second exam and we both passed. Over the time working with Santiago, we formed a close bond. He shared that he and his wife Angelina were having issues getting along. It was frustrating not being able to talk with him as deeply as I would have liked. My limited K'ekchi' was not great for counseling or comforting.

I figured out part of the issue for him was that Angelina wasn't happy that he was away from home so often while helping us in language training. She was having to stay at home alone with their little girl, Josefina, and Angelina was pregnant again. At the same time, she was glad for the money he was able to make while working for us and not have to go off to work in the nasty conditions of the fincas on the coast. Santiago shared how he really hated going to work at the fincas.

This brought back memories of the stories shared during our training with Friends World College and the instructor with World Neighbors. Men such as Santiago would often go off to work at one of the sugarcane, banana, or cotton fincas in the hot coastal areas or to a coffee finca in the highlands. This really was the only means for an indigenous man in the c'alebal to provide additional support for his family, other than being a subsistence farmer.

One of the horrific things we learned about the conditions men faced working on the fincas was that often the owners would spray insecticides on their fields by plane. The men would be out in the fields working and the plane would spray the men as well.

Although DDT was banned in the United States at this time, it was still being sold and used in Guatemala. Julio told us at the Friends class that the level of DDT in mother's milk was the highest of any country in the western hemisphere. It was almost 185 times higher than the acceptable limit.

The men working on these fincas ran the risk of returning home with malaria, some other tropical disease or poisoned from the chemicals. I always wondered if this might have been the cause of José Mariá's boys having birth defects. When the men came home, they would often be sick for weeks and the money they had made went for medicine, if it was even available.

It was a tough situation for Santiago but I reminded him to tell her that we would only be in language study for a couple more months. The money he made would keep him there all winter. He was gone just a few days a week now instead of three or four months off working at the finca.

We came up with another solution. I told Santiago to bring his wife and daughter to Carchá once in a while. The nurses said they could all stay in the room beside their house. He thought that was a great idea. His wife and daughter started to come to town with him about every other week and loved it. Angelina was shy at first and hardly talked, but she got accustomed to the caxlan cuinks and even would help with the language study. Josefina was a doll. She was never scared of us and most of the time had to sit on Randall's or my lap during study time.

One evening Randall and I went to visit Ruth and the nurses, and they had a little early Christmas bundle at their house, a little K'ekchi' newborn baby. The baby's mother had to be taken to the hospital after having complications from giving birth. The nurses kept baby Carolina the first night. It was amazing to see a little K'ekchi' baby only twenty hours old with her full head of dark black hair.

Helen took care of the baby the next day and night. The following day the mother was released and able to come get her baby and go back to her home. There is no telling what would have happened to the mother and baby without the nurses and Helen there to help them.

The two weeks before Christmas, the nurses and Ruth asked us if we would be interested in getting out of the depressing rain for a weekend. We had barely seen the sun since returning from Guatemala City. They told us there was a resort in the dry desert area *departamento* (or state) of Guatemala called *Zacapa* that wasn't too far from Jalapa where Randall and I had stayed on our Friends World College adventure. My first thought was *Jalapa? No thanks!*

Linda reassured us that this place was like a hidden oasis in the middle of the desert. They had discovered it years ago and went a couple times a year to get away from the depressing rainy weather. Two American women, who were teachers for the Baptist missionaries' kids and lived in Cobán, were going to join us. It was very inexpensive and we could pool our resources and drive there in the Land

Rover. We didn't have to think twice and jumped at the chance. We said, "Sure, let's go!"

The seven of us squeezed into the Land Rover and away we went at 6:00 a.m. Saturday morning. We arrived at Hotel Longarone in just over three hours. It seemed like out of nowhere in the desert we came upon the resort, which was surrounded by low adobe walls. Linda turned off the highway and entered through the iron gate. It felt as if we were being transported to a whole new world.

The hotel was set up with small individual huts. They were modest accommodations similar to the roadside motels back home. Located in the dry desert climate, the temperature was in the mid-80s compared to Carchá's mid-50s and 60s with constant dampness and no sun. The huts were air conditioned and very comfortable. There was a large swimming pool with a thatch roofed tiki bar-like area containing refreshments. The hotel had a restaurant that served typical Guatemalan food plus a wide variety of other cuisine. The best part was the fresh fruit. *I will never get tired of mangos and papaya.*

There was hardly anyone else there as this was not their busy season. We spent two days soaking up the sun. We swam and played water basketball. It was perfect weather for drying out after weeks of chipi chipi. Randall wrote to my mom saying, "This was just what the doctor ordered."

The little getaway went by very quickly and we headed back to Carchá late Sunday afternoon. Back for another week of studying and George was coming to visit us. We decided we weren't going to tell him we had gone to Hotel Longarone. He probably would have thought we were being too worldly and wasteful.

Besides checking up on us to see how our language study was coming along, George met with the EMB missionaries to go over details about the MCC/EMB Central America retreat that was going to be held in Guatemala right after Christmas. He also shared details about Randall's and my Spanish language study. George had made arrangements for us to study Spanish for eight weeks. Yes, EIGHT weeks! We would be going to Antigua at the end of January. *¡Muy bien!*

Homesickness settled in a little at Christmas, missing family at this special time of year. With lots of letters from family and friends plus a photo my parents had taken for me, it didn't seem so far away. The missionaries kept us preoccupied and when we weren't studying, we were doing some Christmas activity. We had several nights of choir practice. One night we made cookies at the nurses' and they helped us put together boxes of treats for our host families.

Two nights before Christmas we went to something called a *campaña*. It is a Spanish word that translates into English as "campaign." It was a church revival event that lasted for several days. It reminded me of the tent revivals I had heard about that took place back home. At this campaña, people came from all over the area to attend.

Larry invited us to go with him. Debbie and Ruth went along, too. We left at about 5:00 in the afternoon, and it took two hours to reach the church, traveling slowly over the bumpy roads. The first thing one noticed getting out of the car was the beautiful music. Three men were playing a huge marimba. It was a fun evening of worship that lasted several hours. They had a generator and Larry brought a film (in Spanish) about Jesus' crucifixion, which fascinated all the K'ekchi' parishioners. After the service everyone was served tzu'uuj (the tortillas with beans inside) and coffee. By the time we got home, it was 1:00 a.m. but what a great experience.

During the day of Christmas Eve, Pastors Paco and Rúben invited Randall and me to play basketball with a group of guys from the church. We thought that sounded like fun and a great way to get some much-needed exercise. What a scream it turned out to be!

First, one must remember how short these guys were and that we towered over them. Second, they obviously hadn't played much basketball. Just dribbling the basketball was a challenge and they usually used both hands at a time instead of one. Soccer was their sport and they hadn't figured out a way to use their feet to dribble a basketball. Third, only Rúben knew K'ekchi'. The rest only spoke Spanish and half the time we had no clue what they were saying. Lastly, when they divided up the teams, they put Randall and me on the same team. *Not a wise move!*

The basketball court was located on a hill next to the school and was surrounded by a pasture and lots of pine trees. No green grass was left unused for grazing cattle. The cattle had traipsed across the court at will. The court was covered with pine needles and dotted with cow pies. Many of the pies weren't dried up either. The fresh pies made for interesting dribbling of the ball while trying to avoid contact. We just played around them, trying to stay clear of the pies like they were booby traps. Unfortunately, they were often unavoidable. Players were slipping and sliding. When the ball rolled through a cow pie, nobody wanted to pick it up. We all laughed at the brave soul who did. He would turn his nose up as he wiped the ball off in the grass and the game would resume.

And talk about lousy shots, these guys were horrible. It should have counted as a point just to hit the rim. One guy was a big gunner. Whenever he got the ball no matter where he was on the court, he would shoot. After a while, every time he got the ball Randall and I would start shouting, "SHOOT!" At first he didn't know what we were saying but caught on quickly and with encouragement just kept shooting. Our new friends, Randall, and I were laughing so hard most of the time we could hardly play. However, there was no doubt which team won the game.

After a much-needed shower, we attended the Christmas Eve church service with Paco preaching and Rúben leading the congregational music. Seeing them, we had to chuckle to ourselves about the earlier basketball game. The choir, with Ruth's direction, included Debbie, Linda, Randall, one of the teachers who went to Hotel Longarone with us, eight local people, and me. We sang "Away in the Manger," "Silent Night," "O Come All Ye Faithful," and "Whispering Hope."

The kids in the church performed three little dramas. Chepe's four oldest kids all took part. These plays were a hoot and not like any of the children's Christmas nativity programs I remembered back home. The first skit was about a poor blind girl, getting her sight back miraculously after Jesus touched her. The second skit was the story of the prodigal son. A young actor staggered around the stage drunk, supposedly having left home and partying too much. Then an angel helped him see the light and the son returned home to his accepting parents.

The last skit was the best. It was David and Goliath. After David defeated Goliath with his slingshot, the kids pretended to cut off Goliath's head with a machete. They huddled around the "beheaded" Goliath so we couldn't see while they buttoned the shirt over the head of the boy playing Goliath to look like he had no head. Then they lifted the "headless" Goliath up above their heads and carried him off. The entire church congregation was laughing.

The service started at 7:00 p.m. and went on until midnight. It was a dreary night, cold and windy. The gap below the tin roof allowed the cool moist air to whip through. Off and on it rained so hard we couldn't hear the pastor's sermon and I was even sitting close on the second row.

Late in the service the rain stopped and at midnight it was as if the town blew up with all the firecrackers going off. The event culminated with tamales and coffee. These were the best tamales I'd had so far. There were prunes along with the meat and tomato sauce in the middle of the corn masa. *Delicious!* Even with the nasty weather, it was a fun introduction to a Guatemalan Christmas.

Christmas Day I woke up a little homesick but it was fun to share breakfast with Chepe and his family. I ate my mosh (with some cornflakes on top) and beans with tortillas. I had wrapped the gifts I bought in Guatemala City for the family and gave them right after breakfast. They didn't open the presents in front of me. The kids ran into the next room with the presents to open. Later I found out this was customary to not open gifts in front of the giver. I guess it could help hide the disappointment of just getting socks.

I bought Óscar a book with pictures and stories about animals. I got Rollie some colored pencils and a book that had pictures with the name of the picture dotted below so he could learn to write. The girls got coloring books and crayons. I bought Rigo a little knitted hat that tied below his chin. For Matilde and Chepe I bought sets of new towels for their new bathroom. I also gave them a crocheted cross for their family Bible that I had brought with me from home.

It was fun seeing the delight in their eyes and to get hugs from them all. They gave me a beautiful woven bolsa. Rollie's birthday was December 28 and I was going to miss it since I would be at the MCC/EMB retreat. I went ahead and gave him his present, a fluto-phone (or recorder). He was playing it all morning. I decided, *Probably a good thing I am going to be gone for a few days.*

Later that day before going over to the nurses' and Ruth's, Randall and I exchanged gifts. Randall got me a much-needed new flashlight to replace the one with a burned-out bulb. He also had a shirt made for me with embroidery work done by a local K'ekchi' woman. It had two beautiful quetzal birds on the back flying toward each other and a *Monja Blanca* (white nun) orchid on each front pocket. The Monja Blanca is the Guatemalan national flower, which is quite rare and an endangered species.

I got Randall a K'ekchi'/Spanish Bible and a *tam,* which was a leather strap with holes on each end. The Guatemalan men used a tam and rope to carry their heavy loads. A man would tie the rope to the ends of the tam (or sometimes a piece of cloth). The rope would then be run under the load to be carried. To lift the load, the man would stand with his back toward the cargo, squat and place the tam on his forehead, then lift the load onto his back by using his legs. Once standing, the man would lean forward to balance the heavy load with the tam and rope, keeping the load from falling off his back. Having learned leathercraft as a kid in 4-H from my mom, I carved into Randall's tam, "My yoke is easy and my burden is light, Matthew 11:28-30."

We had made the nurses and Ruth wooden plaques with Bible verses burned into the wood by using a soldering pen. When we were in the city, we bought Debbie and Linda a LIFE magazine that covered events over the past ten years (because they would be leaving for the States in a few months). We added little funny comments here and there, explaining this was to help prepare them for reentry to the States after being gone SO long and being SO out of touch.

They bought Randall and me each a mug that said, "For this I spent 4 years in college!" and filled them with chocolate candy. We were so excited! For them to give us a cup filled with their precious chocolate candy was way more than generous and we were blown away. Joke was on us though because they had filled the cup with black beans and just put a few pieces of chocolate on top. We had a good laugh out of that one.

That night we got together with all the missionaries to celebrate Christmas. There were twenty-three of us in all. We had quite the feast with ham loaf, scalloped potatoes, baked corn, homemade rolls, jello salad, mincemeat pie, orange cake and homemade ice cream. After recuperating from overeating, Millard read the Christmas Story to the kids and then we sang. One hilarious thing was singing "The Twelve Days of Christmas" but we swapped out the gifts in the song with K'ekchi' words.

On the first day of Christmas my true love gave to me
A *patux in a chacach* (duck in a basket)

The best part of the day though was calling my family and talking to my parents and sisters. This was my first opportunity to speak to all of them together since leaving the States. I had spoken to my parents upon arrival to let them know we made it safely and again at Thanksgiving. My sister had called me once as well. It helped to not feel so far away and isolated to be able to talk to them on the phone.

Chapter 25
It's Retreat Time!

The day after Christmas, it was time for the MCC/EMB retreat. Bob had chartered a Pullman and all of the missionaries boarded the bus in Carchá in the early afternoon. The two Baptist teachers from Cobán went with us to babysit the missionary kids. We arrived in Guatemala City and met up with our MCC buddies and there was a group of EMB people from Honduras. They all joined us on our bus, making quite a rambunctious group and chattering away to catch up.

Around 10:00 p.m., after nine hours on the bus, our sleepy group arrived at our destination. The retreat was held at a resort called Likin on a small island just across a canal from the mainland. We had to take a little ferryboat to get to the island. The place had beautiful, clear skies filled with stars. The temperature was so nice and warm, even at this hour. What a great change of weather from Carchá.

The island was on the south side of the country and the resort's beach faced south. The first morning we had breakfast at the resort restaurant and watched the gorgeous sunrise on the left side of the beach. At night we would get a beautiful sunset on the right side of the beach.

The retreat was titled "Development of the Inner Man" and the guest speaker was named Alvin Fry from Canada. It was a very inspirational event and a great time for bonding with others. We received a lot of good advice from those who had been in Central America the longest. Much was shared about being safe with all the turmoil that was going on politically in these countries. Those of us from Carchá felt fortunate that there wasn't strife in the area where we lived. Ken, Carman and Carolyn already had been learning to handle the situations where they lived. We could tell Carolyn was the most worried about things and the retreat benefitted her a great deal.

In the afternoons we had free time to enjoy the beach and swimming pool. Being from landlocked Kansas, I had only seen the ocean once on our family trip to California. This was a totally different kind of beach with black sand. We were told this was due to the volcanic activity that produced the rock from which the sand was created.

Warnings were also given about swimming in the ocean because of a wicked undertow. It could be extremely dangerous. In fact, a couple guys got too far out and couldn't swim back to shore because of the undercurrents. A lifeguard had to swim out and throw them a line and pull them back in. *Now that's scary!*

Not being a great swimmer, I was fine just wading or swimming in the pool. This was also my first experience swimming in a saltwater pool. The salty water made it so one just floated on the surface. It was the strangest feeling but the warm water felt amazing after weeks of cool damp weather, cold showers, and my little room with a wet floor.

In the evenings we had more devotionals with plenty of singing and more sessions with the guest speaker. We learned a lot but probably the most important lesson I learned was to be open about what I was feeling. Being in a foreign country and dealing with culture shock was normal. We all needed to express ourselves openly and freely. A valuable lesson learned after four months of trying to deal with all the mixed emotions—homesickness, loneliness, depression from the crummy weather, feelings of guilt for being so blessed when others had so little (just to name a few). It was a blessing to be surrounded with so many good people and especially a great friend to talk with like Randall. Again I can't emphasize enough, I don't know if I would have lasted without him there.

For three nights the ocean waves crashing on the beach lulled me to sleep. What an amazing and peaceful way to fall asleep. The retreat went by too quickly and it was time to head home. It was another long trip home and we didn't arrive until 1:00 a.m.

Ken, Carman and Carolyn all came back to Carchá with us to visit for three days. Carman and Carolyn had just finished language study and were living with George in Chimaltenango until they found a place to live. They definitely were not ready to go back to George's and happy to come to Carchá for a couple days.

Randall's birthday was January 1 and it was nice for the five original Guatemala traveling buddies to be all together to help him celebrate. For New Year's Eve, Ruth invited us to her house but the nurses were away. They had gone to a church conference in an area north of Carchá called *Sebol*. It was at a much lower altitude there and the temperature was always much hotter.

We were disappointed Debby and Linda missed out on our New Year's Eve celebration and birthday party. The two Baptist teachers who went to Hotel Longarone with us came over to join us so we had eight in all. We made pizzas, coleslaw, and fruit salad. For Randall's birthday we had chocolate cake. We played games and waited for the magic hour. At midnight it sounded like bombs went off when firecrackers were being set off everywhere in town. *Happy New Year, Guatemala!*

It was 3:00 a.m. when we finally forced ourselves to leave. Fog from the firecracker smoke was still lingering in the air across town as we stepped outside into the early morning air. Ken, Carman and Carolyn were staying in the pensión. Carman and Carolyn were shocked that we could be safely out on the streets at this time. They would never have done this in Antigua. We dropped them off at the pensión and said our goodbyes because the three of them headed back to Guatemala City at 7:30 a.m. after very little shuteye.

Chapter 26
A New Year

It was New Year's Day and we were starting a new year of adventures. For Randall's birthday I had Chepe make him a small pouch that would hold his passport. It could be worn around his neck and tucked under his shirt. Chepe did an excellent job. He thought it might turn into a new thing for him to sell. He was quite the entrepreneur and always looking for some way to make more money.

Of course it was another rainy Carchá day and not much fun to celebrate. Randall wrote in a letter to my sister, "It was definitely one of the more 'restful' birthdays I've spent in a while. It rained almost the whole day, so I just stayed in my bed and read and wrote letters. It must be my old age getting to me. Guess I'm just too old for these late-night wild parties."

At my family's house, Matilde made a special New Year's lunch for us with turkey and duck caldo. It was delicious. She also made tamales for supper with the leftover duck meat. However, turmoil erupted in the Xol house that evening. Chepe loved his kids dearly, but he was terribly upset with Óscar and Rollie. The boys must have done something really bad because Chepe's belt was flying. Both of them got a whipping and were screaming and crying up a storm.

That was the only time I heard Chepe raise his voice. He could be stern with the kids and usually it only took a word or a look to get their attention. I didn't ask what the problem was and just hid out in my room. I didn't need a belt lashing either. After the spanking, all got very quiet. I did take note of the fact that the boys were on their best behavior for several days after.

It was back to language study full speed ahead for the next four weeks. We were making progress but the fact that we would be leaving at the end of January for Spanish language training was a little daunting. Randall wrote to my mother with his typical great humor, "I am sure KelLee told you we will be heading to Antigua for Spanish study at the end of the month. It will be a nice change, but I'm not sure my little brain can handle all these foreign languages."

Shortly before leaving for Likin, we heard there was a young, female Peace Corps worker in our area, but we hadn't ever had a chance to meet her. Not long after getting back to Carchá, we finally ran into her at the market. Her name was Cindy and she was ecstatic to meet and talk to Americans. Talk about a hoot, she was a true free spirit but also tough as nails. She was boisterous and her laugh was contagious. She was, as my mom would say, a big-boned gal and made the motorcycle she rode appear to be more like a scooter.

Cindy was working with a large dairy finca outside of Cobán and assigned through the Guatemalan Department of Agriculture. Unfortunately for her, Cindy's hands were tied in what she could do and she was frustrated only being allowed to work with the wealthy finca owner instead of with the campesinos. She also only knew Spanish so was limited in communicating with the K'ekchi'.

We got to know Cindy pretty well over the next month before we went to Antigua for Spanish study. She would stop by my room to visit when in town. It turned out that she was of the Bahá'í Faith. She shared her beliefs and we shared ours, gaining greater respect for each other. She explained that the Bahá'í Faith taught the essential worth of all religions and the unity of all people. I thought that was pretty cool. One day she was very upset because she thought she might have to go home. She shared that riding the motorcycle over the bumpy Guatemalan roads had not done her body any favors and she might even need surgery. Fortunately, she began feeling better and the Peace Corps doctors gave her clearance to stay.

Cindy introduced us to another Peace Corps woman working not too far from Cobán. We had dinner with the two of them one evening at Cindy's. She made quiche, which was my first time trying it, and it was great. They had been in the area a little longer than we had and gave us some great advice and good contacts within the Department of Agriculture.

Sadly, they didn't get to stay much longer in the country. As things got worse politically and with guerrillero activity in other parts of the country, the Peace Corps pulled all of their workers out of Guatemala while we were at language study in Antigua. We didn't get to say goodbye or know how to stay in touch.

In addition, there were a couple of other Americans in Carchá. Two young men were Mormon missionaries. We only spoke to them a few times. They seemed a little distant and didn't appear to be there to make friends with Mennonite missionaries. I had never known anything about the Mormon religion or met anyone who was Mormon. My naivety was quite apparent. I didn't know that most of the younger men and women volunteered before marriage to be missionaries to share their faith.

Randall and I stood out in Carchá being Americans, but these two in their dark pants, white shirts, and ties definitely stood out. The first time we met, we shook hands and introduced ourselves. One introduced himself as Elder Smith and the other said he was Elder Nelson, which they also had on their name tags. After a few pleasantries and quick exchange of where we were from, we went our ways. I turned to Randall after they were out of earshot and said, "That is really strange that they both were named Elder." I thought Randall was going to split a side laughing before he told me that was just the title they all used. *Duh, silly me.*

The first Sunday of the new year, Randall and I went back to Campat for the first time since our initial visit with Bob way back in September. Millard went out to visit and invited us to go along. We were excited to get back and see the people and community where we hoped to work. It was a beautiful sunny day as we drove to the bottom of the mountain and left the Land Rover parked at the little bridge. It seemed we had maybe turned a corner on all the rain. However, we carried our bolsas with plastic-sheet ponchos just in case.

It was still quite the climb on the path up the mountain but with the sun shining and the dry ground, we weren't as fearful of slipping. This allowed us to look around at the beauty of the scenery that we had missed on our first trip. It was breathtaking. There were little waterfalls with water cascading into deep gorges off the side of the path. The deep green foliage was amazing with beautiful wild flowers. The largest blue-tinted hydrangeas I had ever seen were often growing wild along the path. There were even breathtaking, tall poinsettia trees with red flowers blooming unlike any small Christmas poinsettia plant back home.

The winding path would often be shaded by tall cliffs above us or with large pine trees blocking the sun. When beams of sunlight would burst through, it was if lasers were shining on the dense foliage, giving a magical feel. The most tantalizing thing was the sound, or lack thereof. It was perfectly quiet except for the falling water or streams, a few birds chirping, and our footsteps. It was mesmerizing and I thought, *Wow, I get to experience this for the next couple of years.*

We didn't make this excursion quite as fast as compared to the trip with Bob and his long legs. Millard was definitely not the hiker Bob was, but we didn't mind one bit because we were still huffing and puffing. At the summit, Campat looked like an incredible landscape photograph from a National Geographic magazine. Our first view of Campat with Bob was under a shroud of clouds and chipi chipi. We hadn't grasped the beauty of the c'alebal. Millard asked if we had ever seen such a beautiful place and we had to agree it was magnificent.

Two steep mountains were on either side of the deep valley. The valley was huge, probably two miles in length at least. A mountain stream was flowing the length of the valley off to one side. The sun was shining on the mountainside, illuminating the trees that stood tall above the rest of the rocks and foliage. Looking to the far left of the valley, the mountains appeared to merge into one and close off the valley. However, we found out later there was a gap between the mountains and a path that led to the next c'alebal.

The far right of the valley opened up to a large open area. It appeared to be a large pasture and Millard said there was a finca located at the end. It was named *Finca Chilax*. The buildings on the finca were just dots because it was so far in the distance. Unlike most Guatemalan fincas in other areas of the country where coffee, sugarcane, bananas, and cotton were harvested, Finca Chilax raised cattle. Unfortunately, there weren't opportunities for the men from Campat to work there.

We noticed more houses this time compared to our cloud-covered experience with Bob. Little houses were scattered up and down the mountain. Each one appeared to have a little parcel of land around it with very few trees close by. Millard shared that one of the issues for the people was the need for firewood. The mountains were becoming deforested and the men were having to go further and further up the mountain to gather the wood needed.

There were other bare areas on the steep sides of the mountains where trees were cleared. These were their fields for corn and beans. When we were at Friends World College, the instructor made a tongue-in-cheek comment about a saying that every year in Guatemala at least one campesino died from falling out of his cornfield. This seemed like a cruel joke at the time but now seeing these precipitous-sloped cornfields, I thought it certainly could be true.

Being it was January, the fields were covered with just old corn stalks, grass, and weeds. These would need to be cleared by machete and hoe. Then the dried plant litter would be burned before planting season. The spring rains caused the loss of topsoil, as was explained during our World Neighbors' class. The land at the bottom of the valley had rich soil washed from the mountainside. Those who owned that land could raise even better corn. We immediately thought the valley would be great for making gardens.

Banana trees, sugar cane, and coffee plants were more prevalent lower in the valley and often close to the dwellings for easy picking. One could often find a sugar cane press outside a hut. This was like a large wooden clothes wringer and the sugar cane woody stems would be squeezed to extract the juice to make sweetener for coffee or to make the alcohol boj (not popular among the believers).

Dotted across the mountainside were cactus-like sisal plants Sisal (often referred to as sisal hemp) was used to make a strong rope. Another use for sisel was making a tequila-like alcohol, supposedly more potent than boj.

As before on our first trip, there was smoke rising from the modest homes. Usually there were single dwellings spread far from the nearest neighbors, but once in a while there were two or more houses together. We found out these were extended families where grown children with their families lived next door to the parents. Most houses had thatch roofs but a few had tin roofs like the church. If a family was a little more affluent and had a tin roof, they also had a smaller hut beside it for the kitchen This kept the smoke from the fire pits away from the area where they spent most of their time and slept.

We saw something else we hadn't noticed before due to the cloud cover. It appeared that there was some kind of digging going on at the very bottom of the valley and stretched the entire length. Millard explained that indeed it was a project the government was working on to help the c'alebal get water piped throughout the valley.

The people's only water source was the mountain stream that they used for bathing, to wash clothes, and for drinking and cooking. For some it was quite a hike to the stream and then they had to carry the water back to their homes. This project would provide clean water throughout the c'alebal. *Quite an impressive project and good timing for us.*

The steep descent was much easier with the dry path, and we made quick time, reaching the church in about ten minutes. Once again, Pastor José Mariá greeted us and we joined the church service already in progress. It was fun because this time we actually understood much of what he was saying and followed along.

After the service, José Mariá again invited us to his home. We made the little climb of about fifty yards up the mountain. It had a nice view looking out over the valley below that we couldn't appreciate during our first visit in the clouds. His wife served us another nice meal.

We had something new we had never had before. It was called *xut* (pronounced shoot). Smashed beans and hot peppers were stuffed in the middle of the masa dough and wrapped in banana leaves and boiled. It was similar to bland poch but with the beans and peppers added, it was very good. The creativity these people had in ways to prepare corn masa and beans was amazing.

Again, the experience was quite humbling. These people were always so giving and had such big hearts for others. Here they were so poor and with so little, but they gave to us a huge portion of the little means they had. We knew it cost them a lot to feed us but Millard said we would have hurt their feelings if we had not accepted or offered to pay. We did leave a nice donation in the offering plate at church.

I began to ponder over two Bible verses. First verse was Luke 20:45–21:4 "As he looked up, Jesus saw the rich putting their gifts into the temple treasury. He also saw a poor widow put in two very small copper coins. 'I tell you the truth,' he said, 'this poor widow has put in more than all the others. All these people gave their gifts out of their wealth; but she out of her poverty put in all she had to live on.'" The second was Mark 10:35, "It is easier for a camel to go through the eye of a needle than for a rich man to enter into the kingdom of God." Definitely something I think about still today.

The xut and uk'un (atol) drink gave us energy for our climb back to the top of the mountain. We continued to be enthralled by the beauty. As we made our descent down to the car, we noticed a K'ekchi' man coming toward us on his climb up. He was hunched over and had his leather tam across his forehead so we knew he was carrying a heavy load. As we approached, we said the obligatory greeting "Chan xacuil?" With a soft, winded reply, he uttered back "Us, bantiox."

The man was sweating profusely as he slowly continued his trudge up the mountain slope. It wasn't until we passed him that we realized what the load was on his back. He was hauling a bag of cement. *A bag of cement is 94 pounds!* This small man, who probably weighed 120 pounds dripping wet, was about halfway up the mountain with this heavy load. We were always dumbfounded by the K'ekchi' peoples' strength. *No more complaining about our own hike with our light backpacks.*

Chapter 27
Building Relationships

On the drive back to Carchá, Millard, Randall and I talked about the possibility of living in Campat. Millard said we would have to get the elders of the c'alebal to agree to let us come live there once we were back from Spanish study. Our excitement level was through the roof. We also wanted to talk to George about getting a place in Carchá where we could stay when we came to town on the weekends. A place not too expensive but clean, where we could shower and be able to relax when we were in Carchá.

With just a couple weeks of language study left before leaving for Antigua, we finally got to do a little agricultural work. Once I could communicate better with Chepe, I learned he had a small piece of land on the outskirts of town where he planted corn and beans in the spring. He also had a small garden. I showed him the seeds we had bought in the city and asked if we could plant some in his garden. We sure wouldn't have planted a garden in January back home.

Chepe was pleased to let us and we helped him plant some carrots, cabbage, and beets. Since we were leaving soon for two months, we figured we would miss getting to see the fruits of our labor, but it was great to watch the garden begin to take off. Chepe hoped to have vegetables to sell in the market. *Always the entrepreneur.*

On one trip out to Chepe's land we had a surprise. There was a little shack on the property where he kept his gardening tools. It also stored the corn from the previous crop that Matilde used to make our tortillas. Some animals had been eating on the corn so Chepe set some traps and that day had caught a little possum.

The following day he came back from the farm and said he had caught a large possum and a baby squirrel. He kept the little squirrel alive for some reason and brought it back to the house. One of its legs was broken. I wasn't sure what they planned to do with it. The temperature was cool and Chepe didn't think the squirrel could survive the cold. His solution was to shut off the refrigerator and open the door, letting it warm up. Then he put a little blanket in the fridge, propped the door open, and placed the squirrel in the blanket to stay warm.

Now when I was growing up on the farm, we brought a baby pig or two into the house to my mother's chagrin. If a sow couldn't nurse all her babies, we brought the smallest piglets into the house to keep them warm and gave them a bottle of milk. One time we kept a little piglet in a cardboard box in the kitchen by the furnace vent. While we were watching TV, we heard the pitter patter of little feet on the linoleum. The piglet poked her head around the corner and my mom said, "That's it, Miss Pokey, outside!" After that the little piglet became named "Pokey." I thought to myself, *Well, at least we never kept a pig in the fridge.* I never did know what happened to that squirrel.

Each day working with Debbie and Santiago, we seemed to make a little more progress. At one of our study sessions, Debbie and Linda informed us they were going to Campat to weigh babies and invited us to join them. They did this in all the c'alebals periodically to see if the babies were growing and staying healthy. Any babies that weren't gaining weight, the mothers were given a type of formula and medicine, usually for worms.

We were pleased to get to visit Campat again. It was another beautiful day and a great day for a hike. Back to the little bridge we went, leaving the Suzuki and putting on our backpacks with supplies and instruments for the nurses to set up their station. Debbie and Linda took off and Randall and I had to hoof it to keep up. *These gals are in serious good shape.*

After hiking for just a short time, we saw animals on the trail for the first time. Seeing livestock was a rare treat. This day two men had ropes around a couple of scrawny bulls' necks, trying to lead them up the mountain. The bovines weren't being too cooperative and there was a lot of pushing and yelling. I said to the nurses, "I sure am glad I never had to try and lead my 4-H steers up a mountain."

Some turkeys were also on the trail, gobbling at us to stay out of their way. We weren't sure where they came from. *Could they possibly be escapees from a basket on some woman's head during her climb from the market?*

On our previous trip to Campat we had observed the man carrying the bag of cement up the mountain. This day was another first. We knew they must have carried tin for the roofs over the mountain but had never seen it before. Four men were each toting two eight-feet sheets of corrugated tin up the mountain. With the men being just over five feet, the tall pieces of tin stuck out way above their heads. They had to bend over at about a 90-degree angle. *Oh my gosh, what back-breaking work!*

Once we made it to the church, a dozen Campat women were already waiting for the nurses. Santiago, being the health promoter, had informed the people of the c'alebal that the nurses would be arriving that day. It didn't take long for word to spread and more people started coming. Not only did the nurses weigh babies, but they checked people for all kinds of ailments. Sometimes they even had to pull teeth. They paid special attention to pregnant women and gave them vitamins to take.

The nurses' services were free of charge and medicines were sold at cost. The communities chose their village health promoters (such as Santiago) to assure the person was respected and trusted by the community. The promoters went through an extensive health training and were supervised by the nurses to promote and prevent diseases as well as treat the most common illnesses.

The promoters held monthly baby clinics in their communities and taught health promotion lessons. They examined their patients, prescribed the medicine needed, and sold the medicine to the people. Training health promoters was a smart way to have someone knowledgeable in the c'alebal who could help the people get inexpensive medicines and for better health care. The people could not have afforded the medicine in the pharmacy in Carchá, even if they had a chance to go and buy it there.

When the nurses bought medical supplies in Guatemala City, they would purchase medicine in large quantities because it was so much cheaper. Then they pre-packaged and priced the smaller doses, keeping the cost as low as possible for the K'ekchi' people. This assured that prices were regulated and kept at the same price for everyone. Eventually a seasoned health promoter did all the purchasing, packaging and pricing of the medicine with supervision.

The plan was to one day have the health program completely in the hands of the K'ekchi' people. Health promoters were not paid to do the training nor did they receive payment for their time with patients. The trained health promoter would purchase the medicine from the nurses at a minimal cost and then sell to his/her patients at a predetermined price. This would give a small profit to the promoter for his/her time and also improve the life of his/her family.

While the nurses weighed babies, Randall and I took time to study some K'ekchi' and talk with the children. They were fascinated with the caxlan cuinks and *caxlan ixks* (foreign women). Linda and Randall's blond hair was of special interest. We had taken our cameras with us and took lots of photos.

We knew to always ask before taking someone's picture. Non-believers were scared of cameras and of having their photos taken. They believed their spirits were captured in the photo and they could die. Those without fear loved to have their photos taken. We would send the film home to be developed and then get the photos back and share them with the people.

I had learned from taking Chepe's family photos that they would never smile. Using *"Decir queso* (say cheese)" didn't work. They would be stone faced, extremely serious with mouths closed. They didn't want their teeth showing, thinking they were ugly for some unknown reason. Once we got to know someone better though, we could get them to smile. These beautiful people took wonderful photos.

On Saturday we went to another campaña with Millard to an area called *Chitaña*. We were packed in the Land Rover and I was sitting on the hump. It was the most uncomfortable ride and I felt every pothole. The campaña was excellent. Randall and I experienced a new first and felt like we had made a huge success. Though nervous, we got up in front of the people and we sang and spoke in K'ekchi'. Now it wasn't any great sermon or message, but we could communicate and get our message across. The hard work was paying off. Sore butt and all, it was a great night

The longer we lived in Carchá, the more aware we became of the problem with alcoholism. One day walking home from our language class, we came across a man and wife with two little children outside the market. Both the husband and wife were drunk, the wife could barely stand. They tried to talk to us in K'ekchi' and in Spanish. They were a mess and our hearts went out to the children. So little hope for them. Randall and I split up to go to our homes. Before I got to my room, I ran across a man sprawled flat on the sidewalk and out cold.

A few days later, there was a drunk man passed out in front of my room all day. He was blocking my door and I was quite annoyed. Being impatient, I went through Chepe's open door where he was sewing a tarp and asked me what was the matter. I explained and Chepe taught me a lesson in humility that day. Having no idea who this man was, Chepe woke the guy up, got him to his feet and helped him stagger into the house. Then Chepe gave him a place to sleep it off. When the man started to come out of his stupor, Chepe showered, clothed, and fed the man. He said he knew what it was like to be an alcoholic and wanted to help him. I thought, *Who is the true missionary?*

Chapter 28
Kacua′ Marcos

It was just a week before we were to leave for Antigua and Spanish study. I was in my room writing letters when Bob stopped by. He asked if we would like to come to his house and listen to Super Bowl XIV broadcast on Armed Forces Radio. I said, "Heck yes." I ran and showered before heading up to his house. Randall joined us, too. Listening to the game (the Steelers defeated the Rams by the score of 31–19) made us feel closer to home. *What a treat!*

We made one last trip to Campat by ourselves before leaving for Antigua. This was our second solo trip without any of the missionaries. Since we didn't have our own vehicle, we had to take the bus to Chamelco and walk to the bridge, which added another fifteen minutes to our hike.

On our first trip we spent the night in the church. We had brought our sleeping bags and slept on the wooden platform where the preacher gave his sermons. It was not the most comfortable choice and was a little cold, but we survived. We studied with Santiago and his wife Angelina fed us. This final trip we brought food and air mattresses borrowed from the missionaries. This made the boards feel a little softer and we slept much better. It was warmer as well. Getting a good night's sleep helped to make the trip much more enjoyable.

The church had a wooden window that faced the valley toward the Finca Chilax. We opened the window and the sun was shining on the c'alebal. The view was spectacular. With the window framing the scene, it was like the most beautiful landscape painting in any museum.

This trip made us even more excited about the possibility of living and working in Campat one day. The people were so friendly.

As Millard had said, they needed to approve of us living out there though, not just visiting. Hopefully they would feel we had something to offer them by being there.

Once we returned from Spanish study, we would spend a little time reviewing the K'ekchi' we had learned and keep building on it. Then we would come to Campat to start talking to the church members and more importantly, the c'alebal leaders. Santiago was totally on board with us living there and believed we could make it happen. We weren't sure what the leaders would think of caxlan cuinks actually living in their c'alebal or what they would approve of us doing.

Ruth suggested that our ticket into Campat might be through reading. She was swamped with adult K'ekchi' men and women who wanted to learn to read. She used reading materials written by Wycliffe workers. Even though our verbal skills were still very rough, we could read the language quite well. Ruth told us she would help us to teach others to read, and it was a great way to get to know the people and build relationships. She said later down the road we could probably then help in agriculture as we had intended.

This visit to Campat we talked to as many people in the c'alebal as possible, trying to get to know them. Santiago suggested before we hiked out that he take us to meet one of the older men in the c'alebal who was the president of the Campat land committee. I guess the best comparison to the land committee would be the county commissioners back home. It would be the land committee that would need to give us permission to live there.

The man Santiago wanted us to meet was named *Kacua'* Marcos and was highly respected. Just like Na'chin was the term of respect for an elderly woman, Kacua' was used for an elderly man. However, Kacua' had multiple meanings. Besides showing respect for an elderly male, more importantly in the church it meant God. That added to the significance of the title.

At the time we were living in Guatemala, the distinction of being considered an elderly adult was quite different from the United States. Elderly adults in K'ekchi' terms could be anyone over about forty years old, especially for women. This was because in the 1970s and 1980s, Guatemalan indigenous women had one of the lowest life expectancy rates of any women in the world—even lower than Guatemalan men. The entire country's life expectancy (which included ladinos) was fifty-seven years. In 2020 it was a little over seventy-four. So things have vastly improved in the past forty years.

Santiago told us that if we were going to be allowed to live in Campat, we would need Kacua' Marcos' blessing. He was Catholic (a non-believer as Santiago said) and didn't attend the Mennonite church, so we had never met him. Kacua' Marcos' home was quite a distance away from the church at the top of the valley. It was sort of hidden from where we could see it.

We followed close behind Santiago on the narrow, worn path that led us to a tin roofed house, one of the largest we had seen in the c'alebal. Obviously Kacua' Marcos had done pretty well for himself over the years. As we approached the house, Santiago gave his greeting, "Ma cuancat?" Kacua' Marcos responded back and said, "*Us. Ocan, hilan sa' cab* (Come in and rest in the house)," inviting us to enter his home.

Kacua' Marcos was an older man probably in his late 50s or early 60s. It was difficult to tell the age of the K'ekchi' because of the hard work and rough life they led. He didn't rise and appeared a little leery of these caxlan cuinks Santiago had brought to his door. Santiago respectfully introduced us as Herman Rolando and Herman Keli. Kacua' very graciously asked us to sit. His wife brought us coffee from the thatch-roofed kitchen that was located right next door to the main house and we sipped the hot brew.

Meeting with this older stranger was a little awkward at first. Our K'ekchi' was still very shaky but we were prepared as best we could be from what Santiago had taught us. One of the polite things to ask was, *"Ma sa sa' ach'ol?"* This translates into "Are you happy in your heart?" *What an amazing greeting.*

One usually answers back, *"Mas sa sa' inch'ol."* This means "I am happy in my heart." It is kind of like when one asks, "How are you?" Then the person usually responds back without thinking and says, "Pretty good."

Randall asked this greeting and Kacua' answers back, *"Ra sa' inch'ol,"* meaning he was sad in his heart. This was quite an unusual reply and struck a little fear in us. *Oh, oh what have we gotten ourselves into? Is he upset we are here?*

He went on to tell us that his right foot was extremely sore and the reason he was unhappy. His foot was extremely tender and he could barely walk. He apologized saying that was why he hadn't risen when we entered.

Since Santiago was the health promoter, we asked Kacua' if we could look at his foot. Santiago wasn't forward enough or had enough confidence in himself to ask his elder. Kacua' removed his black rubber boot and his foot was a mess and quite odoriferous. Turned out he had a terrible fungal infection, the skin was peeling, and the sores were broken open. His toenails were gnarled and horrible looking. Santiago told Kacua' he had an infection and needed some medicine.

We suggested for Santiago to go back to his home and get the medicine while we stayed there. While he was gone, we tried to explain as best we could that we were *agriculturas* (agriculturists) and hoped one day to be able to live and help out in Campat. We said we had been studying K'ekchi' but we were still learning the language. He complimented us and said for caxlan cuinks we were doing pretty well.

We nursed our drinks while waiting for Santiago. Kacua' didn't seem too enthused about us being agriculturas, not giving much reaction. Trying another route, we planted the idea of possibly teaching reading, which Ruth had suggested. Not much more reaction but we could tell he was giving that a little more thought.

Thankfully, Santiago returned shortly and gave Kacua' some ointment to put on his foot and some antibiotics for the infection. We told Santiago we would like to pay for the medicine and Kacua' thanked us. After finishing our coffee, we said, "Bantiox acue, Kacua' Marcos." We also thanked him for his time and for letting us visit, and we wished for his sore foot to get well quickly.

Once back at the church, Santiago said he thought that went very well and we paid him for the medicine. Thanks to Santiago being both our language informant and the health promoter, we were able to get to know and help Kacua' Marcos. It seemed as if we were supposed to meet Kacua' just then when he needed us. We hoped we had made a good impression with Kacua' Marcos. Maybe he would be in our corner when asking the land committee for permission to live in Campat. We crossed our fingers and said a little prayer as we left to hike out of the c'alebal.

The weather the past couple of weeks had been gorgeous and we put the gloomy chipi chipi days out of mind. We were starting to dread leaving and basically starting all over again with a new language for the next eight weeks. We took our last K'ekchi' test before we left for Antigua and though I felt I could have done better, Debbie said I did fine. *Now to just not forget all I have learned by the time we come back.*

To make sure we didn't forget what we were going to leave behind, it started raining a couple days before our exit. My room's floor was once again soaking wet. I would not miss that when we went to Antigua. Even having to deal with the wet floor, I was going to miss the Xol family. One day Óscar knocked on my door and asked to come in. We sat and talked for a bit. Then he pulled out a note from his pocket and gave it to me. I was very touched when I read it and it said he was very sad that I was leaving and he would miss me. That meant the world to me.

Óscar and I went to Chepe's garden and planted corn, peas, and broccoli. That night at supper we had a great time of fellowship. One of Chepe's friends named Paco had been staying with us all week. He led us in prayer at the dinner table. It was fun to hear him pray in both K'ekchi' and Spanish. I understood almost all of the K'ekchi' but very little of the Spanish. It helped me to get excited to learn more Spanish.

Our final day in Carchá we spent washing clothes at the nurses and packing. Since we were going to be away for two months, we packed the things to take with us and the rest we removed from our families' rooms. The nurses allowed us to store our extra suitcases, sleeping bags, and other belongings we weren't taking to Antigua at their place until we returned. Randall and I hoped to move back in with our families once we returned, if they still had our rooms available.

Saying goodbye to the Xols was very difficult. I was very "Ra sa' inch'ol." Chepe and the kids said they were sad to see me leave and the kids were crying. One of my favorite moments was when I went down to the kitchen to tell Matlide goodbye. Seldom did we ever get the chance for just the two of us to talk, and she was so shy. She smiled and told me she hoped I would be back. I thanked her for all the wonderful food and washing my clothes. I joked about the time I showed her how to cook the raw egg from my orange juice. She held her hand to her mouth to keep from showing her smile and laughing out loud.

We were certainly going to miss the nurses, Ruth, and the rest of the missionaries. They had become family and we were very close to them. By the time we returned, the nurses would have only a couple months before heading home for good.

We fixed one last supper for the nurses and Ruth before we left the next day on the Pullman. They had done so much to help us and fed us so well. In fact when I left Kansas, I weighed a little over 150 pounds, soaking wet. The nurses had a scale at their house and I was at 160 pounds before I went to Antigua. That was the most I had ever weighed. Randall had actually lost a couple pounds and was down to 148. *I guess beans and tortillas and hiking over mountains suit me quite well.*

Chapter 29

Antigua

Not surprisingly, the Pullman broke down on our way to Guatemala City. It was a rarity to make it without a breakdown. The driver was able to get it fixed in about thirty minutes, which wasn't too long a wait. They seemed to be pretty handy at patching up the buses. This reminded me of my dad's lack of mechanical skills but how he would joke that all he needed was some duct tape and bailing wire to keep the equipment going.

Randall and I made our way to the Central American Mission where we spent the night. We were making plans for family and friends to come visit in the coming months and this would be a great place for them to stay. It was very nice, clean, and best of all, very inexpensive. While staying there, we met some missionaries with other groups. It was always great to meet other Americans at the CAM.

The next morning we went out for breakfast and came across a place called Danny's Pancakes. "Heck, let's try it out," Randall said. Inside was a mid-70s older gentleman who hailed from New York. We started up a conversation with him and he shared, "I moved to Guatemala to live and I love it here."

He asked us what we thought about the United States boycotting the 1980 Moscow Olympics because the Soviet Union invaded Afghanistan. We knew this was going on but didn't have much knowledge to share. It turned out this man was a member of the 1926 U.S. Olympic Swim Team. He was totally in favor of the boycott.

While we were eating, a woman came up to our table and started speaking Spanish rapidly. She showed us her Iranian passport then opened up a flag from Iran with the Shah's photo. Then she pulled out a bunch of newspaper clippings. We didn't understand a word she was saying and were glad we couldn't. The Olympic swimmer seemed quite shaken. Thankfully the woman went away. Our older friend, who was extremely bothered by the encounter, left immediately. We never did know what that was all about.

We went to Chimaltenango to see George, Carman and Carolyn. George had a meeting that night so we got to spend the evening with Carman and Carolyn and catch up. They were excited because they had found a place to live. Like Ken, they would live in Santa María Cauqué. Carolyn said they rented an entire Casa Suiza house (all three rooms), including the lot that it was on. They needed to get a stove, furniture, and cupboards plus build a solar shower. Ken eventually moved to a different Casa Suiza where he had two of the three rooms plus use of most of the property.

The following day we headed to Antigua and our new home. George had made arrangements for us to live in the same place where Carman and Carolyn stayed during their language study. The house was hidden behind the wall bordering the street, and it wasn't until you entered that you could see how huge it was. It was made of wood, which made it look like a cabin and unique to most homes (usually cinder block and cement) in Antigua.

We met Doña Rosa, the matriarch and *abuela* (grandmother) of this ladino family. She was extremely nice. Her daughter was Irma and Irma's husband was named Salvador. They had six children. The three oldest were in their twenties (all still living at home) and the others were fifteen, ten and six. The two family members that literally jumped out at us were the family's two dogs. Othello (because he was jealous in nature) was a big German Shepherd, and *Nieve* (snow) was a big white fluffy Samoyed.

Doña Rosa's was definitely equivalent to a middle-class home in the States, with a TV, stereo, cars, motorcycles, modern appliances, and nice furniture. There were several other students studying Spanish and living there, too. Randall and I each had our own room and bath. The big news was we had hot water! *Quite a contrast to our last digs. I think I am going to like this place.*

We started Spanish study the same day we moved into Doña Rosa's home. George had made arrangements for Randall and me to each have private tutors for two weeks. The tutors had also worked with Carman and Carolyn. Working with us for the short time would allow MCC to retain the tutors for when Rich and Martha arrived. Then we would switch to a language school. The tutors came to our house to study. Randall's instructor was named Carlos. Christi was the name of my instructor and she was a great teacher. After the first class I was certain I would be able to have success.

Christi asked me what my parents did. I told her they were farmers and we had cattle and pigs. She asked how many cows we had and I said about eighty head of cows with calves. She said that would be a huge finca in Guatemala and we must be very rich. I had never thought of us as rich but I guess in their terms we were very rich.

She asked if it was cold where I lived. I was able to tell her in Spanish that there was nieve (*Thank you, Doña Rosa and Nieve*) on the ground at home and it was very cold. I had a photo my mother had sent and showed it to her. Christi couldn't begin to fathom snow and had only seen it on TV. She thought it must be terrible to live there and felt bad for my dad to have to get out and feed the cattle every day in the snow. I laughed and thought, *Yes, I'm kind of glad to be here.*

This first day was one we wouldn't forget soon. Early in the day, Randall's upper back started tightening up. As the day progressed, he was in increasingly worse pain. We didn't know if he had pulled a muscle or maybe a pinched a nerve. Our best guess was he hurt it lifting his belongings up on the bus, and the long bus ride the day before didn't help.

Shortly after class was over, he was in excruciating pain and having difficulty breathing. We were panicking because his lips were turning blue from lack of oxygen. I called for Doña Rosa and she came running. Randall later wrote, "I was scared! I truly thought I was going to die. Doña Rosa rushed in, got some salve and just started pounding my back while massaging it. Once I was able to calm down, she found a doctor for me. I remember getting an injection and some muscle relaxers."

I felt so bad for him dealing with this on top of a new living situation and language study. Thankfully, he got better quite quickly and we put this terrifying episode behind us. I thought, *Doña Rosa is his new guardian angel!*

Language study went well but we were always busy with activities George planned for us to do. After class on just our third day in Antigua, he had us go to Santa María Cauqué to see Ken. The contrast to Carchá continued to amaze me. Santa María was a poor town though Ken's living situation was better than average for the village. He seemed to be adjusting to the village well and was happy.

Ken introduced us to friends he had made and we saw a solar shower at the new Appropriate Technology center a couple of kilometers down the Pan-American Highway. All the people in this part of the country seemed less approachable than in Alta Verapaz. Let's just say they were cautiously friendly. This was due to the unrest that was going on in the area and they were scared. I believe some feared being affiliated with gringos and it made them nervous. We were glad to get back to Antigua.

After Spanish classes, Randall and I would walk around the city to take it all in. Antigua translates to "ancient" in English. It was the perfect name. It was a rich city compared to others we had seen, and especially after visiting Ken in Santa María. We fell in love with this beautiful place.

Homes and businesses were behind the seven to eight feet tall stone or cinder block walls covered with plaster. The families on each city block had painted their walls with different vibrant colors. It made for a truly festive look. There were flowers growing everywhere in Antigua. Fuchsia bougainvillea plants with their purplish-red colors were poking over the walls from the homes' courtyards. Beautiful ornate wooden doors built into the walls opened to the Spanish style homes with open courtyards. The mild weather of the Land of Eternal Spring was perfect for this type of house.

To add to the intrigue and beauty of Antigua are three volcanoes—*Volcán de Fuego* (Volcano of Fire), *Volcán Acatenango* and *Volcán de Agua* (Volcano of Water)—that tower on the outskirts of the city, giving a majestic appearance. Volcán de Agua is also called Volcán Hunapú (place of flowers) in the local indigenous language. It is dormant, but in the 1500s there had been water at the top and a break in the crater caused the destruction of Ciudad Vieja, thus the name Volcán de Agua. The destroyed city was relocated to where Antigua now stands.

Volcán de Fuego is an active volcano and can be seen spitting out smoke and sulfur fumes. Fuego is famous for being almost constantly active at a low level. Small gas and ash eruptions occur every 15 to 20 minutes. At night it was an amazing spectacle for us to witness. Larger eruptions have occurred over the years, spewing ash and lava. Thankfully the lava flows away from Antigua. An eruption on June 3, 2018, resulted in at least 159 deaths and over 300 injuries, 256 missing persons and residents being evacuated. La Aurora International Airport in Guatemala City was closed due to the ash in the air.

Volcán Acatenango is one of the highest of the thirty-seven volcanoes in the country. It has two summits, 13,044-foot *Pico Mayor* (highest peak) and 12,729-foot *Yepocapa*. Acatenango blew its top several times in the 1920s, and again in 1972, but has been dormant for more than four decades. However, sulfur gases fizz up through its fumaroles. Together with Fuego, the two peaks are called *camellón* (big camel) by the locals because they look like the humps on a camel's back.

Looking out from the kitchen at Doña Rosa's house, one's view was of her colorful patio with gorgeous flowers and trees with the gigantic Volcán de Agua on display in the background. There were at least six different colors of roses. We would sit out on the patio to enjoy our breakfast and the scenery. Every morning I thought, *Wow, what a view to wake up to! Never saw anything like this in Kansas.*

Doña Rosa was a wonderful hostess. We were fed extremely well. My favorite part was all the different kinds of fruit and fresh juices made in a blender, such as pear, papaya, orange and cantaloupe. A lot of the food—such as tortillas, breads, chicharrones (pork rinds) and fruit—the family purchased from poorer families, who would deliver to Doña Rosa's house. The tortillas were not nearly as good compared to Matilde's right off the grill. *Plátanos* (plantain bananas) were boiled in water, sugar and cinnamon and a real treat. I also had beef tongue for the first time and—to my surprise—it was very good. But I never could quite get past the hair on the chicharrones to eat them.

We had our meals with the other students staying with Doña Rosa. We met a couple named Dan and Elaine from Canada. Dan had been the MCC Canada Executive Director before he and Elaine decided to go to Bolivia as MCC volunteers. They were in Antigua to learn Spanish. They were a delight to know and very supportive. We really enjoyed the time we had with them in Guatemala.

Another couple staying was from Washington state and were in their 70s. They had made the long trek by car from Washington to Guatemala and we compared our experiences driving through Mexico. They were just vacationing and studying Spanish for fun but having a hard time learning it. The amazing part was they were both originally from Kansas. One was raised in Clay Center, Kansas, and the other in Chanute, Kansas. They both went to Kansas State University so we had lots to talk about. *What a small world!*

A younger guy, just a little older than us, had been living at Doña Rosa's house for several weeks. He was from California but he came to Guatemala to teach English in a school in Antigua. He was studying Spanish also. Doña Rosa and Irma would work with us on our Spanish during meals. Obviously something they had become quite accustomed to doing with their student guests.

Our Spanish study was way more intense than with Debbie. Having Christi as a private teacher and several hours of one-on-one study a day was exhausting but I loved it. Spanish was so much easier to learn and pronounce than K'ekchi', plus my little background from high school and college was helpful. We would walk around town and talk in Spanish and learn new words. She would include the history of Antigua. That was my favorite part.

Christi told me that the cobblestone streets were centuries old, laid by the indigenous people after being conquered by the Spaniards in the 1500s. The streets were laid out in a Spanish grid design with streets running east/west and north/south. Antigua was one of the first cities established this way in the New World.

Leading into the town square was the yellowish-orange colored Santa Carolina Arch over the street. Its ornate dome with a large clock in the middle was a magnificent introduction to the city. The story shared with us was that at one time there were two convents, one on each side of the street, the Convent of the Virgin and the Convent of Santa Catalina. The nuns on one side had taken vows of seclusion, but they needed to cross the street to teach nuns at the other convert. They couldn't be walking out in the open so the archway with a secret passage was built so the nuns could travel back and forth, unseen by the public.

Just past the arch stood the obligatory giant Catholic church. We were told that at one time there were thirty-six Catholic churches in Antigua. There were still many active Catholic churches with a definite European design element. The remnants of many of the destroyed churches remained, as well as a couple of convents and monasteries.

Antigua was the third capital of the country. First was *Iximche'*. Second was *Ciudad Vieja* (Old City). Neither of these lasted long as capitals. A devastating earthquake in 1773 practically destroyed Antigua and over the years the city has been hit by many earthquakes.

Christi showed me one thing that was very depressing. In the park there were always lots of young shoeshine boys who were homeless. They carried what looked like old flour sacks that held their nearly empty cans of shoe polish and stained polishing rags. They were dressed in dirty, tattered clothes and their hands were stained with shoe polish. Christi said the boys often sniffed glue and smoked marijuana as an escape from reality because they had no reason to live. It was a huge problem. They would beg to shine my shoes for a few cents. She warned they often were pickpockets and to be wary. Gringos were their favorite targets.

It was quite apparent Antigua was a favorite place for Americans and Europeans to visit. It was such a gorgeous city, inexpensive, and the weather was wonderful almost all year round. It was the tourist industry that helped Antigua thrive. On the streets it appeared to be almost fifty/fifty with foreigners and Guatemalans.

One could tell the locals didn't always have too high an opinion of gringos. Honestly, I couldn't blame them. Some of the younger foreigners were traveling the world on a dime and were pretty dirty and ragged looking. There were a lot of free spirits, making me think they got stuck in the 1960s hippie days. A few of the other gringos carried a little air of superiority and didn't always treat the Guatemalans with respect. However, the locals were used to their attitudes, and for the most part the gringos we met were very nice and respectful to the Guatemalans.

Chapter 30
Unsettling Times

Shortly into our study, Carlos and Christi shared about the turmoil that was currently going on in Guatemala City. The civil war we had learned about in our Friends World College class was escalating. A group of indigenous campesinos organized a protest because of kidnappings and killings in the rural areas. Congress refused to give the protesters a hearing and their legal advisor was assassinated. On January 28, 1980, the day we moved to Antigua, the group briefly took over two radio stations in Guatemala City.

The government of Spain was sympathetic to the cause because of suspicion that Spanish priests were being murdered by the Guatemalan Army. The *Comité de Unidad Campesina* (Committee of Peasant Unity), the *Ejército Guerrillero de los Pobres* (EGP, the Guerrilla Army of the Poor) and a couple other protest groups entered the Spanish Embassy on January 31 to meet peacefully to share their concerns about the inhumane treatment and murdering of campesinos by the Guatemalan government.

Spanish and Guatemalan officials were meeting in the embassy and the group presented the Spanish ambassador a letter. It said they had come to him because they knew that the Spanish were honorable people who would tell the truth about the criminal repression suffered by the peasants of Guatemala. The group had planned a press conference at noon to air their grievances.

According to the Guatemalan police, the protestors in the building had machetes, pistols, and Molotov cocktails (though this was never substantiated) and planned to riot. President Fernando Romeo Lucas Garcia, the Guatemala City police chief, and the Minister of the Interior—despite pleas from the Spanish ambassador to negotiate—decided to forcibly remove the group from the embassy.

After cutting off the electricity, water, and telephone lines, over three hundred armed state agents entered the building. They took over the 1st and 3rd floors of the embassy while the campesino protestors barricaded themselves on the 2nd floor, along with the captive Spanish Embassy staff and the visiting Guatemalan officials, including the former Vice President of Guatemala. The Spanish Ambassador shouted that the state agents were violating international law but to no avail.

A fire was ignited. Some Guatemalan officials claimed it was white phosphorus tossed in the room and that set off the Molotov cocktails. Thirty-six people were killed and only two survived. Those killed included the Spanish staff, the former Vice President of Guatemala, other Guatemalan staff, and the campesinos.

One of the survivors was the Spanish Ambassador (who escaped through a window) and a protester. The protester had third-degree burns and both men were taken to the hospital. The protester was forcibly removed by what was called the Judicial Police. The kidnapped man was taken to an undisclosed location, tortured, and murdered. His body was dumped on the campus of University of San Carlos with a placard placed around his neck. It said, "Brought to Justice for Being a Terrorist" and "The Ambassador will be next."

The Spanish Ambassador escaped the hospital, thanks to members of the diplomatic corps. He fled the country back to Spain. Immediately, Spain pulled all diplomatic relations with Guatemala.

The week after the Spanish Embassy incident, we learned the turmoil was escalating in the area to the north and west of Chimaltenango called Quiché. Eleven soldiers and two guerrilleros (the antigovernment fighters) were killed. Bus transportation was extremely important for the Guatemalan people and the guerrilleros were stopping buses and making the people get off and then burning the buses. The papers reported nine buses burnt in just a couple days. Buses were suspended in that region of the country.

In Guatemala City and some other areas, the bus owners cut back service to 8:00 a.m. to 5:00 p.m., which really caused problems for commuters going to work. Things in the city were deteriorating as well. A few days later there were two military officers and a policeman killed in Guatemala City. Several bombs were set off in retaliation for the embassy killings and all buses were halted for two days. While Guatemala was in turmoil, El Salvador was facing its own crisis with tanks in the streets of the capital San Salvador. Central America was a mess.

Needless to say, this event in the capital was a little unsettling in our first week of Spanish study. George informed us that the Peace Corps workers had been pulled from Guatemala. That was a little unnerving for us. Was it dangerous for us to remain here?

Randall and I still felt safe in Antigua and in Carchá. It was scarier for Ken, Carman, and Carolyn where they lived. It was definitely a possibility that we could be sent packing. George didn't seem to be worried and expressed he thought we would be staying.

Our new MCC Country Director Rich and family were to arrive within the week. He would be the one to assess the situation and make the decision if we stayed or not. The plan was once Rich, Martha, and their two little girls arrived in Guatemala, they would eventually be living in Guatemala City. *What must they be thinking!*

Recalling back living through this experience, I can't help but note how the ramifications of years of United States supported military dictators, injustice, and genocide contribute to today's current immigration problems. People are trying to flee horrible living conditions and violence. With a population of more than seventeen million people, more than half live below the national poverty line of $2 a day. Powerful criminal organizations with gang-related violence are causing people to leave this beautiful country, looking for a safe place to live.

Chapter 31
New Country Director

After coming to Guatemala, Rich and Martha would first need to go through language study in Antigua. Doña Rosa's house was much better suited for Rich's family. It was a perfect place for two little girls. There wasn't room for all of us so Randall and I would be moving to live with two different families. And of course, we also lost our instructors.

Our last day with Carlos and Christi was so much fun. We played Spanish Scrabble. Irma's daughter Fabiola and friend Laura joined us in a game of Uno! After we finished studying, we ate at a Japanese restaurant (which was so good) and then went to a movie. We saw *Rocky II*. It came out just before we left for Guatemala and we hadn't seen it. It cost us fifty cents.

To top off the day, Debbie came to see us. Her parents were visiting and she wanted to introduce them to us and show them Antigua. She took us (including Carlos and Christi) to a little restaurant that soon became our favorite place in Antigua. It was called *Doña Luisa Xicoteneatl* and was a favorite hangout for gringos. They served the best pie and desserts.

Debbie bought a pineapple pie to share. After the exposure to this heavenly place, we made several trips to Doña Luisa's during our stay. This included a few weeks after Debbie's visit when Linda brought two friends to Antigua who were visiting from the States. By far my favorite menu item they served was their granola, fruit, and yogurt with honey poured over the top. It was amazing!

Later that day we packed our bags and said "*Hasta luego* (see you later)" to Doña Rosa and her family. George had enrolled us in one of the Spanish language schools, and they were going to pair Randall and me up with families. We would start school and be taken to our new homes on Monday. We headed to Chimaltenango for the weekend and to greet Rich.

Dan and Elaine went with us to Chimaltenango to welcome Rich and family. At George's we were pleasantly surprised to see Bob, Sandy, and kids there from Carchá. As the EMB Country Director, he certainly would be there to greet Rich and Martha.

Ken, Carman, and Carolyn came and we fixed a great supper as we awaited Rich and his family's arrival. George took the pickup and went to the airport to fetch them. Imagining George, Rich, Martha and the two girls in the cab of the truck brought back memories of George cramming us all in the truck. *¡Bienvenidos a Guatemala!*

It was great to see Rich, Martha, and girls when they came walking in the door. After dinner we had a nice chat, getting to know one another. George seemed a little awkward in trying to figure out his role now that Rich was there. Everyone was exhausted from travel, and we decided tomorrow was another day to continue our discussion since safety was weighing on our minds. We all found places to sleep and had a giant slumber party.

The rest of the weekend was spent discussing the political situation in Guatemala and if it was safe for us to remain there. Rich had assessed the situation and met with us individually to discuss how we were feeling. Dan told us that if at any time we weren't comfortable with staying, we should let Rich know. For the time being, we all felt safe and wanted to stay. Later I was to find out that my parents received a letter from MCC explaining the situation in the country and that if necessary, we would be evacuated. How worried they must have been!

George moved Rich and Martha to Antigua on Sunday, while Dan and Elaine took the bus back. Since we had no place to go, Randall and I spent the night at George's before returning early Monday morning to class. Carman took us to catch the bus, lugging all our belongings to move to our new homes. On the way we almost had a wreck with a guy on a motorcycle and we both veered off the road to avoid colliding. Thank goodness nobody was hurt and no damage to either vehicle, but it was quite the scare. For once we were almost happy to get on a bus.

When we got to our new language school that morning, we found it was way different from having private tutors. There were several other American, Canadian, and European students. We worked individually and in groups. Rotating through several teachers over the weeks was a real challenge.

My first teacher was named Lizette. She was a great teacher, but it felt like we were making slower progress than when I worked with Christi. The school had a set curriculum to follow and we started by going over everything I had already learned. With Christi and Carlos, we were able to work at a much faster pace.

The best part of being at the school (and probably slowed down our learning the language) was meeting all the interesting people from all over. We conversed in English too much, compared to studying with Christi and speaking only in Spanish all day. One woman student was from Milwaukee and was going to be working at a Hispanic health clinic for the poor and needed to learn more Spanish. There was a man from Evergreen, Colorado, who was traveling with his wife.

One afternoon after class I met a couple from Los Angeles and we talked for an hour about the problems in Guatemala. They were not even aware of the turmoil going on. The same afternoon I met a woman from Canada who was attacked by a robber. Her husband broke his heel, attempting to help her. It was a very trying time for them. It made me more cognizant to be careful on the streets at night. Something I never worried about in Carchá.

Chapter 32
Doña Angélica

After our first class, Randall and I were eager to move in with our new families for the rest of our language study. The school administrator came to me just before class was over and asked if I would mind sharing a room with another student for a few days. Someone at the house hadn't moved out yet for me to have my own room. I was kind of hesitant at first but said sure.

Randall and I were taken in opposite directions to meet our host ladino families. My new living situation was not as conveniently located as same as living at Doña Rosa's. The house was on the outskirts of town on a dirt/gravel road. It was a nice but smaller house.

Any worries about my new living situation were for naught. The first thing I found interesting was the family's last name. It was an Italian name, not Hispanic. Doña Angélica, the matriarch of the family, was introduced and her smile and warm welcome told me right away I was going to like her. She also said in Spanish, "Please, just call me Angélica."

She led me down a hallway where all the rooms opened onto the long hall. Halfway down on the right side it opened to a little open-air patio area filled with flowers and plants. Angélica showed me to the bedroom I was going to share. It was a nice size room with two beds and a private bathroom. *Yay! Again we have hot water!*

Angélica told me it had been her son Luis Jr.'s bedroom but he was married now and lived in Guatemala City with his wife and little boy Luis III or *Luisito* (little Louis.) This made me think of home because my brother-in-law was Louie Jr. and my nephew was Louie III.

She lived with her husband Luis Sr., daughter Patti, son-in-law Mario and eight-month-old grandson *Marito* (little Mario). They also had a cat named Bimbo and a parrot that talked and sang nonstop (in Spanish naturally).

There wasn't as much commotion at Angélica's as compared to Doña Rosa's. There were only two other students. Angélica apologized that I would have to share the bedroom for the time being with another student named *Guillermo*. I assured her it was fine. The third student was leaving soon and I could move into her room once she left.

Just before supper my new roommate Guillermo and the two ladies arrived. Guillermo's American name was Bill. He was thirty-one and a dentist from California. Bill was a fascinating guy and I really enjoyed getting to know him. He came to study Spanish because he worked at a health clinic for the poor and had a lot of Spanish-speaking clientele. He was also thinking about moving to Costa Rica. He had lived there with his parents for a few years growing up and really liked it there. He was quite intelligent and aware of things going on in the world and the political situation in Guatemala.

One of the ladies was the student leaving soon. She was an older woman named Gladys from California. The other woman with her, named Rose Anna, was a friend who had come to travel back with her to the States. Rosa Anna was about sixty-five and from, of all places, Wichita, Kansas. She was raised in Seneca and lived in Concordia, Kansas, until her husband had passed away two years earlier. She met Gladys on another trip and they decided to travel together. It was great fun to talk to another person from back home and she was a delight. Bill, the ladies and I had some great conversations about the situation in Guatemala.

Randall got settled into his place. His family wasn't quite as well off as mine but his accommodations still were way better than we had in Carchá. He seemed to really like his family, too. He also had a housemate and of all things, he was from Switzerland and spoke Dutch. Randall was about to bubble over telling me. After the year he had spent in Holland, few opportunities arose for Randall to speak Dutch. We both ended up in perfect situations. *Someone is always looking out for us.*

Angélica was a great hostess. She always had a smile and was happy. She was a great cook, too. She had access to the best produce and meats because Luis was the manager of the city market, a very influential position. Patti and Mario worked for a bank and Angélica took care of little Marito while they were away. Every night during meals we sat around the table chatting. Angélica liked to teach us new words and it was fun to watch her slowly pronounce words and then make us repeat them correctly.

Patti and Mario would share the events that were going on in the country and expressed how worried they were about their safety, especially being a more affluent family. With Luis' position in the market, they feared he or a family member might be kidnapped and ransomed for money. Sadly, it wasn't out of the realm of possibility.

Angélica didn't seem to have a grasp of what was going on politically or why. Being a more affluent ladina woman, her viewpoint leaned toward blaming the campesinos for disrupting her life rather than sympathy for their cause, fighting for a better life. You could definitely sense the fear the family had. Bill and I did try to express the campesinos' side of the issue as best we could without being rude, since we were guests in their home. This led to Bill and me having many more discussions on our own after dinner when we could share in English.

One day Angélica said the family was going to Guatemala City for the weekend to attend a birthday party for Luisito and she was making the tamales. I asked if I could help and she said with her big smile, "*¡Absolutamente!*"

These tamales were a little different from Matilde's. Mostly it was a difference of ingredients that Angélica had at her disposal. Also, she steamed rather than boiled her tamales. Angélica still used a banana leaf to wrap around the outside but instead of two banana leaves, she used some other kind of plant leaf for the second one. The dough was made from corn masa and duck fat for the grease.

The main difference was the filling she put inside the dough, starting with spices she toasted and ground. She added the five ground spices—cumin, coriander seeds, black peppercorns, a clove, and cardamom seeds—in a large pot with melted duck fat and onions. The rest of the filling included garlic, salt, cilantro (which I never liked), Roma tomatoes, chipotle peppers, some lime juice, carrots, potatoes, peas, and duck meat. The best part was we got to try them for supper. They were delicious.

On the weekend, Randall and I went to visit Carman and Carolyn to see their new house in Santa María Cauqué. We helped them build a latrine out of cornstalks and wood. In the kitchen, we stained a counter and worked on a table and moved the pila. It was a good day's work and great to see where they would be living. To catch a bus back to Antigua, we had to walk about four miles to San Lucas Sacatepéquez.

It was great to get back to Antigua and my room to relax. Since my family had gone to the city for a few days, we were on our own for food. Bill and I went to a restaurant called *La Fonda*. I had a really inexpensive steak and it was delicious. We were stuffed but we still went to Doña Luisa's for dessert.

The family returned home and I asked how the trip went. I could tell Angélica was distressed. She said they were quite upset because things hadn't gone as they had planned. They had been robbed at gunpoint while still in their car. The robbers stole their presents for the party, their suitcases with clothes and even the tamales.

Angélica and Patti were quite shaken from the experience, but thankfully nobody was hurt. Bill and I spent a great deal of time talking with them about the incident. Bill offered to help Angélica and Luis if things got worse. He would help them immigrate to the United States if they wanted. It was obvious Angélica was worried and thanked him.

With a new week, I had another new teacher. Her name was Amanda, and Randall's teacher was Pedro. Amanda and I went to the market, which was always a great learning experience. I looked for Luis but didn't see him there.

One day I had mentioned to Luis that I would like to buy one of the wool ponchos made by the highland Guatemalans. He told me ponchos cost $7 or $8, but vendors would try to get gringos to pay way more. He said to barter for the lower price. He said to come by his office in the market later that day, and he would ask one of his friends to sell me one.

I found his office and it was a little brick and cement building with a tin roof in the center of the market. I could tell everyone in the market liked Luis from the way they greeted and waved to him as we walked the aisles. He took me to the booth of one of his friends and I picked out a poncho. He had slim pickings of colors but they were super warm and nice ponchos. I asked him how much one costs. He said since I was a friend of Don Luis, I could have it for $5. I felt a little guilty paying so little and tried to give him $8, but he refused. I couldn't say no after such a kind gesture.

When we left for Antigua, I had brought the peanuts for snacks that Daryl gave us from Cahabón since I figured they would just get moldy in damp Carchá. When I got back to Angélica's, I gave Luis a bag of the peanuts and another bag for his vendor friend. Luis smiled from ear to ear and said, "Muchas gracias."

Amanda and I were able to talk during language study about the political situation and I shared why I was there to work with the K'ekchi'. It was always interesting to get the perspective of the ladino Guatemalans and their feelings toward the indigenous people. Some were very sympathetic and others had a disdain for them. Amanda thought it was great Randall and I were there to work with the K'ekchi' and even more impressed we were learning the language.

Dealing with beggars on the street was one of the most difficult issues for me. I never got used to it nor knew how to handle it. We were told that giving them money often just led to them buying alcohol. I started buying bread and giving it instead of money. One little boy was so appreciative. It broke my heart and made me feel guilty that I had so much by comparison.

I believe Bill's offer to help Angélica's family move to the U.S. struck a chord. They began talking about it more because they were so scared of how things were going in Guatemala. Patti and Mario, who were about my age, had learned some English in school. Though we weren't supposed to talk in English per the school's rules, Patti and Mario would ask me a few things to make sure they were saying something correctly in English.

One day I received a tape from my mother. I asked Patti if I could borrow her tape recorder to listen, and it was sure nice to hear my parents' voices. I encouraged Patti to listen, too, if she wanted to hear the English. Patti commented that my parents had really nice voices and that made me smile. I let her tape a message back to my parents in Spanish and I translated.

Angélica started asking me to teach her some English. She and I would sit at the table and point at objects and we would practice in both English and Spanish. It tickled me because she tried so hard to pronounce English words and then would laugh because she knew she said it totally wrong or just couldn't get the word out. It made me think how I must have come across to Santiago when he was trying to help me say K'ekchi' words. Angélica made a little progress and I bought her a book with translations from Spanish into English.

Every weekend seemed to be filled with some event. After a week of intense study, we needed to get away. Rich and his family, Dan, Elaine, Randall, and I went to Guatemala City one weekend. We took them to the Bavarian restaurant the nurses had shown us on our trip with them to the city.

After a great lunch, we went to the Guatemala City Central Market. The thing at the market that always stood out most was the smell. The meat department was the worst and so gross. Flies were everywhere on the meat that included: beef tongue and stomach, pig's ear, chicken feet, lizard meat, armadillo meat and all kinds of fish!

Later that day Randall and I went to see the movie *Foul Play* starring Goldie Hawn. It cost us a whopping thirty cents. Since it was in English with Spanish subtitles, we used the excuse that it was great language study. That evening we went to a church called *Casa Horeb*, which was an evangelical church that George attended. Little did we know the significance this church would have for MCC and Guatemala in the future.

When I got back from the city to my family's house, Bill had moved out and I didn't get to say goodbye. Angélica said he was going to come back to visit after touring other parts of the country before going home. The revolving door of students continued. A young couple named Randy and Patti moved in. So now we had two Patti's in the house.

As promised, Bill did come back a few days before he returned to the States. He gave his expensive watch to Luis and brought flowers to Angélica. He was such a great guy and I was going to miss him. He gave them his address and phone number in case they wanted to reach him.

One day Luis, Jr. and his wife visited and I really enjoyed meeting them. Angélica made enchiladas that were way better than any enchiladas I ever had back home. They discussed Bill's offer of going to the United States. Luis and Luis, Jr. scoffed at that idea and were not interested at all.

After our trip to the city and back to classes, I had another new teacher named Clara. They just kept rotating. After Clara I had Anna. Language study turned sour when for the second time, I had a major bout with illness. For a couple days my stomach did flips and all the bad side effects that come with stomach ailment. I missed class with Anna for a day but eventually got over it. There is nothing worse than being sick when one is so far away from home. Angélica was truly an angel. She gave me her special blend of tea, mineral water, and lemon juice with Alka Seltzer. It helped me recover pretty quickly.

Much worse though was a couple weeks after Patti and Randy moved in, she became extremely ill and ended up going to the hospital. Angélica feared she had hepatitis. That was one of the diseases we had been given a shot for before leaving the States, and we were told never to drink unboiled water. Randy moved their things out and I never heard how she was doing.

Our last weeks in Antigua flew by. Though we loved Antigua (and I would miss Angélica, Luis, and family), we were ready to get back to Carchá. One thing I wasn't going to miss was Bimbo the cat. He slept all day and often in my room. Then at night he would be prowling and meowing. One night I hardly got any sleep thanks to Bimbo starring in the sequel to *That Darn Cat!* He and another cat were up on the roof of the house, growling, hissing, and screaming at one another. It made a terrible noise, especially on a tin roof.

On one of our last weekends, we had a retreat at Hotel Longarone with the MCC/EMB team. Dan was the speaker and his talk was titled "God's Spirit in Us and Through Us." It was quite thought provoking as we tried to minister to the needs of the Guatemalan people. We had a good conversation as a team about what we would do if there was a revolution and government take-over. Nothing was decided but it was good to be cognizant of the possibility.

Even with the problems at hand, MCC moved forward with plans to bring new volunteers to Guatemala. Two couples would be joining our team. One couple, Phil and Joy, would be working in Guatemala City and the other couple, Dale and Lois, would be moving to Carchá to replace the nurses when they went back to the States.

Seeing all the EMB missionaries at Hotel Longarone made us even more ready to get back to our old stomping grounds. The plan was for Randall and me to move back in with our K'ekchi' families for one month or until we found a place of our own. This was still a sticking point with George as we discussed the type of place where we would live.

Before we left for Antigua, George had found a small room that was an old tienda. He thought it would be perfect for us. I was not too keen on the idea. There was no privacy at all as it was right on a busy street. I felt we needed a little more room and some place a little quieter and nicer for the weekend after spending the week at Campat. The decision once we got back to Carchá would be made with Rich and Bob's input.

The Friday before our last Antigua weekend, George showed up at Angélica's door at 8:30 a.m. and said we had a meeting in Guatemala City at 10:00. We surprised Randall and he joined us in the little yellow car. *Nothing like a little surprise! Classic George move.*

We made it to the meeting in typical Guatemalan fashion at 10:30, thirty minutes late. I don't even remember what the meeting was about. In the afternoon we went to Casa Horeb and spent time talking to them about their garden. They asked us to come visit again before we left Antigua but we never had time.

We made it back to Antigua and dropped by to see Dan and Elaine. Our time with this awesome couple was soon to run out. That night after supper, Angélica and I talked more about the problems in Guatemala. She shared her thoughts about possibly going to the United States, and we practiced a little English before I turned in after a very full day.

Dan and Elaine had a friend come to visit. This man, named Harvey Wegler, had spent many years in Eastern Europe. Dan made arrangements for him to speak at a local church. It was fascinating to hear him talk about the issues those European countries faced and the similarities of what was going on in Guatemala.

Bob came from Carchá to hear Mr. Wegler speak and spent the night with me at Angélica's. It was one of the few times he and I really had some alone time to share. We talked about Campat and what Randall and I hoped to be able to do there. He asked how I was doing physically and mentally. He understood how hard it was to be away from home in a strange land and dealing with culture shock, not to mention the political turmoil. He wanted me to know I could talk to him anytime I needed.

One of the things we discussed was the conundrum of dealing with the horrible poverty we saw everywhere and coping with the guilt feelings, knowing how well off we were in comparison. What more could we do to help? He imparted his wisdom that we can only take one day at a time and just do what we can do. Not to feel guilty for the blessings we have been bestowed but use them to help those less fortunate. His sharing was very reassuring as to why I was there and made me even more anxious to get back to Carchá and our missionary and K'ekchi' families.

Chapter 33
Back to Alta Verapaz

We were down to our final week in Antigua. Randall and I continued to practice our Spanish and felt we had made good progress. Yes, I had another new teacher. This one was named Mario. He was okay but not as good as the previous teachers. He was new and really was just learning to teach.

Just four days prior to my moving out from Angélica's, a new couple moved in. They were a young, unmarried couple named Bill and Yvonne from the States. They seemed like a lovely, free-spirited couple and I was sure they would treat Angélica with respect.

Before we headed back to Carchá, we had two orders of business to take care of. We went to see Carman and Carolyn one more time at their new house and to meet their parents, who were visiting from Canada. The other important thing was to go to Guatemala City one afternoon and get motorcycle driver's licenses. *The dreaded motorcycle!*

George was going to be leaving the country soon and we were inheriting his motorcycle. Getting our driver's licenses was another great example of why it was important that we could at least converse a little in Spanish. I don't think dealing with ladino officials in K'ekchi' would have gone over too well.

It was quite the hassle to get our licenses. We waited in line for a long time and finally were called to the official's desk. We had to show our passports, our U.S. driver's licenses, and fill out some paperwork. Ken shared, "I believe we had a *tramitador* (processor) do most of the work. I recall that we all passed both our written and driving tests with flying colors—of course, without actually doing either!"

Once the man was satisfied with our application, he approved it by stamping our documents about a half dozen times, making it official. We were excited to get back to Carchá and have our own transportation other than the buses. Randall was going to drive the motorcycle back to Carchá and I would take the bus.

The remainder of our Antigua stay, we frequented our favorite pastry shop as many times as possible since we knew our chances were limited. Dan and Elaine joined us for our last Doña Luisa visit and to have pasteles, which were delicious. *Zanahoria pastel* (carrot cake) was so good and my favorite. George stopped by during this trip. He handed the keys to his motorcycle to Randall. Poor George didn't feel very comfortable in a place like Doña Luisa's and didn't appear to approve. But we still enjoyed our last dessert there.

Saying goodbye to Angélica and Luis' family was very difficult. Patti gave me a large chocolate candy bar from Marito. *What a special treat!*

Though it was sad to leave, I knew I would be seeing them soon because I had promised I would come back to visit when my sister Jane came to see me. She was my first visitor and arrived just four days after I returned to San Pedro Carchá. That meant another bus trip to the city, but I didn't mind it one bit.

Randall's trip back to Carchá on the bike went smoothly. Being back on the road was exhilarating for him. Though compared to his Honda 550 journey across parts of the United States, this was a totally different type of adventure. The Yamaha 90cc dirt bike was not really made for long highway trips. It sounded like a chainsaw when revved at a high speed. Randall was saddle sore and exhausted by the time he arrived. I made it just fine on the bus and it was great to get back to Carchá. It felt like "Home Sweet Home."

I moved back in with Chepe and family. Don Antonio was pleased to have Randall back. It was just fine by me for Randall to keep the motorcycle at his house. Not only did it save him the long hike to and from the nurses' house on foot, but also, I wasn't excited about driving the darn thing. I was perfectly content with riding behind him when we went somewhere. I'm sure he was less anxious as well.

While I was gone, the Xols made more improvements to their house by building on an addition. My room was much larger than before and another room was being added adjacent to mine. This was going to be a bedroom for the boys. The plan was for my room to eventually become a tienda for Matlide to sell goods or for Chepe to move his sewing out of the main house.

Getting back into the swing of studying K'ekchi' was a little difficult. We had just gotten to the point where we could think and talk in Spanish. Push that aside and now speak in K'ekchi'. I found myself talking to Chepe more in Spanish than in K'ekchi', but it was nice to be able to communicate better than before. We picked up with Debbie and Santiago, reviewing all we had learned and forgotten. Slowly it started to resurface.

Another challenge was staying healthy. This was not always the easiest thing to do living in Guatemala. It made me realize how blessed we were as caxlan cuinks in comparison to the K'ekchi' people. All my worries about my health and wellbeing were so easily taken care of with help from the nurses and missionaries. We had a huge support system. The K'ekchi' weren't as fortunate but the nurses did all they could to help them also.

Randall and I both had to deal with stomach issues way too often. It was probably caused by too much greasy caldo, hot spices, and coffee. We were always buying Tums from the nurses. I had my third serious case with amoebas when I was back at Chepe's. It really knocked me for a loop. There was absolutely nothing worse than those rotten egg sulfur burps. Again, thanks to the nurses and pills to combat the little stomach bugs, I recovered in a couple days.

For the second time, Randall had a major scare, but this time it was two sores on his arm that became infected. Red streaks started going up his arm. The nurses said it could possibly be either lymphangitis or blood poisoning where the infection is spreading. It could be very serious if not treated and lead to sepsis. They gave him an antibiotic, and thankfully it healed and went away. *Bantiox re li Dios!*

Another smaller issue I had was when my eyes began hurting and bothering me when reading. There was also a white spot on one of my eyes. Never having had problems with my eyes before, it worried me and the nurses said I should go to the optometrist in Cobán. They took me so they could translate and the doctor said I had astigmatism and a small callus on one eye. It was probably caused by the sun and dust. She said it would probably go away but to watch it and wear sunglasses in the sun. I got some drops and never had any more issues with my eyes. *Whoa, another crisis averted.*

I had a disconcerting experience in my last days at Chepe's that made me note how fortunate I was with my upbringing and family life back home. One afternoon I was reading in my room and I heard a slight tap on my door. A young boy, maybe nine or ten years old, named Rolando was at my door. I knew him because he had started selling helados in the town square for Chepe. He was quite poor and didn't go to school like Óscar and Rollie.

Rolando would come early in the morning to pick up the Styrofoam container filled with frozen treats Matilde had made the night before. He wouldn't return until he sold all of the helados unless it started to get dark. He would bring back the empty container and money, and Chepe would then pay Rolando his share.

When I opened the door and saw Rolando, he had a cut on his cheek and one above his eye. Blood was dripping down his chin. He wasn't crying but was on the verge of tears. He was looking for Chepe but nobody was home. He was shy and wouldn't say what happened to him, but I guessed he either fell, got hit by a rock or maybe some-one hit him. He did tell me the money he had made was stolen.

Inviting him to come in, he reluctantly agreed. I had him sit at my desk and told him to stay while I ran to get water. I grabbed the plastic pan I used for shaving and ran to Matilde's pila, filling the pan with water. With a washcloth, I carefully tried to wipe the blood from his face and clean the cuts. He had quite a little bump on his forehead and he flinched a little when I touched it.

After getting him cleaned up, I got some antiseptic and Band-Aids* from the little medicine bag my mother had made sure to sup-ply me with before I left home. Once patched up, Rolando was so appreciative. I was glad I was there to help him. Again, it made me stop and reflect how good I had it and how much support surround-ed me. *I better not be feeling sorry for myself.*

Chapter 34
Semana Santa

After just one week of study, it was time to make the trek back to Guatemala City and meet my sister Jane at the airport. That was a day I will always remember. What a joyful feeling to see her walk into the airport after six long months apart. That first hug was amazing. Her willingness to come and learn about my experiences first hand rather than just being told in letters meant a great deal to me.

I had made arrangements to stay at the Central American Mission the first night. After getting settled in our rooms and catching up on all that had gone on, we decided to go sightseeing. We took the bus system and traveled around to see the city. Her eyes were pretty wide open and she was astonished at seeing the living conditions in this strange, new environment.

The next day we took the Pullman to Carchá and it didn't break down. What a relief! The nurses and Ruth invited Jane to stay with them while she was there. She went with me to meet Chepe's family. Before she arrived, I had sent Jane a list of gifts to bring for my Guatemalan families. She brought photos from the film I had sent home for her to develop.

We gave the gifts and photos to Chepe, Matilde and the kids. The large family photo made them so proud and they were very appreciative. Jane had learned a little Spanish and could express her thoughts a little bit. But she wanted me to tell them thank you for taking such good care of her little brother. They loved that.

I think Jane's favorite part of the visit was when we went to Campat. Randall said we could take the motorcycle but I said "Nah, I don't think so." I don't know who was more relieved, Randall or Jane.

We caught the bus from Carchá to Chamelco and walked to the bridge. That was a piece of cake. I had forewarned her about the hike up over the mountain. She had worked hard to get in shape before coming to Guatemala so she could make the climb. However, the flat terrain in Kansas City hadn't prepared her much for mountains and higher altitude.

It was a struggle and we had to make lots of stops to rest. Each time she would ask, breathing hard, "How much further?" I would say, "Just a little bit more."

After the umpteenth time she told me if I said a little bit further, she wasn't taking another step. I laughed and told her it really wasn't much farther. When we reached the top, Jane gasped as she took in the view of the beautiful Campat valley. I thought, *Her face says it all!*

Santiago knew Jane was coming to Guatemala and wanted to meet my sister *Herman Juana*. I had told him when we would be coming to Campat to visit. He and Angelina had huge smiles on their faces when we arrived and warmly greeted us. Angelina gave us caldo and coffee, treating us like royalty. Jane was so humbled. She had brought gifts for them and photos I had taken. The best time was taking more photos and getting Santiago, Angelina, and Josefina to smile. It was such a fun day.

I took Jane to see the church and where we had spent the nights in Campat. Of course, we were quite the spectacle and people came to greet us. We met José María's wife on the trail and she had her wooden washboard and laundry on her head. Jane was astonished seeing this. We stopped to talk to her and she asked if we would take her picture. Jane had brought a polaroid camera so we could give the photos we took immediately. They were so amazed watching the photo appear and come into focus.

We were having a great time but I told Jane we better start hiking back up the mountain. She looked at our climb and shook her head in doubt, but we made it. It started raining on our climb down. The temperature was warm and we were hot and perspiring from walking. We didn't mind the rain a bit. It felt good. We timed it just right to catch the bus for the return trip home. Once on the bus for Carchá, Jane was worn out and said she would never make that trek again, but I was proud of her determination and for making the hike.

During her stay in Carchá, each of the missionary families invited us for dinner. Jane said I was blessed to have such a wonderful support system and a relief for her to know. It was time to go back to Guatemala City and on to Antigua. I wanted to introduce Jane to Doña Rosa's family and Rich and Martha. All the family was away except for Doña Rosa. We were able to take a great photo of Doña Rosa on her patio. Rich and Martha were studying so we didn't get to talk very long, but we had dinner with them and the girls one night during our stay in Antigua.

From Doña Rosa's, we walked to Angélica and Luis' house. I had told them before what day we would come to visit. Angélica answered the door with Marito in her arms. It was so good to see them again even if it had just been a week. Marito was no longer shy around me and he wanted me to hold him. Angélica handed him to me and then gave Jane a hug.

Luis, Mario, and Patti soon arrived home from work. Jane had brought gifts for them and Angélica and Patti gave Jane a beautiful huipil (blouse) with hand stitching. Earlier Angélica had told us we must stay for dinner. She put on her usual feast. Jane teased Angélica that she fed me so well I wouldn't ever want to come back home. Angélica beamed.

The week Jane was in Guatemala was *Semana Santa* or Holy Week and Easter. What an amazing time to visit. This was also my first Guatemalan experience of this most special of holidays. We spent a couple nights at Hotel Antigua and were able to take in Good Friday. Semana Santa in Antigua was something to behold.

In the cobblestone streets, the people would create beautiful artwork called *alfombras* (rugs). These pieces of art were designs with intricate patterns made from organic materials such as sawdust, pine needles, flower petals, and palm leaves. Some used spray paint to add additional color to the sawdust. The designs would often include religious and cultural images, combining indigenous and Christian beliefs. The rugs would be built three to five feet wide in the middle of the street and could be just a few feet long or continue for several blocks, as far as the eye could see. The people living in the houses along the streets would work together to create these masterpieces.

Throughout Semana Santa, processions were held carrying statues of saints through the streets to the churches, similar to what we had seen in Guatemala City months before. The procession would walk through the alfombras, destroying all the hard work. But the rugs were the people's way of paying homage to their religion.

Some of the statues being carried were on huge platforms and as many as a dozen men or women would be on each side. Jane said that in a way the alfombras reminded her of when we were kids and our family went to the Rose Bowl parade in Pasadena with all the beautiful floats made with flowers.

Jane and I spent our final day in Guatemala City just touring together. I felt bad we never made it to visit Ken, Carman, and Carolyn but we just didn't have time. We went to a small market and bought several Guatemalan gifts for our family back home. Jane left on Easter morning and now my first visitor had come and gone. It was a sad goodbye, knowing it would be some time before seeing her again.

Chapter 35
Our New Home

Once back to Carchá, I knew we were close to being able to start work in Campat. Our first order of business was finding a place to live in town when not in the c'alebal. With Dale and Lois joining our team, we needed to find a home for them as well. They needed a larger place because they had three small boys.

Bob and George helped find a house and attached was a little room that had been a tienda. The little addition had its own bathroom and that would be great for us when we were in town. It needed a lot of work but it was perfect! Even George was delighted in the place. It was going to work out. *¡Gracias a Dios!*

Over several weeks we spent numerous days and nights in Campat. Having our motorcycle really helped cut down on travel time since we didn't have to take the bus to Chamelco and hoof it. Marcos, who lived in the house by the bridge, gave us permission to leave our motorcycle at his place whenever we went to Campat.

The people in Campat were getting used to seeing us there. Our next move was to go back with Bob to talk to Kacua' Marcos and set up a meeting with the land committee to bring up the idea of us living there. The talk with Kacua' Marcos went well and I am sure our initial visit with him helped. He told us his foot was much better and was appreciative of what we had done for him. We were able to make plans to come back in two weeks to meet with the committee.

Before we had our meeting with the land committee, Campat had a *nink'e* (festival) to celebrate the completion of the c'alebal's water project that we had noticed on our second trip to Campat with Millard. The project was part of the government health department's plan to provide clean water to campesinos.

For Campat, they tapped into the valley's natural stream that created a water source high up on the mountainside. They built a cement collection and storage tank. It was sort of the same idea as the water towers built back home but the mountain provided the height. The men of Campat dug the ditches by hand the length of the valley where the plastic pipe was laid. The pipe went all the way to the school at the far end of the valley.

At long last the project was finished. There were *chorros de agua* (cement stations with faucets) scattered down the valley. The cement bags to make the chorros were all carried up over the mountain. Each chorro had a place for a person to set his or her container under the faucet and fill it up. The flow out of the faucets was very strong thanks to gravity pushing the water through the pipes from the collection tanks high up on the mountain.

Dignitaries from Alta Verapaz, including the governor and officials from the Health Department, gathered at the school. They had come by vehicle to the Finca Chilax and then walked the long distance in the flat valley to reach the school without having to go over the mountain. Kacua' Marcos had invited Bob, Randall and me to attend as well.

There were two marimbas and a man playing a flute. They sang the Guatemalan national anthem and raised a flag. The *jefes* (bosses or dignitaries) spoke (mostly in Spanish) about the accomplishment of bringing sanitary water to the people of Campat. It truly was a big deal that they had done this for such a remote c'alebal. The land committee and people of Campat were very happy.

Women from Campat made caldo for the celebration. We were told to sit with all the big jefes to be fed. They appeared to be pretty full of themselves and it was a little hard to take. We felt awkward being linked with them and got the impression they didn't understand or appreciate why we were there. It was interesting and very humbling that Kacua' Pedro (one of the elders from the church) and

Kacua' Marcos introduced us and shared appreciation for our being there.

Back in Carchá, it took several days for us to get the keys to the new house, as was typical to accomplish most things in Guatemala. Patience was a virtue. Something I didn't always have a lot of to spare. Nothing EVER moved very fast there.

The family living in the house who was moving out took their own sweet time to leave. The day to receive the keys kept changing and we were getting frustrated. While we waited, Randall and I were totally immersed in language study and continued to live with our families. We both were getting cranky, thanks to eight days with no sunshine and lots of rain, cold, and mud. This was unusual for this time of year. It was just plain depressing and we were so ready to get moved.

At last we got the keys to our house and we changed the locks first thing. We began cleaning and painting our room. It had nice red and white tile floors so no more cement and damp floors. The missionaries came over and we helped them clean and paint the rest of the house for Dale, Lois, and the boys. We were finally able to move into our new Carchá home. I wrote in my journal, "We still have a lot of work to do in our room but it was nice to be away from the mice, trucks rumbling, and neighbors making noise at Chepe's."

Little did I know one of the first issues we had to deal with in the new house was worse than mice, there were rats. Thankfully, rat poison seemed to take care of the problem before Dale and Lois moved in.

In our little rectangular-shaped room, we built a cupboard/room divider with shelves for storage of food, dishes and clothes. We bought some green and turquoise checkered cloth (which matched the newly painted green walls), and Priscilla sewed some curtains to hide things on the shelves.

Dan and Elaine had finished language study and had come to visit our team in Carchá before leaving for Bolivia. It was always such a delight to see them. Elaine made curtains for the windows. We used some cinder blocks and boards to make a bookshelf.

At the beginning, we slept on cots with our foam mattresses but eventually we built two beds and bought a table and two chairs. We even bought a little hot water heater so we could have a hot shower. We justified the purchase in that after a week in Campat (with no shower) and our long hike (often in the rain), we needed a hot shower just to warm up.

Getting our room together was a slow process but was shaping up to be a cozy little place. We eventually bought a stove that used propane gas. The market and store in Cobán carried all the other things we needed like a cast iron skillet, pans, and dishes.

For our first home cooked meal, we had quite the celebratory dinner with rice and beans. We purchased tortillas in the market to have an authentic Guatemalan meal. Millard and Pris were our first guests, and they bought us fresh baked bread and homemade *mora* (blackberry) jam.

Chapter 36
The Big Question

Once we had settled into our new room, Randall and I started spending even more time in Campat. One of our first agricultural adventures was planting corn with José Mariá. It was spring and planting season. He asked if we would like to help, and we jumped at the chance. Oh, did we have a lot to learn! My days of planting acres and acres of corn back on the farm did little to prepare me. The eight-row corn planter and tractor would have been no use on a mountainside.

Being very poor, José Mariá didn't have much land compared to some of the others in the c'alebal. His land had been cleared from weeds, old corn stalks, and dead bean plants with a machete. The dried plant debris was then burned so the soil was covered with a fine layer of black ash. Some "plowed" their fields with hoes, turning over the soil and others just planted right into the ash-covered ground.

This corn planting was a learning experience for these two college-trained caxlan cuinks. José Mariá showed us his corn planter. It was a stick about six feet long and two inches in diameter. He had used his machete to chop a point on the end of the pole.

We carefully watched as José Mariá modeled how to plant. He would use the stick to poke a hole in the ground about five or six inches deep. He had corn and bean seed in the bolsa around his neck and would drop four or five kernels of corn in the hole and a bean seed or two. The beans were a climbing variety and would grow up the corn stalks as they matured. Then using the pole, he would cover up the seeds with loose soil and move about a foot to make the next hole.

First of all, we were amazed at how he could take the seeds from his bolsa and drop them in the hole without even bending over. He cupped his hand and let the seeds slide off his fingers right into the hole. Second, the field was at the very least a forty-five-degree angle. He had one foot solidly stationed below the other to keep him from slipping down the mountain. Try walking across a loose-soil field on a forty-five-degree angle to dig holes and plant seeds. *Yes, I definitely understand how someone could fall out of their cornfield.*

There were five friends from the church who were there to help. Randall and I were each given a planting stick. The men stood about a yard apart up the steep, sloped field. In other words, we WERE an eight-row corn planter. José Mariá took the lead and worked his way around the mountain in his field as we followed along.

It was obvious the Campat men had a distinct advantage over the caxlan cuinks in being so much closer to the ground, but they still never missed the dang hole. Needless to say, Randall and I were constantly bending over, picking up seeds after missing the hole. The men would tease us but were very kind and patient with us rookies.

Once we reached the end of the field, we would move up the mountain and start back across the field again. That day my appreciation for the farmers in Campat grew exponentially. It was backbreaking work and we were worn out afterward. Once we got back to the church, I told Randall, "I am going to be so sore tomorrow."

The two-week wait for our meeting with the land committee went by quickly. Dan and Elaine were still visiting and wanted to go to Campat with us. We knew the hike would be too much for Elaine and discouraged her from trying. She reluctantly gave in but Dan went with Bob, Randall and me to our meeting with the land committee.

The meeting was held at Kacua' Marcos' house. It was supposed to start at 4:00 p.m. so we arrived in plenty of time. In pure Guatemalan fashion, the meeting started at about 6:30 or 7:00. As the committee members arrived, it was a little intimidating to stand in front of these revered Campat men. We knew some of them but several we had never met.

Bob took the lead in explaining that we were with the Mennonite church mission and that we were agriculturas. We wanted their blessing to come to Campat to live and work. He asked them if they would be interested in helping to build a place for us to live and after we left, the building would belong to the c'alebal. We would supply all the materials if they would help build it.

The committee questioned exactly what it was we would do there. Randall and I shared how much we enjoyed our visits to Campat and hoped that we could provide help in any way. We talked about helping with gardening and small animals, like chickens and rabbits. We made sure to mention the possibility of teaching adults to read. We emphasized adults because we knew we had to stay clear of teaching children because of the school being available, even if it wasn't doing the best job of educating the children of the c'alebal.

The school at the far end of the valley had a ladino school teacher who would hike out over the mountain to the c'alebal to teach, at least when it was convenient for him. One never knew if he would show up or not. The boys and few girls who attended would make the long trek each day to see if the maestro did come.

The young teacher was studying at the *universidad* (university) and was required to teach in the c'alebal in order to graduate. He spoke only Spanish and most of the youth spoke only K'ekchi', a conundrum for certain. However, most of the K'ekchi' felt it was important for the boys to learn to speak Spanish because in the larger market places in Cobán or Carchá mostly Spanish was used in trading goods. As adults, if they needed to travel to other areas of the country to find work, Spanish was essential.

We had noticed that on days the teacher was present, the children and teacher were often out on the makeshift soccer field playing fútbol rather than studying. Though we would have loved to have held classes for the children, we knew we would butt heads with the teacher and Department of Education. It was better to stick with teaching adults. We didn't need that drama.

José Mariá had joined us and shared with the land committee how we had helped with planting. Kacua' Pedro spoke up for us and encouraged the men to let us live there. The fact the government had just helped the c'alebal with the water project, and it was such a success, might have also been in our favor.

We had no clue which way it would go by looking at the faces of the land committee members. The men asked to discuss the matter amongst themselves. When we were called back, we were pleasantly surprised when the elders said yes but on a trial basis.

The Kacua's were aware of how important being literate was for their people. They expressed that many in the c'alebal wanted to learn to read and if we really wanted to help, teaching the adults how to read would be of great service. Accepting the challenge to teach reading wasn't a difficult decision and we said yes. *We can do this!*

Neither Randall nor I had any teaching experience but Ruth shared with us the reading primers she used to teach her students. These primers were written by the same two American Wycliffe workers (Fran and Ruth) who had written the English instructional manual we used to learn K'ekchi'. We had become friends with Fran and Ruth and dined several times with them. Once when we mentioned that we might teach reading, the two K'ekchi' master teachers were excited and encouraged us to do so. They emphasized it was such a need and was also a great way for us to keep learning the language.

Fran and Ruth had devoted their lives working with the K'ekchi' and at that time were in their late 50s. They transcribed the previously unwritten language, wrote a K'ekchi' alphabet, and translated the Bible into K'ekchi'. They had created the reading primers for teaching the K'ekchi' how to read and had taught hundreds of students over the years. Fran and Ruth helped print over 100,000 K'ekchi'

Bibles and worked with the K'ekchi' for fifty-eight years. Fran was eighty-six years old when she decided to return to the States due to her health issues.

With access to the reading materials we needed, we could help others to learn to read. We could read K'ekchi' even if we didn't know all the words. It was a lesson in humility because we ourselves were still novice K'ekchi' speakers and had so much to learn. Fran and Ruth were right, teaching reading turned into a great learning tool for us as well. As noted in the old Latin principle *Docendo discimus* – by teaching, we learn.

The land committee said they would consider building the house but for the time being suggested we live in the church's kitchen and get accustomed to living in the c'alebal. Wise decision to see if these caxlan cuinks would stick it out. We tentatively set the date of May 8 to move to Campat, which was about two weeks away. It felt like we had won a small victory and Bob was very pleased. It was an anxious but exciting time. We hiked out of the valley with a spring in our step. *We are going to be working in Campat!*

Chapter 37
Preparing for Campat

We had a lot of work to do in the next couple of weeks before moving to Campat. Dan and Elaine were still visiting so we took them to *Balneario Las Islas* (The Island Spa). This was a place everyone talked about in Carchá but we hadn't had a chance to experience yet because of the weather.

In the spring and summer once it warmed up, people would go to play in these series of little islands that formed in the middle of a pool more than 50 meters long. Las Islas was every bit as cool as Oceans of Fun but was a natural water park. It was gorgeous with the cascading water, blue pools, and green scenery. It was a little chilly though in April but we had a grand time.

George wanted another gathering at his place for us to meet the new Guatemalan MCCers. Dan and Elaine made the trip with us back to Chimaltenango. They would soon be leaving for Bolivia. This time we had to catch a bus at 3:20 a.m. on Saturday morning. Going so early was a pain and it wasn't a good trip with the bus breaking down along the way.

We eventually made it to George's place and met Phil and Joy, who would live in Guatemala City after language study. We also met Dale and Lois, the new MCC nurses we would be sharing a house with in Carchá. Dale was going to be the main person working with the K'ekchi' because Lois would be plenty busy taking care of their three boys. The boys were Justin, Lance and Zach—about eight, five and two years old. Our MCC team was increasing in size from just George and the five traveling amigos to now twelve adults and five children.

After the short MCC weekend, we said our final goodbyes to Dan and Elaine. We would miss them and wished them well in Bolivia. I headed back to Carchá alone on the bus and Randall stayed in the city to await the arrival of his first visitors.

Randall's college roommate Joe and new bride Kathy came to Guatemala on their honeymoon to see him. Sadly, he wasn't there for their wedding but what a lovely gesture showing their special friendship by coming to visit. Randall made sure to give them the royal treatment on their honeymoon and grand tour of the country, including coming to Carchá. They spent about a week in Guatemala.

One of the funniest things happened while Randall was away. I went out to Campat by myself and I started talking to a K'ekchi' man and he called me Herman Rolando. I told him I was Herman Keli. He apologized and laughed, saying, "Oh, all you caxlan cuinks look the same to me." *Really? You have to be kidding. Randall has blond, straight hair and blue eyes and I have brown, curly hair and hazel eyes. Plus I am several inches taller. Maybe it is our moustaches?*

The nurses, Ruth, Randall and I had a great laugh over this since all of the K'ekchi' men were about the same height, brown eyes, and straight black hair with the identical haircut. They ALL looked alike to us. Making it even more difficult, Linda added that they all seemed to wear the same clothes. She joked, "You know the guy, the one with the blue pants, white shirt, and a hat."

During the time Randall was gone, Ruth gave me a lesson on teaching reading in K'ekchi' and shared the primers we could use with our students in Campat. I found it fascinating that I could read all the words but there were some words I didn't have a clue what their meaning was and had to ask. It truly was a great learning tool.

I also went with Ruth to a c'alebal called *Pocolaj* and taught my first reading lesson. She went there a couple times a week and had twenty students. She paired me with an elderly man. He was really struggling to grasp the connection between letters and sounds. Even still, I felt like he made some progress and that was quite encouraging. Ruth said I did a good job, which boosted my confidence that we could actually do this in Campat.

It was May Day when Dale, Lois, and their boys moved into the house. That was a huge change for all of us. First order of business to help Dale and Lois was to find someone to do laundry. We hired a lady named Yolanda to wash their clothes and Randall's and mine. She was a huge help to us and we didn't have to spend all our time washing clothes. It also provided some much-needed financial assistance for Yolanda's family.

To wash our clothes, Yolanda used the pila in the back of Dale and Lois' house that was protected from the rain with a little roof overhead. Dale rigged up a long clothesline that used a pulley system. One pulley was attached to a pole next to the pila and the clothesline ran out about 25–30 yards to another pulley tied to a huge tree in the backyard. Brilliantly this allowed the clothes to be reeled out from the pila into the sunshine and brought back in quickly when it started to rain.

After having toured the country, Randall brought Joe and Kathy to Carchá for the last couple of days of their visit. The day Randall left to take Joe and Kathy to the airport and just days before we were to move to Campat, we heard some startling news. Two gringos were killed close to Carchá in a town called San Pablo.

It was a little scary for all of us. We hoped it was just a rumor, but I decided not to go out to Campat by myself. Later we found out it was a Guatemalan man and woman killed in San Pablo. However, there were gringos murdered but in the *Departmento de San Marcos* (a department along the Pacific Ocean and along the western Guatemala-Mexico border to the west of Antigua). A fourteen-year-old Guatemalan was also killed. It occurred much closer to our MCC colleagues. We never did find out all the details, but it put us all on notice to be cautious.

Randall returned safely from Guatemala City after taking Joe and Kathy back to the airport. We were making plans to start spending entire weeks at Campat. We made a couple trips out to Campat to check things out. We were able to talk to Kacua Marcos and Kacua Pedro. They both said they wanted to learn to read but needed glasses to read the print. I thought, *We have to talk to the nurses.*

We also discovered the church kitchen was being occupied by a very poor family so we had to make changes to our plans. After talking to the people of the church, we decided to move on May 12 and live in the back of the church.

We had plenty to do to get ready. We had to figure out what items we needed to take to live in the c'alebal and what supplies we could carry in our two large backpacks to last from Monday until Friday. After eight months, we finally were going to begin what we had been sent to do. It was a very exciting time.

Chapter 38
The Big Day

On the big day of the move to Campat, we had our cots, sleeping bags, and a little kerosene stove for cooking. Our backpacks were filled with extra clothes, food, candles, and other supplies. In addition, we needed to take one of our suitcases to store things when we went back to town because they would have church services on Sunday.

Bob offered to take us out to Campat. With everything loaded in his Land Rover, we were embarrassed by our wealth of belongings (thinking all were necessary to survive) and how little the K'ekchi' had in comparison.

I rode with Bob and all our stuff while Randall followed behind on our motorcycle. Once to the bottom of the mountain at the bridge, we had lots of help waiting. Santiago, José Mariá, and two other church members (Tomás and Luis) were at the bridge to help us haul things up over the mountain to the church. Bob wished us well and left to go back to town. Hiking up and up, we were a little caravan and got lots of strange looks from people we met on the trail. *What a fun day!*

When we arrived, we were mauled by kids from the c'alebal excited to see us. Everybody was so kind. It was as if the c'alebal's "Welcome Wagon" was there to greet us. The wife of a man named Domingo gave us food (tortillas, beans, cooked squash, and sugar cane.) Others brought us potatoes, *raxtuls* (a prickly green chayote squash), bananas and coffee.

Their welcome was overwhelming and they so freely shared the little they had. Their gifts to us were so much more than what we could ever repay them. We just hoped that our being there would be beneficial to them.

People knew we were there to teach reading and began asking if we would teach them. Earlier we had talked with Ruth about who would want to learn to read and worried it would be hard to find students. Our worries were for naught. We had guessed only the men would be interested, but we found out quickly that young, married women were anxious to learn to read.

Depending on their family situations, young girls in Campat were not able to attend school for very many years if any at all. Older daughters had less opportunity to study while their younger sisters might get to go a year or two longer. A girl's role from an early age was to help her mother at home and take care of younger brothers and sisters until her suitor came calling for marriage.

At the end of this first day, we were exhausted but felt content and hopeful. To our delight, we each had four students sign up. Better than we could ever have dreamed. My students were Tomás, Luis, Santiago's wife Angelina, and a man named José. The beautiful people of Campat had welcomed us with open arms. *This just might work!*

The children were so special, each with their own personalities—loving, shy, needy, caring, jealous, boisterous, jokesters. Mothers brought their babies with matted eyes, bulging tummies, and dirty faces. That night in the candlelight I wrote in my journal, "Why was I born an American? Why was I blessed with my parents who have so much? How can I repay my good fortunes in some small way?"

In the morning we woke to watch the sunrise as it shone on the c'alebal. It was as if the mountain and valley were glistening from the sun rays bouncing off the dew. I decided God had never created a more beautiful place. It was perfectly quiet except for the bubbling river. The morning air was fresh, crisp, and clean. The only thing more beautiful was the fantastic evening sunsets with the orange, pink, and red colors lighting the western sky over Finca Chilax at the far end of the valley.

We taught each student one-on-one for about thirty-minute sessions. Within two more days, I was up to eight students, including Tomás' wife and two other women. It kept us very busy. Initially we taught our students in the church, but eventually we started going to their homes. When we weren't teaching, we were talking to these proud, loving, and generous people and assessing what we could do to help better their lives.

We also didn't have much privacy. Being the first caxlan cuinks to ever live in the c'alebal provided a lot of curiosity and entertainment for the locals. We had very close neighbors who had moved into the little kitchen (what was to be our initial home) that was owned by the church. We never knew the circumstances as to why a man named Eusebio and his family, who was one of the poorest families in the c'alebal, had moved in there.

It was such a small hut and poorly constructed, since it was built to just be the kitchen for the church. Eusebio was rail thin and didn't appear to have much motivation. We thought possibly he had been sick from working away at one of the fincas. When he spoke, he mumbled and was hard to understand. His wife was short and rotund but that might have been because she was always pregnant. The family had somewhere between five to seven kids, we never could get a good count. *Old Mother Hubbard has nothing on her!*

All the children were barefoot and in dirty, ragged clothes a size or two too small or really large and baggy, obviously handed down from one child to the next. One little boy named Ernesto was crossed-eyed, missing his front teeth, and had a perpetually dirty face. His little button-down shirt was stretched so much by his growing body that his belly button was always showing. His brown striped pants were so baggy that he had to hold on to them to keep them from falling off.

It didn't take us long to realize that the church's rough-cut plank boards for walls had several knotholes. These made perfect little peep holes for the neighbor children to watch these two caxlan cuinks. Ernesto seemed to be the most curious and courageous. He would often peek in through one of the knotholes. If we noticed him, we would wave or say something to him. He would scamper away, giggling and hiding behind bushes or a banana tree. We got pretty good at playing "Peek-a-boo, I see you."

The best though was when one of us would keep watch outside for Ernesto approaching and let the other inside know. Just as Ernesto would peek in a knothole, the person inside would look out so both were eye to eye and scare him. He would burst out laughing and run as he held onto his pants not to lose them.

At night Eusebio's family would sing around the fire in their hut and it was heavenly music, even when not on pitch. Quite often a family member would bring us coffee or tortillas. Talk about another lesson in humility. When we would leave for the weekend, we would be sure to leave any leftover food we had brought out for the week with them. Often we brought out eggs and made sure we had a few left to give to them. The missionaries gave us some of their kids' old clothes and we brought them to Eusebio's wife for her little flock. She was truly appreciative.

After several months of living in the back of the church, Larry went with us to approach the c'alebal land committee to inquire about building the house we had talked about in our initial meeting. We reiterated that if the people would help build our house, it would belong to the c'alebal and could be a community building. We were so excited when Larry convinced the land committee it was time to start building our house.

There was a community plot of land where our little house could be built. Randall shared about the experience, "Then they told us they could start in three weeks. We were totally baffled. They explained that they needed to wait until the dark of the moon (new moon) to cut the corner posts because that was when a termite-type bug would not be burrowed into the wood. If the posts were cut during the full moon, the bugs would be in the wood and would eat the wood. I know I was just flabbergasted when I heard that."

Some theories about cutting wood at different phases of the moon are tied to how much sap is in the tree. During a new moon, the sap is supposedly down in the roots. While in full moon, the sap flows up. So during the full moon, the bugs are burrowing into the tree to get to the sap and would be there when the tree was cut for posts.

It would take over three months to build our little one-room house. *Ugh! Nothing happens fast in Guatemala.*

Chapter 39
Erlinda

Fast forward and it was now almost exactly a year from when we first moved to Campat. We had been in our little house for about four months. Erlinda had been my student for only a couple months when her brother Antonio came to our door asking for help that was way out of my knowledge and comfort zone.

Sitting in the home of Erlinda and her husband José Tuc Coc, my mind was racing the whole time, thinking *What the heck am I going to do to help Erlinda? I have pulled baby calves and delivered baby pigs but a human baby!*

With Erlinda in labor and now standing with José's help, Na'chin encouraged me to eat the caldo and tortilla she had given me. Here I was sitting about five feet from the poor woman in pain and I was eating chicken. *How surreal!*

José shared that the c'alebal health promoter Santiago had been there an hour or more before me, which was going to be my first question. They said Santiago had given Erlinda a shot for the pain and wanted them to take Erlinda to the hospital in Cobán. *The nurses' hard work is paying off in training the health promoters!*

Going to the hospital was scary for the indigenous people for several reasons. The K'ekchi' were often looked down upon by the ladino doctors and nurses and not treated with respect. It was intimidating to not speak Spanish well, if any at all. The hospital staff usually didn't speak K'ekchi' and even if they did, probably wouldn't use it. It was beneath them. Campesinos also feared that if they went to the hospital, they would die because that's what happens when you go to the hospital. An ill person usually waited too long to go to the hospital and there was nothing the doctors could do. Thus, the hospital was equated with death.

I encouraged José to take Erlinda to the hospital, but it was an hour and half to two-hour hike up over the mountain to Chamelco—without being pregnant or in labor—and then a thirty-minute bus ride to Cobán. José said all the rest of the family members were off planting corn on the other side of the valley and there was no one to help carry her up over the mountain.

Erlinda was back crouching and the contractions didn't seem to be as strong. She said the pain wasn't quite as bad after the shot Santiago gave her. They decided to wait and see how things went. I was there for about an hour and the sun was peering over the mountaintop. I told Erlinda and José I would check back throughout the day to see how she was doing. I thanked them profusely for their hospitality and made my exit.

Since I had already had breakfast, I went back to my house and got ready for the day. I had several students to teach. I stopped after my first student to see how Erlinda was doing. José had left shortly after I had. He went to help his family plant corn. Even with his wife in labor, corn planting was a high priority for survival.

Erlinda appeared to be in a little less pain and was sitting up. Again, I talked to her about going to the hospital and suggested it would be good to go now. I could get a car and come get her while it was daylight. No dice, especially with José not there and she didn't want to bother him. She said if the baby didn't come that night, she would go then.

After checking on Erlinda, I went to teach a couple more of my students. By noon I had taught three more students and had three additional cups of coffee. I stopped again to see how she was doing but still no baby. After lunch I had a couple more classes and each student blessed me with another gourd or cup of coffee. I was going to become addicted if I didn't float away first.

After my last class at 3:00 p.m., I went to see Santiago. He had been off planting corn with his family all day. He was back home and

I wanted to seek his advice concerning Erlinda. He was worried and agreed it would be best if she went to the hospital now. We went together to see Erlinda.

José had just returned from planting. She was no better and had no strength. Now I am thinking it has been about twenty-four hours from when she had gone into labor and she was exhausted. We again stressed we felt she needed to go to the hospital and there was still enough daylight. I suggested they let me go get the car in Carchá and meet them at the bottom of the mountain at the bridge.

Together Santiago and I didn't carry any more weight. José said they still didn't have help to carry her and she was scared of the hospital. He said they would wait until morning. If still no baby, his family would be available to help him carry her over the mountain. It was so frustrating because there was nothing else I could do.

Right after getting back to my house from Erlinda's, our neighbor Alfredo Acte stopped by to visit after *calec*-ing all day. To calec was using hoes or machetes to clear the land of weeds and grass before planting. He had just acquired a new piece of land that needed to be cleared. We developed a great friendship with him and he stopped to visit most evenings. His story was quite interesting. He spoke fluent Spanish because he had been *chapoced* (or grabbed) and was made to serve in the Guatemalan Army. He saw and experienced a lot of horrible things he didn't want to share.

Alfredo had a brilliant, inquisitive mind. He was always asking questions. One of my favorite questions was when he asked if men had really been to the moon and how did they get there. He wanted to learn some math and we taught him what we could. He picked it up very quickly. Alfredo also wanted to learn English so we spent a lot of time teaching him words and phrases.

After Alfredo left, Luis and Albina stopped by. Then Marcos came by and brought me freshly made tortillas for supper. Not long after Marcos left, Tomás and Matilde visited and stayed until about

8:30 p.m. There was never a dull moment in Campat. It was so wonderful to just talk and get to know these beautifully spirited people.

That night I didn't sleep well, thinking about Erlinda's situation.
Knowing the need to go check on her early, I had just slept in my
clothes. At 3:00 a.m. I heard someone again at my door call out "Ma
cuancat?" I knew immediately it was José. I jumped up and answered
to see if there was any news. José looked panicked and said they
wanted to go to the hospital. Erlinda was in terrible pain and there
was still no baby.

It was raining and pitch dark out. I knew it was too dangerous
to try and get her up over the mountain in these conditions. Also, I
wouldn't be able to get the Land Rover that early anyway and there
was no bus running at this hour. I told him we would have to wait
until 5:00 a.m. and hopefully the rain would let up. It would be close
to dawn and we would be able to see the path better. He agreed and
went back to his house to wait. It was a long couple of hours with no
sleep.

The rain let up but there was still chipi chipi. I put on my plastic
sheet poncho, grabbing my bolsa, flashlight, and motorcycle keys before I went over to José's house. It was still dark out as I maneuvered
carefully over the slick path. There were four men from José's family
there waiting. José said Erlinda was hurting and scared but ready to
go. I still didn't know how they were going to carry her. But I told
him I would go to Carchá and get a car. José thanked me and I took
off as fast as I could up the dark, slippery, steep slope of the mountain. My adrenaline was pumping.

Once reaching the peak of the mountain, the long descent awaited me. The chipi chipi made the path much slicker than when it was
just flat out raining. After all of our trips up and over the mountain,
we were getting pretty adept at the climb and descent without slipping and falling. Besides a sore bottom and hurt pride, mud-soaked
pants made hiking much worse after a fall. I jogged down to the

bottom of the mountain as quickly as I could without landing on my tush. Reaching the bridge at the bottom of the hill and Marcos' house where I had parked the motorcycle, I put on my helmet, jumped on, and took off for Carchá.

Driving the motorcycle on the mud road from the bridge to San Juan Chamelco reminded me of riding my horse Queen in the pole bending races back home at the Tall Corn Festival. You had to dodge and weave around the potholes. Here though one strived to avoid hitting a hole, getting splashed with mud and potentially being thrown off. I made pretty good time, even though I never was comfortable driving that motorcycle. It was so early even the kids along the route didn't come out to wave like they normally did.

Once I reached Chamelco, the road became gravel and I could make much better time. The worst thing was when a bus was coming toward me and I had to get over to the side of the road to avoid being hit. I would pray the bus didn't hit a pothole with perfect timing and spray me with mud. That did happen more than a few times over the years. Once hitting the blacktop outside of Carchá, I beelined home and it was about 6:30 a.m. This had to have been a new record for me to make the trip that quickly. To my great relief, Randall was back from his trip to the city. I woke him and explained the situation. We were able to borrow the Land Rover.

I was an exhausted, nervous wreck. Thankfully Randall drove us back out to meet José and Erlinda. Once we got back to the bridge, all we could do was wait, which seemed like an eternity. Randall and I caught up on all that had happened that week and I heard about his parents' visit. It was great to have company visit us. But there was always the letdown when they had to leave, knowing it would be a long time before seeing them again. We had been waiting at the bridge for a couple hours when finally at about 9:00 a.m., we saw a group of men come around the bend and down the last incline toward us. It was José and his family. Erlinda had arrived!

Not knowing how they were going to carry her over the mountain, we flipped out when we saw them. José and his four family members had taken turns, one at a time, carrying Erlinda. They crossed the little bridge, stopping at our car. When they arrived, José was the one carrying Erlinda. She was sitting in a wooden straight-back chair and tied to the chair to keep from falling off. A piece of blue plastic was covering her to protect her from the rain, which thankfully had stopped. José had a rope running under the seat of the chair. The ends of the rope were tied to his leather tam that rested across his forehead.

José was bent over with Erlinda in the chair laying back at about a 45-degree angle. Sweat was pouring down his face and he was exhausted and in pain. The other four men all looked worn out as well. We helped them remove the plastic rain protection from Erlinda and José slowly knelt down as the four men helped lower her to the ground. It had taken almost four hours to carry Erlinda (while in labor) down the mountain with the chipi chipi making the trail treacherous. However, they never fell!

Erlinda was hurting and scared. After being untied from her awkward mode of transportation, we helped her get into the back of the Land Rover where she could lay down. I figured Erlinda had been in labor for about 36 hours. We were so afraid the baby was dead. José thanked his brothers and cousins, and he climbed in with us. The engine roared as Randall turned the key and we were off for Cobán. Every bounce Erlinda winced in pain. The shock absorbers on the Land Rover were pretty worthless. On this day, our joke that we weren't sure it even had shock absorbers wasn't funny.

It took about thirty minutes to get to the hospital. Randall put the pedal to the metal as they say. The fact that two gringos brought her to the hospital probably helped Erlinda get more attention from the nurses in admittance. We had heard horror stories of how long people often had to wait to be seen. But we got her right in and they examined her. *The baby is alive!*

Erlinda had really high blood pressure and her legs were terribly swollen. Go figure! The doctor gave her a shot of oxytocin and she was taken to delivery. We were told to return at 2:00 p.m. and that we couldn't wait in the hospital.

We took José back home with us to Carchá and we went to the pensión to get something to eat. He was not one of the men from the church in Campat and he didn't know us very well. It was quite a different experience being around him compared to others from Campat with whom we had developed close friendships.

José was very quiet and reserved because he wasn't used to conversing with caxlan cuinks. When we walked down the street, he would walk behind us instead of beside us. We tried slowing down to get him to walk with us and he just slowed down. No matter how much we encouraged him, he would stay behind. He was polite and thankful for our help but exhausted and worried about his wife. We ate, rested a little bit, and then at 1:30 headed back to the hospital.

When we arrived at the hospital, great news! Erlinda had delivered a healthy little girl. Both Erlinda and her baby were doing fine, however, the doctor had to use forceps and the baby's head was swollen terribly. José was really worried and asked if the doctors could fix it. The doctor comforted him saying the swelling would go down. As we were leaving, Randall asked me if I had thought about what day it was. In all the angst, I hadn't really thought about it being Good Friday. *What an Easter blessing we received!*

José came back and stayed in the back room that Dale and Lois had for guests. The next morning he was up early and ready to return to the hospital. We knew it wouldn't be open that early so we fixed breakfast. Since we didn't have tortillas and beans to give him, we made some oatmeal and scrambled eggs with *Protemás*˚ (a dried, soy protein sold in Guatemala that sort of tasted like meat). Protemás was something we found was light to carry in our backpacks to Campat and a decent replacement for real meat.

We shared our homemade breakfast and our version of coffee, including pan we had purchased in the market from a baker. He seemed to enjoy his breakfast but who knows what he said when he got back home. "You wouldn't believe what those crazy caxlan cuinks gave me to eat."

We took José back to the hospital and more good news—the swelling was down. Erlinda had the prettiest baby. The Guatemalan indigenous babies all had a full head of dark hair and were so cute, unlike many bald gringo babies. José was beaming and so proud. Erlinda seemed to be doing well and was happy.

We were told that mother and daughter would be released from the hospital after a couple of days. Nervous José decided to go back to Campat to wait. We told them that after Erlinda was released, they could stay at the Dale's until she felt ready to go back to Campat. That never happened. José, Erlinda and baby took the bus to Chamelco instead of Carchá and returned back home to Campat with Erlinda hiking up over that mountain just a couple of days after giving birth to her baby. *They are tough, strong people.*

The following week when we went to Campat, we stopped to visit them. It was customary for the women to lay in seclusion for a couple weeks after giving birth so we couldn't see Erlinda. We figured that was a custom the women took full advantage of with all the work they normally had to do.

Na'chin was there to take care of Erlinda and the baby during this time. José was so proud and said mother and baby were doing just fine. He thanked us again. Na'chin was smiling from ear to ear and gave us each a cup of coffee. Thankful that her daughter and granddaughter were okay, her words said it all, "Bantiox re li Dios."

Epilogue

The miracle of Erlinda and her baby surviving was just one of many experiences that filled our three years in Guatemala. The time spent in Campat with the K'ekchi' people taught me invaluable lessons about the good of mankind. It was an incredible life experience and will always be a part of me. The story shared to this point only covers about nine months out of nearly three years in Guatemala.

The nurses Linda and Debbie left to go back home and were sorely missed. Dale, Lois, and the boys became part of our new family in Carchá and were so much fun. Over the years, people went on furloughs for months at a time or home for quick visits. New EMB and MCC missionaries joined the Guatemala team while we were there—Barb, Charlie, Linda, Brent, Theresa, Allen, Doug, Phil, and Pam. We were blessed also with many visitors. Randall and I were able to travel to Haiti to visit Dwight and Sandy, but that adventure is to be told another time.

Relationships continued to develop and blossom in Campat. Santiago's brother Pedro and his wife Adela became entwined in our lives through their children, Victor and Fidelina. Their bravery and love for their children was a true testimony to parenthood. The young couples Luis and Albina, Tomás and Matilde, and Alfredo and Albina and others forever touched our lives. Their stories are to be told next.

Photo Gallery

MCC Orientation Group September 1979

Rich, Martha, and girls
(Photo courtesy of Martha Sider)

Carmen

Carolyn

Ken

George, MCC Country Director

Debbie, Linda, and Ruth
(Photo courtesy of Linda Witmer)

Don Chepe Xol Family

Bob, Sandy, and children
(Photo courtesy of Linda Witmer)

Larry, Helen, and children
(Photo courtesy of Linda Witmer)

Millard, Priscilla, and children
(Photo courtesy of Linda Witmer)

Daryl, Rhoda, and children

Doña Rosa

Luis and Angélica

Mario, Patti, and Marito

Alfombra in Antigua during Semana Santa

The trail to Campat begins

My sister Jane on the trail

Lois, Dale, Zach, and Lance

Justin way ahead on the trail to Campat

The last ascent

The c'alebal of Campat

Santiago and Angelina

Angelina, Josephina, and Santiago

Kacua′ Marcos

Visiting Campat on laundry day

Boiling the corn for tortillas (cua)

Grinding the boiled corn for tortillas

Patting tortillas

Tortillas on the grill

Chicken caldo

Tamale time in Campat!

Planting corn

Luis, don't slip and fall off the mountain

Erlinda and her daughter

About the Author

KelLee is the author of *My Little Valentine, Mansion on a Hill,* and *More Voices of The Willows.* These books tell the story of his mother and birth grandmother's reunion and about The Willows Maternity Sanitarium in Kansas City where his mother was born in 1925. Through the people he met and the friendships he developed after sharing about his mother's story, he decided to write about his own life-changing experience as an agricultural and literacy missionary in Guatemala. This three-year period of his life (1979 to 1982) took place between his undergraduate degree and completion of his graduate studies at Kansas State University. *Mountains of True Peace* is the first of a series about his adventures and personal growth while living and working in Guatemala. KelLee currently resides in Manhattan, Kansas.

Randall Loucks (left) and author KelLee Parr (right)
San Pedro Carchá, Alta Verapaz, Guatemala, 1980

Don't miss out!

Visit the website below and you can sign up to receive emails whenever KelLee Parr publishes a new book. There's no charge and no obligation.

https://books2read.com/r/B-A-HBG-BMLTB

BOOKS 2 READ

Connecting independent readers to independent writers.

Did you love *Mountains of True Peace*? Then you should read *My Little Valentine*[1] by KelLee Parr!

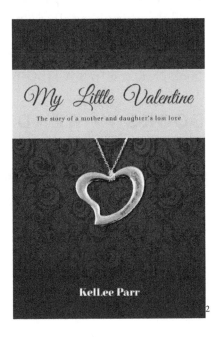

This is the true story of lost love between a mother and daughter. In 1925, a rural Kansas teenage girl found herself in the "family way" and unmarried. She was sent to The Willows Maternity Sanitarium, a home for unwed mothers, and gave up her baby to be raised by strangers. She was devastated but had to promise to never look for her baby. Though kept a secret, she never forgot and always hoped her baby girl was happy. Adopted and raised by a wonderful Kansas farm family, the daughter always wonders the who and why about her birth mother. After 66 years they are reunited and this is their story.

Read more at www.mylittlevalentinebook.com.

1. https://books2read.com/u/3GlEKm

2. https://books2read.com/u/3GlEKm

Also by KelLee Parr

A Guatemalan Journey
Mountains of True Peace

Standalone
My Little Valentine
Mansion on a Hill
More Voices of The Willows and the Adoption Hub of America

Watch for more at www.mylittlevalentinebook.com.

57377461R00156